The Hidden Library
of Tanith Lee

The Hidden Library of Tanith Lee

Themes and Subtexts from Dionysos to the Immortal Gene

by MAVIS HAUT

McFarland & Company, Inc., Publishers
Jefferson, North Carolina, and London

On the front cover: A photograph of Tanith Lee taken by Alan Dudley (UK).

Frontispiece: Red Queen, inspired by a short story titled "White as Sin, Now"

Library of Congress cataloguing data are available

Haut, Mavis, 1936–
    The hidden library of Tanith Lee : themes and subtexts from Dionysos to the immortal gene / by Mavis Haut.
      p.   cm.
    Includes bibliographical references and index.

    ISBN-13: 978-0-7864-1085-9
    softcover : 50# alkaline paper ∞

    1. Lee, Tanith—Criticism and interpretation.   2. Fantasy fiction, English—History and criticism.   3. Horror tales, English—History and criticism.   I. Title.
PR6062.E4163Z69   2001
823'.914—dc21   2001030516

British Library cataloguing data are available

©2001 Mavis Haut. All rights reserved

No part of this book may be reproduced or transmitted in any form or by any means, electronic or mechanical, including photocopying or recording, or by any information storage and retrieval system, without permission in writing from the publisher.

Manufactured in the United States of America

McFarland & Company, Inc., Publishers
   Box 611, Jefferson, North Carolina 28640
   www.mcfarlandpub.com

For my expanding family

Acknowledgments

My thanks are due first to Tanith Lee for her unflagging patience and supplies of hard to obtain books. Thanks to Woody Haut and Sabina Spier for their steady encouragement, and to Barbara Levick, whose seminars in *Gender Studies: The Ancient World* were extremely helpful. Thanks to Dr. Juliet Wood for her seminar paper and to John Clute for advice about publication. Finally, thanks to Andy Sawyer at the Science-Fiction Foundation Library, to David Cowperthwaite for his booklet, and to Robert Cross for rescuing my text from cyber limbo.

Contents

Acknowledgments — vi
Preface — 1
Introduction — 3

1. ACQUIRING IDENTITY
   The Birthgrave, Vazkor, Son of Vazkor (Shadowfire, 1)
   Quest for the White Witch (Shadowfire, 2) — 7

2. VIS—RACE AND MYTH
   The Storm Lord, Anackire, The White Serpent — 27

3. THE FLAT EARTH—MORTALS AND IMMORTALS
   Night's Master, Death's Master, Delusion's Master,
   Delirium's Mistress, Night's Sorceries — 37

4. IN THE STEPS OF THE GODDESS
   A Heroine of the World — 71

5. REALITY, LOVE AND OPPOSITION—SCIENCE FICTION
   Drinking Sapphire Wine, The Silver Metal Lover,
   Electric Forest, Day by Night — 90

6. THE FATAL OBJECT—THE SECRET BOOKS OF PARADYS
   The Book of the Damned, The Book of the Beast,
   The Book of the Dead, The Book of the Mad — 105

7. FOLK, CLASSIC AND FAIRYTALE
   Kill the Dead, Cyrion, Sung in Shadow, Volkhavaar — 125

8. WORKS FOR CHILDREN
   Prince on a White Horse, The Dragon Hoard,
   Princess Hynchatti and Other Surprises, Shon the Taken,
   East of Midnight, Companions on the Road,
   The Castle of Dark, The Winter Players, The Black Unicorn,
   The Gold Unicorn   138

9. EVEN ANGELS ARE SUBJECT TO CORRUPTION
   The Blood of Roses   141

10. ENTERING A MORE FAMILIAR WORLD
    Sabella, Lycanthia, Heart-Beast, Elephantasm   158

11. THE BLIGHTED FUTURE
    Eva Fairdeath   173

12. THE BLOOD OPERA
    Dark Dance, Personal Darkness, Darkness I   177

Conclusion   186
An Interview with Tanith Lee   187
Tanith Lee: Biographical Notes   193
Notes   195
Bibliography   211
Index   215

Preface

The more than sixty books of Tanith Lee form a storehouse of submerged materials relating to history, folklore and literature, and to many myths, religions and customs of various ancient cultures. These materials are not included simply for decoration, atmosphere or reference. They arrive with existent systems of meaning already attached to them. These systems then interact with Lee's own wide range of narratives and settings.

As resonances are produced between the overt intentions of a narrative and its buried counterpart (or counterpoise or counterpoint), Lee's unexpected usage of esoteric contents often disturbs the conventions of genre fiction. Even while she appears to be representing seamlessly precise settings (whether these are entirely fantastic or located in more recognizable contexts), she may well also be creating simultaneous, subtle ruptures by inserting the odd, deliberate anachronism, prolepsis or juxtaposition. Subversive insertions also characterize Lee's forays into contemporary or future times, revealing that here, too, much cultural content has a quasi-mythological or ritualistic character, often in the shape of science-specific mythopoeisms. This book hopes to identify additional layers of meaning in Lee's texts by examining the interplay between various currents in her work.

Lee's work attracts frequent comment on her rich and poetic prose style, her acute sense of the strange and unexpected, and her striking imagery and use of color and texture. It is to be hoped that some of her more writerly qualities will make themselves apparent of their own accord as this book proceeds, even without resort to detailed commentary. The reader requiring more general discussion of Lee's work will find reviews of her books in appropriate magazines, periodicals and encyclopedias of sf and fantasy.[1] Elsewhere, different authors observe different particularities: her recurring motifs (for example, the tower),[2] her evocations of archetypes (such as anima and animus),[3] her emotional range,[4] her language skills.[5]

Sarah Lefanu brackets Lee's work with Angela Carter's as she examines her particular position as a woman writing science fiction and fantasy, her unusual deployment of the "traditions of romance fiction" and her deeply nonconformist interpretations of vampire and fairy tales and traditions of swords and sorcery.[6] Joan Gordon discusses Lee's use of the vampire convention to examine power and control using "themes from post-colonialism through ecology, religion, and sado-masochism to symbiotic feminism."[7] Lillian Heldreth confirms the accuracy of certain sources in Lee's creations, notably her ethological exactitude concerning wolf communities in her representations of werewolves. Heldreth also shrewdly observes Lee's "facility for moving from a visual image ... to a philosophical or psychological principle, and back again."[8] And finally, Lee has herself written an interesting preface to a collection of her own short stories, *Women as Demons*.[9]

Introduction

In spite of the great quantity of her work, which includes fantasy, science fiction, horror, books for children and even a historical novel, Tanith Lee exhibits a scrupulous distaste for formulae or templates. However, although her polymorphism is as considerable as her output, with each book evolving according to its own internal process, themes recur and cross-references accumulate. The common nucleus of some continuing preoccupation will branch out into disparate forms as it is repeatedly questioned and tested in different contexts. The resolution reached in one book may be reconsidered from another angle in the next, or perhaps even put into reverse. Images become overlaid with their negatives or opposites, and the resulting ambivalences and contradictions mean that no answer is ever final. As Lee's preoccupations remain both very much alive and in a perpetual state of flux, the cycle becomes the omnipresent blueprint beneath ever-altering appearances. This book will focus particularly on the many forms that certain basic themes take in her work.

Lee's resistance to permanence is resolute, sometimes even ruthless. The fixed, the changeless, or simply that which lives too long is dissolved by such transformative events as death and renewal, or reincarnation/resurrection, and carried away in the continuum of narrative. The myth of Dionysos, "breaker of chains," an Eastern sacrificial fertility god (which means he dies and resurrects himself recurrently), appears again and again, either through his function or in the many oppositions that pervade Lee's writing.[1] Lee's first published book for adults, *Birthgrave*, contains repeated deaths and resurrections. Later, the Flat Earth sequence portrays immortals finally yielding to a humble acceptance of the cycle of human death. In *The Blood of Roses*, a semi-angelic being outlives his proper span and is utterly corrupted by it. Everything of Lee's harbors its potential opposite, and Dionysian qualities make her characters supple enough to contain contradictions without strain or discomfort. Even wickedness becomes ephemeral in the larger pattern, so that evil characters may be treated with compassion or even humor. Duality and contradiction pervade sexual definitions also. The sexual aspect of Dionysos[2] emerges in a partly magical child who oscillates between sexes, adopting the gender it believes will give most pleasure to others.[3]

Sometimes Lee uses literary models. At times her source is plain, as in her versions of works by Chaucer and Shakespeare, but there are subtler echoes: the Bible, Milton, Donne, Blake and many lesser writers. Folktale is embraced as warmly as the classics, and animated discussions, developments or even antitheses of ideas and structures contained in the originals can result from these literary presences.

Though describing herself as "intuitive," Lee anchors her work firmly to existing signifiers in contexts of myth, religion, superstition, folklore, history, geography, social practice, methods of war, and so on. But even while she is encouraging suspension of disbelief by invoking familiar things, she may be simultaneously dismantling the symbolic order to which they belong. Her writing on madness, which imbues ostensibly random objects with bizarre but unmistakable symbolic significances, can be particularly unsettling and ambiguous. In *The Book of the Mad*, a deranged mind becomes a frozen labyrinth that links different timestreams and forms of madness. But generally Lee's texts are laced with sly Brechtian reminders that they are only fiction, and with small-scale directives on methods of reading. Mildly counselling the proper textual approach, a character muses, "...with any legend, one must read between the words, being skeptical but not too much so, sifting and rejecting and searching...."

Of course, fantasy and science fiction can claim special dispensations. As Rosemary Jackson has noted, "Fantasies image the possibility of radical cultural transformation through attempting to dissolve or shatter the boundary lines between the imaginary and the symbolic." This symbolic is "that social order constructed by discrete units of meaning, by a network of signifiers.... It is opposed to the imaginary, which is without (before) signifiers. To break the symbolic ... is ... a radical, subversive activity."[4]

As she reanimates elements of ancient symbolics or reinvents modern ones, Lee often prefers the "parallel" (her word) world, a place that is simultaneously strange and familiar, like Paradys (which is an alternative Paris). Though she also uses purely imaginary contexts—as in *Drinking Sapphire Wine, Electric Forest, Day by Night*—more often she locates her work in familiar systems and ideas where, if these happen to be abandoned, their restoration is detailed. Her playful Flat Earth floats on a sea of chaos and is populated with the djinns and demons who conventionally belong there. *Malice in Saffron* (*The Book of the Damned*) has a Medieval setting that functions according to a dynamic that inserts visions and apparitions where we would now perceive plainer dreams and hallucinations. Such substitutions focus on a mythopoeic aspect of history in which historical fact matters less than the revitalizing of discarded spaces.

In myths, boundaries constantly blur and overlap. Made up of accretion and fluctuating repetition, myth produces stories that are both already known and not known. As Lee saturates her narratives with repeated fragments of myth—usually traditional, sometimes of her own making—oddly familiar outlines gradually emerge. The *Birthgrave* sequence painstakingly restores an imaginary version of a possibly never-existent symbolic located in the mists of a prehistoric past. The story of a girl in a fictitious, a historical moment also retraces the outlines of a semi-mythological goddess religion.[5] The girl becomes simultaneously ancient and a chronic, and the strange anomaly of a spaceship in the final pages of this book—along with references in subsequent volumes to a "curious" belief that the earth revolves around the sun—reinforces the singularity. In her many games with time, Lee uses chronological discrepancies like metaphors.

Myth is easily reified and readily parodied, and therefore oddly vulnerable to manipulation. Paradoxes inevitably cluster thickly as Lee sets about reviving the meaning that underlies the signifier.[6] This text hopes to locate certain signifiers and trace some of these processes.

With strong leanings towards the dualism of Gnosticism, Taoism and various strands of Eastern religious thought, Lee's broad, non-affiliated, transcendental framework permits much diversity as she works endlessly towards moments of reconciliation between dark and light. She represents many different shamanistic experiences: death and resurrection, flying, transformation into animal shape, madness and illness, coexistence of different places and times. A Gnostic and Zoroastrian fascination with angels and light surfaces repeatedly as an angelic Lucifer/Christ and a dual or androgynous god appear in several texts. *The Blood of Roses*, an epic work on the Christian religion that traces worship from its numinous, pagan, forest origins through early Christendom, attaches light to *gnosis* or direct religious experience, dark to greed for spiritual power.

Lee's characters, who may not all be human, or not all-human, inhabit a range of fictional contexts. They love, hate, betray; need food, sleep and solace; seek power; crave admiration, love and wealth; and fall foul of conspiracies or treacherous lovers or into error. They may contrive to master adversity, gain experience and strength, even dull the edges of their perpetually gnawing curiosity. But above all, even if often unawares, they are getting wisdom, and alongside their struggles, another half-recognized world, where death is merely a phase between lives, flows on. Many seem to find survival oddly trivial, though not apparently because of their powers of self-resurrection. Death may be casual, comic, nostalgic, even erotic or desired as an end to suffering, but as an inescapable part of transformation and renewal, it is always linked to desire and to creation—a theme expressed with a particular beauty in *A Heroine of the World*. Of course, this elicits all kinds of responses from Lee's headstrong characters. For the most part they display a normal, healthy resistance. They bridle and refuse; they cling to life, steadfast ignorance and immediate pleasure; wisdom must be wrung from them. Some of them may be kin to gods or goddesses, even evolving into the Goddess herself, but their reactions still seem profoundly human, and their split natures form a crack through which comedy often bursts irrepressibly out.

But though they make much of personal freedom, these characters do not really choose their destinies. They finish either badly or by accepting that they are only moments in a larger cycle. The task is as much to know as to alter themselves. In *Anackire*, the protagonist's prayer is *"Not what I lack, nor what I desire, but give me only what I am."*

Since Lee's work develops in a non-linear manner, this text follows the emergence of themes in preference to chronological order. For example, the last volume of the Vis trilogy, *The White Serpent*, was written ten years later than the earlier two volumes, with many works falling in between. A bibliography supplies the necessary dates. A brief list of the themes that will unfold themselves gradually in the text to come includes: growing up, transgression, transformation, rebirth; hubris, immortality, nature and death; the goddess, albinos; demons and androgynes; likeness, difference, attraction and incest; repression and madness; religion, institutional and otherwise; art, magic, transformation, love and play; creativity and boredom; blood, pollution, sacrifice and vampirism; instinct, animals and shape-changers; fatal and transitional objects. These may often overlap or seem contradictory, but the unifying subtext of a cyclical reality is generally constant.

Some accounts are more detailed than others. The *Birthgrave* sequence, coming at the start, is dealt with fully; the Vis epic receives more cursory attention, focussing largely on its differences.

A final remark, concerning Lee's use of names: The reader should not only be on the lookout for buried resonances, but also for frequent changes of name, sometimes slight, sometimes major. A change in name indicates a shift in identity. In *Birthgrave*, the nameless heroine borrows the name Uastis from a healer as she herself learns to heal. In *Drinking Sapphire Wine*, constant body changes make characters recognizable only by name. Name changes become crucial in different ways.

— 1 —

Acquiring Identity

The Birthgrave, Vazkor,
Son of Vazkor (Shadowfire, 1),
Quest for the White Witch (Shadowfire, 2)

Rewriting Oedipus

A woman/goddess gradually emerges from a miasma of self-hatred and a belief in her own inherited evil (though in Lee's hands "evil" is often a term in search of a definition) to an eventual understanding of her true identity. The sole survivor of a dead race, she is awakened and expelled from the terrestrial womb of an underground cave by a volcanic eruption. Death preceding birth immediately establishes the parameters of the narrative of Lee's Birthgrave trilogy.

The protagonist narrates her story in the first person. She wakes in ignorance of who or what she is, and acquires memory, consciousness and autonomy slowly and painfully. Lee carefully locates the process inside the natural order: "I lay like an insect in a chrysalis, awaiting some wrenching calamity to break my cocoon, and turn me out, half-formed."[1]

Not yet known to herself, she remains nameless for the greater part of the book. A succession of titles serve her instead, first goddess, then Imma (small one), she becomes known as Uastis (healer), inheriting the title from an old healing-woman. Her winding journey towards self-discovery leads her to many barbaric places. Amidst violence, loss and death, she forms liaisons with a series of men in whom, despite wide moral and personal differences, she sees an uncanny similarity. As she acquires traditionally masculine skills, she also discovers the feelings particular to women, including a sense that love is a form of enslavement or loss of self.

In accordance with the heroic model, she garners consciousness through conflict and error; she is marked out by fate and passion, and does not accept her destiny easily. She is greatly surprised as the abilities associated with female divinities resurface, such as powers to heal and reanimate the dead. Then she self-resurrects, repeating the original awakening motif. The weaving together of different aspects of herself, especially the masculine and feminine sides, relates as much to the conflict between essential cultural polarities—the patriarchy and the matriarchy—as to her own personal struggle. Lee, however, avoids simplistic or moralizing gender divisions. Women may prove obstructive; male characters may serve as helpers and protectors—though sometimes at a price. With the exception of Vazkor and the ghost of the dead high priest, who surreptitiously urges her towards self-loathing and suicide, moral baseness and folly are fairly randomly distributed between the sexes. Speaking of war, an old woman says:

> "It is man's work."
> I laughed. "I too have fought and killed, Kotta. It is the work of fools, not men."

In this hostile setting, Uastis is both heroic and vulnerable, irrationally brave and strangely unconfident. When the power-seeking Vazkor recognizes the potential she consistently fails to see in herself, he takes steps to suppress his female rival. He falsely persuades her that he is her brother and she conceives a child by him.

Though many components are altered or reversed, the Oedipal content is unmistakable, as Lee makes use of concepts like fate and hubris and matriarchal residues of the Sphinx, Jocasta, the Furies.[2] As the last survivor of an ancient race, and still widely worshipped as a goddess, Uastis fears that the hubris of her ancestors offended Nature and inspired the mysterious plague that annihilated them. The birth of her son marks the moment when the underlying Oedipus myth comes fully into the open. Like Tiresias, the blind midwife Kotta sees what others cannot see and is aware of the boy's real ancestry. As the son sets out on his long quest of revenge against his birth mother, the inevitable is already casting its shadow over him. After giving birth, Uastis escapes from the tribal camp and leaves her son to be reared by a woman whose baby, born in the same tent on the same day, has died. The abandonment of her child and continuing pursuit of her destiny is precisely what allows Vazkor to secure his son as an instrument of retribution.

This is no simple retelling of an ancient legend. Lee rewrites the story freely. As Sophocles's play opens, parricide and mother-son incest have already happened. Jocasta is the lingering, tragic cipher of a matriarchal culture which Oedipus has a sacred duty to uproot, regardless of his own personal attachments. But Lee's sequence reinstates the goddess of the matriarchy.[3] Though at first the heroine's past appears to have been erased, the mother-goddess slowly revealed herself in her and is consciously separated out from the prevailing patriarchal code.

The Oedipal son dominates the two subsequent volumes. The first traces his youth and search for his true ancestry. In spite of an unusual sensitivity—he is cast as a mother's boy—and the influence of Kotta and his foster mother, he has been deeply indoctrinated with all the responses expected of him in a male-empowering, tribal community.

From the instant that he is mistaken for his dead father, to whom he bears a striking physical resemblance, he becomes obsessed with him. His hatred for the mother who abandoned him at birth, "that wild cat who sloughed me and left me behind like excrement," is rationalized when he is informed that she was responsible for the death of his father. Adopting his father's name, and thus his identity, he allies himself firmly with patriarchal values. This will become central to his struggle.[4]

Though the powers he develops are clearly inherited from his mother, he resolutely construes them as the legacy of his father. His relations with women are initially negative, compounded of lust and contempt, but he begins to develop personal feelings for a city woman that have no possible origin amongst the androcentric tribespeople with whom he was reared. Love and tenderness towards women conflict painfully with the ethos of fatherright to which he is committed.

Shadowfire 1 ends as traces of his mother shake his belief that she is the embodiment of evil (the view she herself had once held). The paths of mother and son cross repeatedly. He finds his own powers of healing when he revives the daughter of a man Uastis had once saved from death.

Quest for the White Witch[5] commences with the hero walking upon water. His blossoming supernatural abilities fill him with disbelieving astonishment. In the southeast[6] he becomes involved with people of different races and religions, the Masrians[7] and, in strong contrast, the dark, lustful, semi-troglodytic Hessek who inhabit the swamps. In return for power and money he exploits his talents. He engages sexually with the mother of a young man who has adopted him as a brother. Incest is once again making itself felt.

As in the Thebes of Oedipus, the Hessek witch, stealing Vaskor's power as he boastfully exhibits his magicianship, conjures up a plague of flies.

Vazkor manages to burn the witch, but dies. It is the end of a phase. After lying dead for several days, like his mother before him, he resurrects himself. Appalled by the annihilating consequences of his powers—"Bar-Ibithni had had a surfeit of the dark"—he is moved to remorse by the death of a baby. He discovers that a shrine commemorating a rustic goddess is a memorial to his mother, begins to doubt the validity of his revenge and sets out once more to find her.

His long journey concludes on an island, where he meets a woman whom he assumes is his half-sister. He overcomes his revulsion towards brother-sister incest (expounded earlier in his rather prudish lecture) as they are drawn irresistibly together, but suffers a momentary horror when he discovers that she is his mother. Later, seeing no meaning outside the presence of the woman who is his natural complement, he returns to the island to stay. It is a return into both nature and the goddess. He says:

> It was the abstract nature of the world that brought her back to me. The sound of waves breaking on a clear cold shore, the moon coming up through a cloud of trees, the silver bird that cries for dawn, the spring, which was flowing over the land at last.[8]

The Quest for Identity

Lee has an apparent liking for the transitional character of the bildungsroman. In *Birthgrave*, the inexperienced adolescent Uastis-Karrakaz, who is about to enter a male-preferring, adult world, starts out with unusually low self-esteem. She has been severed from childhood by a wholly dormant (latency) period and born directly into young womanhood. Haunted by blurred and often unintelligible memories, it is difficult for her to distinguish between the real and the imaginary. Her contacts with the opposite sex are bruising and full of confusion and contradiction.

With great effort she learns to control her rebellious passions. She affects a studious bravado to mask her lack of confidence, but even at her most naive it is precisely her inability to resist her instincts and desires that is the foundation of her integrity. As she pieces herself together according to her own wayward nature, she is also piecing together a lost matriarchal culture. Often misreading the signs, she finds small fragments of this culture in shrines and ruined cities, but her struggles, embedded in an unenlightning and repressive patriarchy, seem hopeless. Uastis's initial belief that she is an incarnation of unalleviated evil is only gradually exposed as deliberate manipulation by a patriarchy that is doing its utmost to subvert the meaning of the woman-centered culture it has recently displaced. Throughout Uastis's long passage into maturity, Lee underlines her incoherent but indestructible "loyalty to those henceforth abandoned clearings across which higher and lower worlds once passed."[9]

Without memory, the protagonist is ultra-suggestible. She awakens in an underground cave so void of identity she is not at first sure if she is even human—"whether a thing with legs and arms, or a beast, or a brain in the hull of a great fish...." Both evolutionary and embryonic development are implied here. Immediately, she is forcibly expelled into the world, and the first voice this newborn creature hears tells her: "...you were a little child, and had not yet properly learned the ways of evil. But now you have grown to womanhood in your sleep, and you will learn ... you are cursed and carry a curse with you...."

Some simple villagers associate her with their goddess and force what she perceives as a false identity upon her: "...I felt their grasping fingers on my soul...." She attributes miracles of healing to their credulity rather than to any powers she could possess, and only when her first lover, the bandit Darak, unmasks her without revulsion does she begin to believe she may not be a monster. "I saw that he had set me free of something, with him at least, but chained me too, of course."

Other women, resentful of her refusal of the constraints that bind them, also limit her freedom; and when she is forced to kill a rival in self-defence, the death destroys the last constraints of conventional female identity. Alongside Darak, a boyish aspect of herself emerges. She learns about physical courage and the supposedly male skills of fighting and horsemanship, and, refusing a segregated or subordinate role, she forces herself into the midst of the men's discussions of strategy. "The skills were there in me, in my dreams and recollections ... women and men had not been separate races as they were in this world around me."

Apart from veiling her face, she dresses like a man, fights like a man, treats sexual encounters with casual, male inattention and later astonishes a crowd by acting as Darak's archer in a chariot race. Living among bandits, she is well placed for assaults on convention, and the renegade Darak positively encourages her transgressions. Close to nature, instinctive and spontaneous, he is a natural ally of women. Sexual jealousy can rouse his hostility, but the grimmer part of male dominance is absent. Darak sees no need to excise her "masculine" characteristics, or to remake this able and unusual woman in any way.

Uastis's youthful freedom is instructive but short-lived. She enters the next stage of her life scarred by many killings, both those she has perpetrated and the deaths of Darak and her other companions, but she has acquired strength, courage and a limited knowledge of a world controlled by men.

Coming to understand men is crucial to her own development. Each of her lovers represents a new stage in her discovery of herself and the world. When one of her casual lovers betrays Darak, Uastis avenges Darak's death by killing the traitor according to the bandit code. But she is also grief-stricken. Her rejection of open emotion is over; masculine and feminine responses are beginning to overlap. During a quiet interlude, she begins to want to become herself for herself. She tells Uasti, the healer of the caravan people, "I have lived with men in the stamp they have given me which was not of my choosing.... I will not run between the shafts anymore. I must be my own and no other's."

During this time she receives some training in healing from the old woman, who observes her latent powers, saying, "...in your way you must get power over others. That's your heritage ... you must take it, and learn to control both others and yourself."

Vastis begins to regard human relations in a newly introspective way:

> I thought I had been one with Darak in my fashion, forgetting oneness does not come from the body alone.
> Now I became one with the strange old woman of the wagon people—by an almost imperceptible process that sprang from understanding.

It is this interval in the company and protection of a woman who, as a healer and magician, can lay claim to being a soul-kin of some sort, that leads to the next phase of her existence. When the wisewoman is murdered, there is a curious fusing or embrace of personalities: The protagonist takes on both her title and the qualities it describes. Soon her sufferings will be of a kind more traditionally associated with women, though understanding will still be miserably lacking when she meets her next lover, a man who embodies naked power. This lesson will be painful. A long time will elapse before she can imagine any moral exercise of power.

During her stay in the city of Vazkor, the masculine loses its easy charm and becomes alien and oppressive. Even the goddess in Vaskor's misogynistic city is angry, dark and subterranean. For Vazkor, gender division is absolute. Female pollution must be rigorously excluded. Uastis's fierce argument over her right to wear boyish clothes may seem childish, but self-representation has a symbolic value for her. However, she fails to recognize Vazkor's urgent political need for her as a symbol.

Vazkor is all cold calculation. Feeling and the female—especially a female as powerful as he knows Uastis to be—must be suppressed. Pleasure withers at his touch. For Uastis, their relationship is sexually negative and filled with dread: "There was a fierce terror in me that his being would absorb mine." When she is forced to couple with him, she recalls a rape. Uastis seems able to dismiss rape that is exclusively physical in a fairly off-hand way. Emotional violence and abuse—attacks on her inner being—contain much worse horrors for her. With Vazkor, her deepest distress comes from the involuntary arousal of her own sexual responses:

> I had forgotten he must touch me, I had forgotten he would be clever in what he did, I had forgotten his weight on me would feel like Darak in the dark ... there was a kind of opening in me I could not help, and yet I hung above it, watching my own responses as if it were a dream.

But, though at first in the form of self-alienation, during this painful intrusion Uastis is beginning to observe her own separateness. Her detached attitude towards physical violation does not, however, extend to the treatment of other women. She prevents soldiers from raping a village girl. But at this stage the intervention has no personal content. Uastis still feels greatly distanced from the less heroic problems of ordinary mortals. Still somewhat in the grip of hubris, she acts, "because it was a woman they were hurting. Certainly I felt nothing for her as a living creature."

In her system of values, sexual freedom expresses female autonomy, and Uastis has no scruples over promiscuity. But though she understands rape as the subjection of the female, she is still unable to differentiate between men. Each one seems cast in the same likeness—which is, in fact, imposed by a repressed memory of the ghostly priest. In reality, each of her lovers contains a different meaning and serves a new purpose. As a thief and appropriator of the property of others, Darak teaches her how to appropriate the freedom that supposedly belongs exclusively to his sex. From Vazkor's icy manipulations she learns the twisted ways of political power. She also learns the vice of hubris. Not all lessons are good ones.

From a forced and unconsummated marriage with the boy-king Asren, Uastis has a brief experience of maternal feeling. The feeling appears to be displaced from her own unwanted pregnancy with Vazkor's child. Watching as Vazkor cruelly disables Asren, she finds the will to destroy him.[10]

The birth of her son is another turning point in *Birthgrave*, releasing Uastis from any further obligation to serve the interests of man or myth.[11] As she disposes of the corpse of the child that properly belongs to the tribe, she is burying her own male-dominated past. This is the moment when her chains are loosened. "I was free ... for the first time since I had come from the Mountain, I had acted alone."

When Rarm lifts Uastis up into his spaceship, he restores her lost memories.[12] His ship is equipped with a technically advanced computer, programmed to respond to individual psychological needs. The last pieces of the jigsaw are set in place by this mechanical angel in a machine as it accesses a complete account of her life, including what has been forgotten. After sharing this account with Rarm, she dares for the first time to confront her own face in a mirror and discovers to her astonishment that she is alarmingly beautiful. True identity can only be recognized through confirmation by another. "It was not a demon I fought, only myself. Yet so terrible, so real to me."

She has been slow to understand it, but autonomy has always been her goal. There is no sexual alliance. She loves Rarm without any "fascinated hatred." When he departs for his own different world, Uastis remains behind musing, "I have no Dark Prince to ride in my chariot, to walk with me, to hold me to him. I have no one. And yet. I have myself, at last, I have myself. And to me, at this time, it seems enough. It seems more, much more, than enough.'[13]

Father, Mother, Son

From the start, Vazkor's sins have legendary proportions. He crosses the world, pursuing matricide (the worst crime known to the matriarchy), then commits incest with his mother (the worst possible offense against the patriarchy).[14] Still the goddess appears to favor him. As a child he is immune to harm from her emblematic animal and recovers from the bite of a fatally poisonous snake. Busy with boyish pursuits, he sees no special meaning in this.

Vazkor does not take up his mother's moral struggles, though he does misread his destiny just as she did. Embittered by his abandonment amongst the red warriors, he militates against the loss of his birthright. Though his stance is stoutly worldly, it is as a misfit that he eventually grows to be capable of free choice and moral decision. Primed to hold women in contempt, he believes his gifts are an inheritance from his father. When he learns this truth about his origins, he instantly switches from fidelity to the woman he had believed to be his mother to dedication to the man he now knows to have been his father.

The tribespeople jeer at the child's love for Tathra and imply incest. His passionate feelings for her are stressed and he makes frequent reference to her beauty. Even after he discovers the identity of his real mother, he still feels that, "Tathra was yet my mother. Though not my flesh, though I had not been shaped in her body, still it was so. Her breasts had fed me, her arms rocked me before I ever knew it."

It is the eternal mother that he loves. Nakedly Oedipal from the start, it is no surprise that by the time he is removed from the tribe, Vazkor has already committed parricide, admittedly upon the person of his foster father, but in the belief that he has killed his natural parent. In an inversion of the original Oedipus, he enacts his crime in full and conscious hatred for his putative father—"...that red pig grunting for my mother's flesh. Supposedly it is the oldest hate of man, but always new." Although at this point he balks at its literal practice, incest becomes increasingly crucial and increasingly actual throughout his story.

When he severs his connection with his (surrogate) bodily parents, his "spiritual" destiny can begin. At this time, however, Vazkor is not in the least interested in spiritual destinies. He prefers whatever is most immediate and requires least thought. His remarkable resemblance to his father gratifies his ego, and he convinces himself that his magical powers are all inherited from his father. But he is not a warrior. In boyhood, when his body rejects tattoos and in dismay he says to Kotta, "Without the tattoos I am not a warrior," she tells him, "Just so, you are not." Though he kills his tribal father with sheer mental power, even that damages him severely.

Vazkor never disputes the tribespeople's belief in a history that eradicates the mother goddess: "...one tale, discredited at once, was of a goddess risen on earth. More to the tribal taste was the notion of a powerful and ambitious man." When he enters adult existence, he becomes the captive of male instincts. His undividedly male identification is summed up when, facing his enemies, he feels a great rush of hubris:

"Such a scalding wave of pride swelled me that I feared none of them. It would have been more prudent to fear.... I could remember only my inherited gift of magic power, which must come from him.... Godless so far my entire life, Vazkor became my one true god."

Unobtrusively, the action has moved onto the divine stage.

Snatched from execution by the tribal people, he falls into the vengeful clutches of the elite city-dwellers, the people of his father. He is sentenced to a slow death in punishment for his former "hero-deed"—when he had single-handedly rescued tribesmen taken as slaves, killed many of the "masks" and, worst of all, abducted the noble city-woman Demizdor. But he is stolen from his captors by a wealthy lord, who hopes to breed self-healing super-warriors out of him.

In an unaccustomed "feminine" position, Vazkor is turned into a sexual object. Captive in a luxurious limbo, "...the panther was safely locked in his tasteful cage—if he had ever been out of it."

Though Vazkor has fathered thirteen tribeschildren, the city women are barren and the breeding project fails. Ironically, he can remark, "Each city and its might had come to ruin. This made me arrogant as I climbed the hill to find them, the children of that perished glory, still clutching at history like a rotten plank in the river," but still fail to see that the plank of his father's glory is not only rotten but a deliberate fraud.

The captive Vazkor is officially appointed as a "horse tamer." In fact, he is a stud. He breaks free of his enslavement only after healing a poisoned horse intended to kill him, and rashly dispatching Demizdor's lover. Demizdor admits her impossible love for him and helps him escape at the cost of her own life. For Vazkor, Demizdor becomes a person in her own right. He begins, belatedly, to understand her position. The offer of friendship that he makes to her is a new development, belonging to an emerging feminine aspect.

But with this all-male hero, resistance is to be expected. Lee deals with this neatly. As his quest takes him to the dark Hessek witch Lellih, her powers are clearly seen to be fueled by energies coming from Vazkor himself. Vazkor's negativity towards the feminine is inscribed in the repellent, swamp-dwelling Lellih. Though his earlier meeting with the black witch Hwenwit seemed to suggest that he might have succeeded in ridding himself of his loathing for the "dark" and "feminine," his hatred of his mother is still intact, and when Vazkor, hallucinating, sees the witch as a white goddess, he instantly imagines it to be his mother. Reflecting his state of mind, the whiteness of this figure is so extreme and deathly it conjures up the realm of darkness:

> Her whiteness was the whiteness of torches congealed to flesh, so white it made me queasy to look at her, as if at something bloodless, unhuman.... Beneath the veiling, what? A cat's head or a spider's?

Bit-Hessee is starkly opposed to the Mazrian "light."[15] Vazkor can accept Mazrian warriors, taxes, commerce and worldly values without qualification, but ambiguities linger on. An inner life lurks among the depraved Hessek, and Vazkor sorely lacks inferiority. This gives his own dark self great power over him. The Hessek perceive him as Satan, Lord of the Flies, and, like Oedipus before him, his ignorance causes a plague of flies. Even when he realizes he is confronting Lellih rather than his hated mother, her "darkness" easily overwhelms him:

> My viscera scalded, but my flesh was like a layer of wool. I could barely see or hear.... She had crawled up to my mouth, and fastened there as if she would drain me of my life.

Lee inserts the personal into the overall narrative as the burning of the witch simultaneously purifies the Hessek of evil and Vazkor of his fantasies and excessive desire for worldly advancement. He spends a long period alone in an icy region of the southern hemisphere.

> I had ... commenced reflection in the form of those huge symbols of infinity, or the invisible symbols of the nadir.... I grew very calm, a calm I had never known before.... It seemed to me I fathomed the innermost secrets of myself and of everything ... the wilderness washes off for a moment, or forever, the mud and the clay....

This wilderness is foreshadowed in the Wilderness that Vazkor crosses in the company of the nomadic Sri. Uasti's sojourn with the waggon-woman is recalled as Gyest befriends Vazkor. Both these marginal figures are detached from the social conventions. Choosing to veil their faces, Sri men adopt utopian socialist attitudes towards gender restrictions: "...in matters of sex our laws do not fetter us ... children are not mine or thine among us. They are Sri."

Vaskor develops filial feelings towards Gyest: "I never had the father with whom most men expect nature to equip them ... he was the closest I got maybe." It is Gyest who defines his bondage to his father, naming it *Shadowfire*, and to whom Vazkor confesses some loss of incentive to murder.

"I don't even know that I hate her still. I am weary of hating her. Gyest,' I said, 'I may never play the sorceror again'."

In fact, he is more or less true to his word and avoids major sorcery, despite pressures to exercise his powers. He finally tries his magic powers against his mother's to discover who she truly is, and finds that each one can match the power of the other. Neither dominates. The war is over. A balance between female and male power is achieved at last.

Incest and Oedipus

Sacred incest implies lingering traces of a mother goddess. Extreme attention to the link between brother and sister also signals matriarchal culture. The shared womb is an indissoluble bond that obliges a maternal uncle to be responsible for the welfare of his sister's children.[16]

Birthgrave meditates lengthily on sacred incest. In matriarchal terms, the elder Vazkor's claim to be Uastis's brother gives him both rights and duties, but Uastis takes no pleasure in her supposed link with him: "It seems it should have been joy I felt to have found this 'brother' ... I felt nothing, only an overbearing sorrow and bewilderment...."

Although she perceives Vazkor's need for authentication through her— "You cannot ride into Za without Uastis"—when she first refers explicitly to their kinship, it is only to get her own way in the insignificant matter of how she intends to dress. Her argument seems personal and childish— "'Brother,' I said, using against him that kinship he had used against me, 'we must not quarrel over such trivia'"—but trivial disputes serve to keep Uastis from appreciating the political and symbolic stakes. Vazkor's tenuous hold on power depends on displacement of the goddess. It is some time before Uastis fully formulates his fragile position:

> "Every City," I said softly, "here and in the desert, and at Sea's Edge—each one worships a woman. There are no gods for Vazkor to say he is, only goddesses." ... I am not sure why that revelation came to me then.

The reader, however, is aware that this revelation occurs immediately after Uastis sees an unveiled statue of the angry goddess. Semi-consciously, she has understood the reasons for the goddess's anger.

The elder Vazkor's pretense to be a brother is unpardonable, implying a commitment he has no intention of meeting. He plots against his "sister" and, in seeking vengeance through him, imposes patriarchal codes on his son. But although Uastis's struggle is exacerbated by his misrepresentations, it is precisely his attempt to destroy her through her son that restores the primary mother-son icon.

The mother-son pair is integral to the matriarchy, incorporating the male sex without the power struggles that an adult father would introduce. There is no struggle for possession of the child; the son has always been one with the mother.[17]

Although love and sexuality are linked in Lee's sequence, she differentiates between them. Sexual license exemplifies the generic fertility of a mother goddess, appearing in this sequence in temple prostitution and in a recurring reptile. Love is the means through which a person is transformed and realized as an individual. Each suggests a different level of development, but there is no essential contradiction between promiscuity and love. It is lack of concern for the person that Lee abhors. Vazkor coldly announces his plan to have a child from her, and Uastis replies, "I am I.... A woman perhaps, but not a vessel of your pride." She comments, "He was indifferent to my individuality. It had no place in his scheme of things."

The sexual abandon and rape in the younger Vazkor's early life are different. They are "games" played in a struggle to assert himself within a context where rife misogyny normalizes rape. After raping a girl, the youthful Vazkor comments, "When I was done and found her bleeding I was sorry for a moment." In his absolute ignorance he seems to manifest an innocence that clings to him irrespective of his deeds. It marks him out as the perpetual child, always searching for the mother, always denying or mistaking the nature of his search.[18]

Parallels between their lives stress the cyclical character of myth. As the goddess is reinstated in Uastis and the son through his mother, the androgyne or complete, unseparated human is reinstated in the mother-son pair. The pair represent the perfect union of the sexes, reenacting the fact that they have already been literally one flesh. Without this sexual duality, the mother-daughter pair signify a single identity, one and continuous even if apparently multiple.[19] Vazkor's error, when he supposes his mother to be his sister, acknowledges this mother-daughter identity. Sisters and mothers are interchangeable in sacred incest. The mythical goddess is always one and the same no matter what manifestation or parts she may split herself into.

Jung describes the purpose of mother-son incest as "...the strange idea ... of entering into the mother in order to be reborn through her. But the way to this goal lies through incest."[20]

The desire to be reborn from the mother is not, of course, exclusive to the male. Rebirth is a prevalent theme in Eastern or matriarchal systems.[21] Uastis, in her long, incoherent search for the goddess, is also seeking for a way to be reborn: To merge with the goddess is also to be reincarnated as the goddess. To fully realize the goddess in herself, Uastis must incorporate a male aspect. The boyish Imma serves this need until the new incarnation of the goddess begins to long for the son who will complete her.

Lee's relationship to her sources reveals more interest in structure than surface. Shifting names force us to recognize divine personages by means of character and attribute, and to understand their evolution through change of name. The different names of the heroine of *Birthgrave* indicate both her stage of development and her cultural context—first "goddess," then "small one," then "healer," Uasti, which city pronunciation converts into Uastis, meaning "the goddess." In her slave days she has no name. Her last name, Karrakaz, belongs to the reincarnated goddess. Her son follows the many variants of this name littering her trail across different countries and masks his identity with the name of Zervarn when he finally locates her. Underneath the story, both history and myth are at work.

This is also true in Sophocles' Oedipus play. The name Laius is simply a title meaning "the king," and "Laius's murder is a record of the solar king's ritual death at the hands of his successor."[22] The king-god must ensure the fertility of the queen-goddess, and failure carries the penalty of death and replacement by another consort.[23] However, according to the evidence of Frazer, Graves, Harrison and others, the matter is more complex. In many ancient systems the killer and new "king" is the *son* or *twin* of the deceased one, and whatever form—sister, mother, wife—the goddess, or her priestess, adopts, she is one and the same, so union with her automatically becomes sacred incest.

Bachofen, writing of Oedipus and his role in replacing preceding matriarchies, tells us that Oedipus is an "embodiment of the male fecundating principle ... prevailing in the tellurian sexuality of the swamp.... In this stage ... the mother is also seen as the wife, even as the daughter of the man who fecundates her: each generation of men in turn fecundates the maternal matter of earth."[24]

The life and education of the incestuous Vazkor (son) is largely constructed from sexual activity and relations with women.

Both Vazkor (father) and Laius are clearly unsuitable consorts for the great mother/goddess. Laius, already tarnished by a homosexual scandal, initially refuses sexual union with Jocasta; a single drunken episode produces Oedipus.[25] Uastis's son is born from a single loveless bid for power, and the narrative makes it plain that to love a woman would be entirely out of character for Vazkor (father). The murder/sacrifice is inevitable.

When Laius commands the death of his infant son, Jocasta ameliorates this to exposure and returns her son to the uncertain but still maternal mercies of Nature. The desertion of Tuvek (later also known as Vazkor) amongst the tribespeople also does this. The resemblance is also physical: Jocasta, meaning "Shining Moon," reflects the semi-albino Uastis.[26]

Jocasta was descended from the Spartoi, the "spurious" ones, who didn't know the identity of their fathers.[27] The Thebes of Jocasta's father was dedicated to the mother goddess. Jocasta's clasp indicates worship of the goddess. Creon rules in Thebes in his capacity as maternal uncle or brother to the priestess-goddess. All this indicates a lingering matriarchy. Only as a brother is the elder Vazkor able to claim authority over Uastis and become her husband. Her utter fury when she discovers his claim is false is explained in this light.

The Sphinx also has matriarchal origins. She derives from "...the winged Moon-goddess of Thebes ... to whom the new king offers his devotions before marrying her priestess, the Queen. But the Sphinx, overcome by Oedipus, killed herself, and so did her priestess Iocaste."[28] Graves continues: "Was Oedipus a thirteenth-century invader of Thebes who suppressed the old Minoan cult of the goddess...? Under the old system, the new king, though a foreigner, had theoretically been a son of the old king whom he killed and whose widow he married; a custom that the patriarchal invaders misrepresented as parricide and incest."

As lion and woman, the Sphinx merges magically with the natural world. Uastis's lynx mask associates her with the Egyptian great mother, Hathor, whose destructive aspect is lion-headed like the Sphinx. Vazkor confronts a snow-lion just before he finally meets his mother, evoking Oedipus's meeting with the Sphinx outside the gates of Thebes.

The plague of flies in Bar-Ibithni is unarguably Sophoclean. The Hessek witch rises from beneath the earth to punish those who worship only light and the sunlike, a Fury or primitive female power of death and Hades. Echoes of Jocasta's suicide also run right through *Birthgrave*, as Uastis is constantly tempted to kill herself by the evil priest who urges her to believe she is loathsome and guilty. Jocasta quietly hangs herself when convicted of incest—or, in another version, hurls herself off a cliff and into the sea like the Sphinx before her. But Uastis is drawn as if by instinct towards self-assessment as well as self-obliteration, and refuses to submit to her fate. Both heroines acquit themselves with dignity and an acceptance of personal liability, but where Jocasta removes herself from life, Uastis withdraws discreetly to a wilderness where the goddess can survive in peace. The sense of a possible return survives along with her. This is not the story of the triumph of patriarchy over matriarchy.

Sacred Places, Snakes and Masks

Sacred places proliferate in this sequence. Legend, myth and religion have always endowed certain places with special significance. A place may continue to resonate with particular events, and thus become "holy." The practice of building churches and temples on sites already sacred in earlier times is widespread.

Caves are often consecrated to birth, death and reincarnation, and associated with the great goddess, as at Eleusis, Delphi, Cumae and many other sites. In the *Birthgrave* sequence, rebirth, acquisition of powers, alterations in character, strange new realizations frequently take place in caves, tunnels or crypts. Uastis's awakening, her murder of Darak's betrayer and the killing of Vazkor and the boy-king all take place in caves and cellars. The goddess' temple at Ezlann is undermined with a labyrinth of passageways. Uastis passes through a "tunnel-womb" to a Stygian Water which brings her to death, resurrection and irrevocable change. As Demizdor sends Vazkor down the ancient tunnel called Worm's Way, knowing her own death will follow, the image is of a mother giving birth. Both Uastis and Vazkor are interred before they resurrect. The Hessek practice underground rites. Vazkor's transformation in the Wilderness takes place in a cave.

Other sacred spots traditionally lie in wild regions, often alongside springs or streams or in ruins or forest clearings. These may be designated "evil" places and be shunned by men, but Uastis, and Vazkor after her, come by power and knowledge in such locations and are instinctively drawn to them. Sometimes they provide sanctuary, as when Uastis is awaiting attack:

> "Don't worry that they'll come for you here...." He pointed to the leaning stones across the stream. "That place," he said casually, "an altar of sacrifice—old as the ravine itself. I've heard them say some black god or other still broods here...."

Alone in a forest clearing at night, Vazkor mixes dream and reality:

> A stream bubbled from the earth here, and some thousand or so years ago they had built a basin to receive it, and put a marble girl on the plinth above. I think she was the goddess of the stream or of the grove.... It must have been the time and the oldness of the wood, but I half got an idea that I should have her, that she would come off the plinth and put on flesh for me.

Unawares, Vazkor is glimpsing the goddess, and thus also his mother. This image of the goddess is gentle and beautiful, but she may equally well be savage. After leaving the tribe, Uastis bathes in a stream in company with a wildcat and sees a familiar mound of stones. She has returned to the same "altar of sacrifice—old as the ravine."

Bodies of water are also sacred, and, like springs and streams, the sea claims mysterious healing properties. Uastis describes the sea:

> ... the boiling cauldron, seething, limitless, seeming to curve with the round shape of the world, banded with every color of the changing sky.... I understood then that I had known the sea before.... Huanhad touched my shoulder softly.... "The sea," she whispered. "You will be better here."

Vazkor, at his first sight of the sea, finds a reflection of his own mental state: "I had reached the sea unexpectedly.... Like a sort of madness itself, it seemed to complement my own bewildered wandering ... like an oblique figment or expression of my mental process."

In sacred places beauty may fuse internal and external or mind and the natural world. Faint residues inhabiting places and things can evoke transpersonal memories linking past and present. Lee uses these motifs to make a psychic geography that maps ancestral traces. Alone near a bandit camp, Vazkor sees an apparition of Darak with his mother:

> I was waking up. Visions, truths, reverie, leading me back to consciousness and feeling, to involvement, to life, where, perhaps, I was reluctant to go.

Memories also linger in the many deserted cities of the trilogy. Hallucinations materialize amongst ancient ruins. Visiting a ruined city at night, Uastis has a vision of her people's past. "Dimly, softly, I heard their voices around me ... they had come, but only as ghosts. Many men and women, and their children, friends and lovers...."

The ancient road leading to Vazkor's city contains memories in its stones, causing dreams which are not personal to the dreamer. Sleeping beside a pool, Uastis dreams in the person of a male ancestor as he drowns and rapes a young girl. Understanding this as a historical event, she forbids her men to drink from the pool. As dreams begin to participate in history as well as myth, the two acquire a common, if chaotic, identity that is one of the essential characteristics of the epic.

Snakes are an insignia or even alternative form of the great goddess as Kundalini. Bringer of knowledge to the human race, symbol of reincarnation, the **snake or serpent** is ubiquitous in myth and religion. In a vision at another ruined city Uastis watches a woman perform an erotic dance with a snake. When a version of this dance is repeated at a banquet, she wonders, "Where had they got this ritual? Had they remembered it unknowing? Did the corruption still live in them?"

Amongst a primitive people, she also witnesses a ritual where young girls copulate with a huge lizard.

> It seemed I was looking into my past, or my future, or at a painted picture, which forever changed itself, and yet retained its basic elements ... pale hands reached for me and there was the old and ancient laughter of the dead who had not died, but lived on in the corruption of all who had come later.

This passage comments on how time may corrupt and debase mythological content. In the *Birthgrave* sequence, images of reptiles generally seem to represent the evil aspect of dead ancestors. Uastis's struggles conclude as she fights a giant lizard. In the Vis sequence, however, the snake will take on a different aspect.

Masks, or animal-headed gods, are familiar from carnivals, balls, pagan celebrations such as Halloween, and many events when an element of ritual or sacrifice is present. Torturers, executioners, inquisitors, klansmen, etc. are often masked.

Masks play a fundamental part in the *Birthgrave* sequence, but their role is especially important in the first book. Aristocratic city-dwellers wear masks that indicate position in an impersonal and hierarchical society. Metals—gold, silver or non-precious—signify rank, and different animals seem to signify differing character or function. Removal of a mask betokens respect.

With her face always hidden, Uastis is masked from herself; and before she is finally able to confront herself, she passes through several different stages of concealment. Before adopting the mask, she wears the shireen, or veil. This sinks her into an undifferentiated collective, appropriate to her youth and undeveloped sense of identity. By invoking tribal superstition she avoids exposing the face she believes to be that of a gorgon. When she puts on a mask she assumes a more specific outer identity or "persona." Masks represent artifice, not nature.

The elder Vazkor gives Uastis a mask representing a lynx. Until the moment when she drinks from a stream (cited above) alongside a big wildcat, the lynx seems to signify evil. After she pays her dues to nature by giving birth, and the penalty for hubris by a time of nameless slavery, she leaves the mask behind in the tribal camp. But it is a trace of herself and causes a breach between the young Vazkor and Tathra. It aligns him with Uastis when he chooses it from a huge hoard of treasure and suggests that he may not be Tathra's son. Later, Gyest makes a copy of the lynx mask as a meditational device to help Vazkor in his search for his mother.

Uastis is not masked for the blind Kotta, who sees in her, "Something I have not seen before. Put your hand into cool water when the day is hot. Beauty which is a fire and does not burn." But her vision is premature. Uastis will need more time before she can remove her mask and complete her task of self-discovery.

Hubris, Nature and the Goddess

Exhilarated by supernormal power, Uastis exclaims, "...I could defeat everything that troubled me, bit by bit, and by my own will alone. I *knew*.

Elation." She also immediately confesses to extreme stupidity. "Strange that when we feel we understand all things, we understand nothing." She is describing hubris—contempt for beings of unequal power—a failing custom-made to tempt immortal gods and goddesses as they choose between healing and killing.[29]

When Uastis avenges Darak's death she is barely aware of her magic powers and kills with hypnotism and a knife. This is not cold justice; it has an intensely physical, semi-involuntary quality.

> Within the icy shell a scarlet bird tapped its beak to be free... The shell burst, and it filled me, flowing warm and bright from my guts into my lungs, heart and brain; and from my brain into my arm, my hand, my knife.... It burst from my mouth in long bloody streamers of sound, and the horse, terrified, bolted.

Depletion and sickness follow excess. The aftermath of her rage leads her to take up the profession of healing. But when she kills again, the stakes have risen, and she makes deliberate use of supernormal powers. Uncontrollable fury grips her as, newly risen from the dead, she willfully destroys the guilty and innocent together. The atmosphere is charged with supernatural dread, and this time her surge of rage creates a kind of fusion between passion and hubris:

> I felt no compulsion, only great anger and great Power.... A white heat rose from my belly and filled my brain. I felt my skull would split open if I could not let it free. A blinding white pain gushed from my eyes.... I rose in the stirrups, my whole body arched and straining as I screamed after them the single word.

This mass killing causes her much retrospective remorse. Hubris apparently has damaging effects, and the cost is considerable. Her son, too, will be afflicted with loss of magical power and sickness after similar events:

> ... the murder had brought its own punishment. As if in the throes of some violent illness, I swung in my saddle, sick, half-blind, half-deaf, shaking uncontrollably, my body running, my clothes and my hair dank with icy sweat. But still the sense of Power; no defeat.

In spite of this experience, Uastis is intimidated by Vazkor.

> So he taught me—their customs, their beliefs, their dark dreamings, And he taught me how he would use me as the instrument of his power.... And he taught me to fear him too.

Perhaps her fear is partly an unwitting fear of hubris in herself, but even at her worst, when she has gained divine powers but no corresponding sense of responsibility, Uastis is never without human warmth, and as she develops the qualities of a goddess she also becomes less arrogant. Too human for a goddess, too powerful to be only human, Uastis is often an ambiguous figure, but the paradoxes of divinity become approachable in her. She is a white goddess, but also a black one. She heals and restores life as she kills and destroys and as mother goddess abandons her only child. Light enough to fly, she is also the subterranean goddess of caverns. Virginal and promiscuous, strong and fragile, human and divine, we hear echoes of her in many places.

A great goddess subsuming all goddesses exists in polytheistic religions, notably Hinduism. "Since Devi was the goddess *par excellence*, she accrued many different epiphanies. Each form of Devi had a somewhat different aspect or function...."[30] Devi is goddess of rivers, mountains, light, caves and darkness. Bringing fortune or misfortune, life and death, she is mother and mistress, warrior-maid and goddess of love. Karrakaz, the true name of Uastis, echoes Kurukulla, the South Indian goddess of caves, as also Kali and Kauri and other names too: Kybele, Kore, Keres...

Lee emphasizes this multiplicity without losing the single character. Uastis suffers much inner conflict, and her abilities fluctuate alarmingly. She is unreasonably weakened by her menstrual cycle. In pregnancy her magical powers disappear and only reappear after the birth. But, however preternatural, she remains within the scope of nature. Nature as seasonal cycle reflects the long dormant period that precedes her rebirth. Nature as science explains her revival when an influx of air results from an earth tremor. Giving birth expresses nature, but it also exercises the "divine" powers of regeneration and fertility. Nature equates readily with the goddess. It may even *be* the goddess.

In these ways a human Uastis can also be divine without perishing from hubris. Perceiving her powers as given by Nature, she can raise Fethlin from the dead without thought of personal power or glory. This moment contrasts sharply with her son Vazkor's raising of the empty, mindless corpse of Malmiranet from motives of personal aggrandizement: "No longer confined by the natural laws of the world. Now and again the whisper had come, and I had put it aside in fear. But I was beyond fear at last, and beyond half-doubt. Vazkor had mastered death."

Lee conceives of hubris as a humanly motivated disregard for "natural laws" and the attempted assumption of "divine" powers.

In subsequent texts Lee will often be busy with these themes.

—2—

VIS—RACE AND MYTH

The Storm Lord, Anackire, The White Serpent

History, Race, Myth and Hero: The Epic

With its sense of history paramount, the Vis trilogy has all the traditional components of an epic. The fates of nations depend upon heroic individuals who renew the legends of their forebears. Destiny outstrips personal desire. The goddess reaches down to intervene in the affairs of men and, if events demand it, walks the earth again. Wars—hearts too—may be won or lost according to transcendental designs. Private and public interests conflict in political alliances; strategic marriages override private loves; offspring fulfill divine intentions. Races, cultures and religions clash as the world is witnessed struggling to bring itself into balance.

This history of a continent centers on the dark, warlike Vis and the semi-albino, visionary race of Lowlanders, but lesser nations exemplify radical regional variations and cultures. Rituals and ruins disclose pre-histories, and animal remnants of an earlier evolutionary phase survive in remote jungles. The discovery of a forgotten sister continent illuminates developmental differences.

Each part of the sequence adopts a different perspective. **The Storm Lord** recounts the slow awakening of a non-violent and long-enslaved people as Raldnor, goaded by his conflicting, mixed race origins, leads an Amanakire rebellion. **Anackire** takes its title from the name of the goddess. Since she is life itself, this goddess requires nothing, and neither punishes nor rewards human actions. Sunk in pettiness and greed, people seldom understand her and look askance on her devotees. Her Lowland followers translate her dispassion into stoical acceptance of their own extermination. Eventually Anackire intervenes to halt war between nations. In a less classic mode, **The White Serpent** disgards former hierarchies. Interest shifts from hereditary royal rights to power struggles among more emancipated and common men. A world enlarged and sophisticated by population movement is seeking racial balance. Lee uses the device of the continuance of the reincarnated soul to slice through pretensions to racial purity and separateness.

The heroes of all these narratives have certain common features. Each is ignorant of his father's royal identity; each feels he does not belong where he is. Growing up amongst Lowlanders, Raldnor is isolated by his lack of telepathic abilities: "...he stood, unconscious and mute, on the fringe of their society, a tolerated idiot—outcast, not by them, but by his own deformity." Though he does eventually learn to use telepathic skills, as a boy he is also handicapped by his urgent sexual needs and ready anger; he is a warrior set down among mystical pacifists.

Rem is cruelly abused by his mother. Sensitive, solitary and marginalized by homosexuality, he becomes a soldier. He is subject to visions, but prefers to be flogged rather than confess to this aberration. Then, unexpectedly, he falls in love with the wife of his half-brother, the king. Finally, captured by the enemy, tortured and tipped into madness, he is restored by the goddess and lives to fulfill her designs.

Rehger does not endure such acute hardships. Though he is torn from his beloved mother in early childhood and sold as a slave, he comes to enjoy fortune and fame as a successful gladiator.[1] In the end, however, he remains the least realized of the three, spending only a short time pursuing his true vocation as an artist.

With all their differences, each of the men is born into the typical circumstances of the hero: "...the child of destiny has to face a long period of obscurity." On coming of age, he "may precipitate a considerable crisis.... Earlier patterns break to fragments or dissolve.... Yet after a moment of apparent havoc ... the world takes shape again ... crucifixion-resurrection can be illustrated either on the body of the hero himself, or in his effects upon the world."[2]

Raldnor is crucified upon his double heritage. To identify with one side is to betray the other. Consequently, he betrays both in turn. When he takes up service to Amrek, he "had lost half his blood, half his soul. The schism of divided race had finally resolved itself, and the Lowlander was eclipsed by the dark-haired man." When these same betrayals lead him to integrate the opposites in himself, they become the means through which he can unite opposed nations.

Lee does not, however, permit a simplistic outcome. A Lowland priest comments, "You have given us hubris.... You have hatched the serpent's egg.... But it is the double-edged sword. After you have taught us to be cruel, can you teach us to be humble once again...?" Raldnor replies with bitter, self-knowing humor, "I am the golem of the goddess."

Raldnor is a hero constructed by and for an era unquestioningly embedded in the divine. He never considers obstructing its purpose or putting his private concerns before those of destiny. Rem's situation is more complicated. Rejected by both parents, he is a perpetual outsider and object of mistrust. Accusations of conspiracy continue to hound him when he is united with his brother. Even after he is captured and tortured, he is still rumored to be in alliance with the enemy. He doubts himself profoundly, and doubts the goddess too. Entrusted with Ashni, the tiny incarnation of Anackire, the baby seems to him like "some purely spiritual hugeness, trapped there in the small and helpless shell"; and when she is stolen, he is prepared to spend some eight years searching for her. Yet later he tells himself that "he did not now believe in her anymore. He had no faith in her goddess."

In his moments of renegation, Rem briefly seems to resemble the enemy adventurer-king Kesarh, but, though a certain attraction exists between them, the two men are polar opposites. Where Rem lacks confidence in his own experiences, Kesarh negates spirit altogether. He fails to appreciate that the goddess has returned in the baby Ashni, where as Rem responds immediately to her. Kesarh craves worldly power, even if murder and treachery must be the means of securing it; Rem takes on the lineaments of the dead king Rarmon. Both men love intensely, but Kesarh's love for his sister causes her death. Rem's conversion from homoeroticism to the love of a woman is not a comment on sexuality or sexual politics but a turning towards a source of life.

This part of the trilogy reflects an era of diminishing spiritual certainty. The madness sent by Ashni to alleviate Rem's sufferings, or the mass hallucination through which total war is averted, reflect a new need for divine communication. Rem only becomes able to communicate properly with humans after his bout of divine madness.

Rehger's true identity is frustrated. In his career as a gladiator he only *performs* the hero. The days of the true epic hero are over: He can neither live out the old legend, nor take root in the new. He finds purpose only in the realization that he has no purpose: "...he had lost himself forever. Rehger, like Amrek, was gone into the past."

Neither Rehger nor his lover Aztira submit willingly to fate, and up to the last moment his personal will conflicts with the will of Anackire. Through their opposition to the will of the gods, a more modern perspective comes into play. Rehger's endless discontent reaches a point of spiritual crisis at the remote city of the Amanackire, where he sees there is nowhere further to go. He recognizes that "What had driven him was not pride or hate, or rage, or love. If he examined himself, it transpired that he had never validly undergone any of these states, these justifiable emotions of humankind." Aztira apparently also understands that the man she once preserved from his appointed death can get no further in his present lifetime. When she takes him to witness a reincarnation in progress, she is giving him the faith and courage to confront both death and the worst pain of subsequent rebirth. As he evaporates mysteriously from the pages, leaving only an empty boat behind, this disaffected and deeply skeptical man is giving himself up to life by the act of killing himself.[3]

Lee admits the difficulty of distinguishing between inheritance and reincarnation. And both possibilities may be painful to accept. Despite the bracelet of scales that marks out certain of Amrek's descendants, Safca expresses doubts that she is his daughter. When she refers to the mark on her wrist as "the curse of Anackire," Yannul comments, "Maybe it wasn't a curse. Only an emblem. It hasn't harmed you. Could Amrek have misunderstood?" Some physical characteristics bear clear witness to past incarnations. The rare crimson hair of Astaris also adorns Val Nardia, the mother of Ashni. Manifestations of Anackire are recognized by their white hair and a face that some statues of the goddess represent exactly.

As faces or physiques of kings reappear, they do not signify that moral character will be repeated, but there are often residues. Looking back, it becomes clear that, as a thwarted sculptor, Rehger has something in common with Amrek, a man also forced into an unsuitable role and made king through the machinations of his mother. Rehger has also inherited some aesthetic sensibility from him. Amrek's death becomes retrospectively poignant: looking at the snake which wraps itself about him, he asks, "How can I fear this thing? ... Something so beautiful." Even Amrek's father, Amnorh, is perversely expressing a love of beauty in the women he collects for his underground Bluebeard's gallery.

But Lee's heroes in this sequence are merely mortal and will serve only their given time. Sometimes they are permitted to return into the obscurity of ordinary life. Even Raldnor, who has been an "icon" and a "god," declines to be king and escapes the people who do not want "to see a god reduced." When he finds Astaris, they slip away "like peasants" into the forest together. Lee interprets this departure in explicit terms: "...it was not legend, but the forests that had swallowed them. Though it was legend that would preserve their names thereafter."

The true reality lies in what goes unremarked by the world at large. In *Anackire*, Rem's heroic deeds are not conducted in the public eye, and his Zakorian torturers are careful to leave his face undamaged so that he remains usefully recognizable. He has not become an icon, and thus takes on the throne without the handicap of being likened to a god. The child that Aztira conceives before Rehger's departure is, "A covenant between your race and mine. Between reality and hubris." Panduv's tiny infant will grow up to become a sculptor and Rehger's second chance. In time, human desires will escape from divine intentions. Epic reality will pass away.

Women, Mothers and the Goddess

Women are major influences on the three heroes, and, for good or ill, they all have formative relations with their mothers.[4] It takes much of his lifetime for Rem to recover from his mother's malice and abuse. When he is taken to her house after his nearly fatal flogging, he falls to his knees and vomits at her feet, as if to a venomous goddess. He is only reconciled with her in a posthumous vision, a moment so important it coincides with the restoration of his sanity. Raldanash, Raldnor's other son, is so exclusively mother-identified he forbids the naming of children after his father. Despite intense hatred for her, Amrek also is obsessed with his cruel and dominating mother. Relations with Val Mala seem to be at the root of his attempt to exterminate the Amanackire.

But this wicked queen is also shown to be a childhood victim of "the sexual customs of her house." The text often illustrates abuse or exploitation with images of dolls. By painting her face a blank white, Val Mala is not only imitating Anackire, she is deliberately making herself into a doll, and is on several occasions compared to one. Astaris, mute until Raldnor can coax her into communication, seems "like a puppet moving very gracefully on strings." The heroic Raldnor becomes "an icon" and Rehger, burnished and gladiatorial as he models for a statue of Rarmon, is also an object of spectation. Lowland women, sent to a Vis banquet in order to kill the invading soldiers, are "rag-dolls." Amnorh creates a secret museum of dead-in-life doll-women. "You pack me off, maybe to my death, like a doll you are tired of," says Kesarh. His sister replies, "...that's how you think of me...."

But neither Tibo nor Panduv are in the least doll-like. Practical, undeceived and powerful mothers, they put the welfare of their children before ordinary notions of morality. They lie eagerly to protect their sons, and Tibo, effecting justice, avenges the selling of Rehger by pushing her brother-in-law off a cliff. When she turns to the goddess to support her at her trial, her expectations are honored. The heated statue of Cah produces no incriminating burn as she lays her hand upon its foot, and from this moment the goddess endows her with special powers. Raldnor's foster-mother is another anchoring maternal presence; relations between Yannul's Lowland wife and her sons are loving and kind; the simple Berinda, with her houseful of happy children, is an exemplary good mother.

But though the goddess has common features with positive mothers, her cult may also produce jealous children. Rem's road back to the city is blocked by a group of Amanackire. The reconciliation of nations and the recognition that Anackire transcends divisions between both men and gods is already developing weak spots. Rarmon (Rem) "...disliked them, so cold so pale. Not Lowlanders anymore, but something novel and quite alien.... They did not care for him either, or that he, not they, had wedded the psychic storm. They jealously wanted to be gods, gods in the ancient manner: Men who were paranormally superior to, and held sway therefore over, other men."

Lee's phrase "gods in the ancient manner" is clipped: compatible with rationalist thought, yet simultaneously including the transcendental. But the seeds of *The White Serpent* are already sprouting, the Amanackire are already manifesting hubris and people in the city are "everywhere discussing the wonders of gods and sorcery, and everywhere ignoring them. Trade and commerce flourished." The sacred prostitutes or Daughters of Anackire go about "bare-breasted, their nipples capped and rimmed by gilt, gold in the yellow veils of their skirts, their hair bleached, topaz in their ears and navels...." They contrast sharply with Anackire's daughter, Ashni, emerging naked from the wild: "...the little breasts had blossomed on her ... whiter than the albino wolf ... a diadem of flowers on her head ... the fey, unhuman child."

But Anackire is not a god; she is a first principle from which nothing is excluded. Anackire is Nature, and human extrapolations proceed "from a unique source of being that transcends and reconciles all polarity."[5] As humans perceive Anackire in the form of a goddess, or perhaps in a handmaiden or priestess, each person's perceptions are different. A lady-in-waiting is puzzled as she tends Ashne'e who seems too frail to give birth yet possesses power she is unable to refuse. A hill-woman takes Ashni for a nature-spirit when she appears as a mute child-goddess and wordlessly requests to be taught "to be human." Safca, who buys her as a slave, becomes deeply attached to her and is taught to play with the snakes which filled her ancestor Amrek with such excessive horror. She learns to listen to "the element which was mother and teacher to the lesser element" (i.e., to the presence of Anackire in herself), and when Ashni is sold to a trader, Safca recognizes exactly who she has been harboring. In turn, the trader faints from the sheer intensity of his ecstasy when she reveals a little part of her divinity to him.

The mystic Raldanash sees the full range of her different aspects.

> He had already learned without tuition, all she was, or all that he could understand she was. The soul of Raldnor's daughter in an envelope of flesh ... growing to the likeness of a young woman.... Her consciousness was older. Older even than itself.... She began to talk to him.... In the end he knew death as a little thing, and in the end also ... he was not amazed or discomposed to find Ashni as she really was, a summer being limned by gold, taller than heaven where the stars were branching in her hair, her eyes like suns, her plated tail coiled with a wonderful economy.... Ashnesea, Ashkar, Anackire.

When finally the epiphany of the incarnate goddess comes to an end and Ashni departs the world of men, the event is watched by a peasant priest. Through this eminently sane person we glimpse the goddess at her most accessible, an Ashni who is not the special property of heroes or kings.

> The jargon of the priests—the transcension, the chariot of flame that takes the god into heaven ... miracles are nothing—... there's the fact beyond the miracle ... what we are and must become....

As he cooks his mundane breakfast sausage, he sees that she is gone: "She was gone to be a peasant in Thaddra, or to run with wolves./ He grinned at the sky, crying with joy./ 'And yet,' he said, 'Ashni, you are also the Morning Star.'"[6]

Of course, Nature or Anackire also possesses a terrible aspect. Her fearful interventions appear mostly in the effects of weather and natural disasters. There are several earthquakes, not only the strategically decisive one that gives victory to Raldnor and is definitively an act of the Goddess, but a lesser tremor that throws Raldnor and Astaris into each other's arms. The tidal wave that wipes out Saardsinmey is a disaster on a scale with the miracle of the vast suspended wave against which visions of the many gods of Vis appear to the different nations assembling for battle.

Nor does Anackire preserve her earthly ministers from suffering, though she may sometimes provide them with the means to endure it, as when she eases Rem's pain with madness. Her little handmaiden, Anici, is apparently sacrificed to waken Raldnor's conscience. Kesarh's sister kills herself in shame at the incest that fulfills the Goddess's purpose. Even someone like Amnorh, who believes he can cheat the Goddess, is unwittingly carrying out her designs. When Ashne'e takes him into a cave to see the eight-armed statue of Anackire, he recognizes what each one represents: "The arm of deliverance and the arm of protection, of comfort and of blessing, and also those terrible arms of retribution, destruction, torment and the inexorable curse." Yet he still steals gold and jewels from the Goddess and, along with them (and unawares), an invisible burden of "spiritual wealth" that makes him into a twisted devotee of Anackire and the means by which Raldnor and Astaris can depart the public stage.

During the big earthquake the same statue is dislodged by underground water pressure and projected through the air on the crest of a water spout. In a semi-comic excess of showmanship, this flying Anackire incites a terrified mob to wholesale religious conversion, though they only perceive "the eight *maledictions* of her arms...." In their reading of the natural phenomenon of an earthquake as a preternatural force, Lee sets up a paradox that straddles the deeper and undisturbed mystery of Anackire's power.

As in *Birthgrave*, certain sites are specifically sacred. Forest devotees of the Goddess on the sister continent live in utmost simplicity, naked, eating berries and fruit, engaging in healing and telepathy; but in Ankabek, the island temple of Anackire, magic is practiced among formal rituals. These variations in local belief and practice also serve the secular aspect of the narrative by revealing people through them. When a Vis man finds a Lowland girl making offerings to the goddess Corrah, he says in amazement, "The worshipper of Anack the Serpent goes to the dirt-heap of the unbeliever to *offer*.... And won't the snake woman enviously strike at you for it?" The Lowland girl replies, "Anackire has no jealousy.... Anackire is the name we give the State of Life, of existence, body and soul, earth and eternity. But you give it the name *Corrah*." The man protests that, in her system of belief, Corrah does not exist. The girl continues, "All things exist. Look at that pebble lying there. You might call it *um* and I might call it *oom*. Isn't it still a pebble, and lying there?" Though offerings are not required by Anackire, the girl politely offers to Corrah because she is a goddess who expects offerings.

Summoned to Ankabek, Kesarh is deeply skeptical, and even after witnessing a miracle he tells the priest, "I don't value your religion." Rem's experiences there are entirely different. Though he is deeply uneasy and still regards the visions to which he is prone as shameful, the place itself opens unexpected possibilities. He is attracted but convinced that "They would not let him in. He was neither worshipper nor acolyte." But the doors swing open before him and he remembers "what they said of the goddess. Seek Her, you will find Her. Seek Her not, She is not." Overwhelmed with visions and taken to the chamber of the goddess, he expects punishment. "It occurred to him that he expected punishment in every avenue of life ... this might be a fatal flaw." He begins to see himself, and "some part of Rem told him he had already seen Her, long ago, far away. Before he was even born." Religious experience is not restricted to the individual perceptions of a single lifetime.

The goddess is indisputably situated in cycles of reincarnation. A priestess, about to propose a mass-suicide before murderous pirates can reach Ankabek, makes an explicit speech to her community. "Death is not death. So the rituals of the goddess have taught us. Dying is only change. The flesh is left upon the ground. The spirit is born again out of the husk. And this She has taught us by her symbol and her image which is the snake, who, casting its skin, pours from the husk alive, that we may know we too shall live beyond a cast-off skin, alive and beautiful as the stars."

Lee also includes more disbelieving analyses. Rehger prevents his father from killing the political agent who is about to forcibly enlist him, saying, "He didn't owe his death to me, or to you." Yennef replies, "*Lowlander* talk. Repayments for past lives? Debts for future ones?"

The Amanackire, in relation to death, "did not mourn. Ruthless in their faith and pitiless, certain all men lived forever. What was death? Having only just participated in the lesson, they had missed it. Physical life was also sacred, and to be saved."

The process of rebirth seems full of pain, far less gentle than death. Though Raldnor draws Astaris back into life with comparative delicacy, he is haunted by an image of her disintegration: "She raised her arms, and long cracks appeared in her body—ink lines on amber. Then she crumbled all at once in blazing ashes, and the ashes blew away across the moon."

Aztira describes the procedure at length:

> I shrieked and rent myself with my nails. I didn't know my name or Who—or *what* I was. I thought myself an animal, a fish, a serpent.[7]
> I thought that life was death.... The body weighs like lead. To breathe is to suffocate. Anguish, agony. To die is better.

The Amanackire have Nietzchean ambitions to usurp the powers of godhead.[8] Rehger addresses his resurrected lover as "The Goddess Aztira." "We are gods," she confirms, as she describes the almost limitless powers that the Amanackire will achieve before their eventual downfall. She also insists that he "must be got out of this unclean, sorcerous city." She tells him, "It's said we were winged ... that we rode ... in chariots like stars, and will reclaim many kingdoms ... until ... our wings are broken and our season finished.... We are gods. But Anackire is not a god. Anackire is everything, and of this the gods are only part."

Anackire appears in many more forms than the more specific goddess of *Birthgrave*. Ashni is Ashtoreth or Ishtar, meaning "star." She emerges in the black goddess Cah as a male fire and sea god and as the double-sexed deity Zarok-Anackire. When Raldanash finds "himself in conversation with the goddess," she defines herself:

> I am the symbol and the name. In Omnos I am Zarok. In Zakoris I am Zarduk and Rorn. Outside the world, I am all others. In sleep, the dream. Beyond death, the emblem of awakening.

But she trims her definitions to suit their recipients. The non-mystical Rem needs to believe in a divinity that trails clouds of plain humanity. Ashni tells him, "men themselves are gods. But, fearing their own greatness, they send it from them to a distance, and must give it other names." Far off in Zor, Safca dreams of "a pillar of light which did not burn," and Lur Raldnor in the Lowland city dreams "of a black monster and a red, and Rem in the midst of fire, and his face was a screaming skull."

As history and religion overlap again and again, the reader begins to see a degree of interchangeability.

> In the beginning, which was before the beginning as they remembered it, the people of this continent had been universally white-skinned and pale—Lowlanders. But the Vis races ... had come. The pale races had already sunk from their personal apex. It seemed they had been witches, but had abused the gift, which finally withered. They gave in to the invaders, who in turn gave in to their own weakening.

Religion is equally subject to cyclical and evolutionary forces.

"Yannul wanted to laugh with anger. He was close to weeping, too. The supernal authority which had picked him up and flung him through the mirror of destiny, that monster clutched him yet, had never let him go, or any of them, live or dead."

His experience is the reverse side of a particularly memorable prayer to Anackire: "Not what I lack, nor what I desire. Give me only what I am."

In reality, there is no other option.

—3—

THE FLAT EARTH —MORTALS AND IMMORTALS

Night's Master, Death's Master, Delusion's Master, Delirium's Mistress, Night's Sorceries

---

Space, Time and Storytelling

Lee plants the inhabitants of Flat Earth, human and otherwise, in a consistent and self-conscious fiction. They comment lengthily and often comically on the nature of reality, time, space and sundry philosophical issues. They may also suffer the logical consequences of their views. As stories rather than histories are repeated self-reflexively throughout the texts, belief gains new prominence. "Storytellers," a chapter in *Delusion's Master*, details how a disguised Azhrarn, who corrects a garbled story about himself (originally an event in *Night's Master*), sparks a heated discussion about belief among a group of pilgrims and is accused of blasphemy.[1] A story has implications beyond itself.

This sequence is sometimes compared with *The Arabian Nights*, a text that also gives weight to story—keeping death at arm's-length—but Lee's storyworld has no external point of reference or Scheherazade. Lee makes the four corners of her little earth—or playroom—into a space able to include a cosmos simply by invoking the fastidious logic of play.[2] Earth, the divine and demonic realms of Upperearth, and Underearth and Death's kingdom of Innerearth all operate within their own continuums, as a welter of humans, demons, djinns, gods all interact according to their different natures. Fluent and contradictory, Azhrarn's lives and deaths evoke both Christ and Ahriman, Dionysos and any dying god. Lee's references come from all points of the compass. Myth, religion, folk and fairytale merge into pure story. Repeated themes and the echoes or continuing presences of certain characters provide a pathway through extreme complexity. The interconnected stories in *Night's Master* become continuous narratives in *Death's Master*, *Delusion's Master* and *Delirium's Mistress*, reverting again to stories loosely connected to the preceding material in *Night's Sorceries*. *Night's Master* centers on Azhrarn, demon ruler of Underearth. His dark beauty is irresistible to both men and women, and he itches to meddle in their affairs. As much a prototype of a child as of the son-god Dionysos, he is sexually fluid, seemingly semi-androgynous and somewhat polymorphously perverse.[3] Self-obsessed and willful, his consuming curiosity about humankind overrides concern for the consequences of his actions. He adopts a beautiful mortal baby, who grows up to become his willing catamite. But the boy pines for the sun, which is fatal to Azhrarn. Granted a day on the Earth's surface, Sivesh responds ardently to Earth and Azhrarn jealously brings about his death. The other key element in this book is Azhrarn's death, volunteered to save the world from itself. Azhrarn overflows with contradictions.

Death's Master tells the childhood stories of Simmu and Zhirem, abandoned in a monastic orphanage where they form an intense friendship. Simmu has the same apricot-colored hair as Sivesh. Rendered amoral by years spent among the magical Eshva women of Underearth, he understands animal speech, can change fluidly from one sex to the other and has a profound love of beauty. The dark-haired Zhirem, emotionally maimed by immersion in the fires of invulnerability, is his opposite—fixed and withdrawn by nature. When they grow up, Simmu, helped by Azhrarn, founds a city of immortals but becomes despairingly bored there. Left behind, Zhirem changes himself into Zhirek, an evil magician. When they meet again, Zhirek condemns Simmu to endless torture in the flames of invulnerability and retreats into a crevice in a desert rock. Simmu is eventually rescued by Azhrarn and becomes an Eshva. A sometimes kindly figure of Death also wanders in and out of the narrative, a reminder that death is less perverse than human desire.

In *Delusion's Master*, attraction and opposition between Azhrarn and his red-haired "unbrother," the Lord of Madness, cause large-scale disturbances.

Azhrarn falls in love with Dunizel, a half-mortal woman, who gives birth to a daughter. Dunizel is killed when Chuz sends a horde of pilgrims mad, and Azhrarn declares immortal enmity. As Chuz tries to entice her away, Azhrarn removes his baby daughter to his kingdom.

Delirium's Mistress is Sovaz, the daughter Azhrarn pointedly renames Azhriaz. She lies entranced in an enchanted palace but continues to grow in her sleep. Disguised in the person of a mortal youth, Chuz manages to gain access and elopes with her. Azhrarn tracks them down and challenges Chuz to take his punishment, which is to become mad himself. Chuz deserts Azhriaz. She follows after him, then accepts her fate as Azhrarn's earthly minister, a beautiful, terrible, deeply sad Goddess. Angered, the gods of Upperearth send three mindless angels to destroy her, but Azhrarn arranges her escape and wrestles with one of the angels until the fatal moment of sunrise. His body is left lying in a cave in Underearth. Azhriaz flees off the edge of the world into chaos and returns with the mind of the child her early circumstances had disallowed. The angels abandon their murderous mission. Later, Soveh-Azhriaz again meets her lover, Chuz, but decides to become mortal. She grows into an ancient wise-woman and is finally reconciled with her father. Of an evening, the ageless immortals Azhrarn, Chuz, Fate and Death come to visit the ancient, mortal woman who has become the "mother" of them all.

Only one story in *Night's Sorceries* does not fit retrospectively among the earlier texts. Chuz and Soveh are reborn into a much later world, the girl with marigold hair and the slightly mad prince, dark and handsome. This time their happiness seems lasting.

Flat as a map of itself in its illusory space, this earth is small and stylized, mock-heroic rather than heroic. Lee's torrent of narrative abounds with poetic conceits and verbal plays. The language is highly patterned. Comment that a first person narrator might have provided now drops with deliberate artifice from the lips of an author who subverts the immediate "reality" of the story by making her presence consciously felt.

The fictional storytellers who wander through these books are less random than they may seem at first. A dead father takes the form of a dilapidated vagrant to tell his son a story that guides him to save himself. Stories develop an almost physical presence ("stories gathered around her like flocks of birds"), many belonging to our own childhood as much as to the Flat Earth. Fairytales pop up at will. A Sleeping Beauty lies unconscious in the daughter of the Demon; a happy accident appends the identity of Cinderella to a simple peasant girl.

The Flat Earth is a tiny-seeming stage, put together with delicate exactitude. The precise location of a potential leak from the heavenly cistern of immortality may be pinpointed. This earth can be compacted into a single drawing. "The desert became a tawny chart, where features were marked in blots and smudges ... poured to the horizon." Simmu's dainty model of the Flat Earth uses the author's own technique—by reducing scale it creates a peculiar coexistence of both distance and proximity:

> The huge board counterfeited the earth, seas of blue glass scales, land masses cut from the polished wood of many trees, with mountains upraised and here and there painted with crystal snows. Cities were modeled on the board too, miniature but marvelous, while ships the size of beetles sailed the glass oceans.

Spatial paradoxes proliferate in the sequence. The little, measurable earth is sandwiched between heaven and hell. Though heaven has the atmosphere of a convent parlor, and hell, like a cowboy town, seems to have only one main street, ideas, emotions, characters are not correspondingly reduced. Nor is scale the only means of dislocating everyday perceptions. The sequence spans millennia, not years. Through constant juxtapositions and exchanges between the timescales of the spirit and human worlds, Lee dissolves all normal sense of time. Azhrarn may visit the human world—though only by night, since sunlight is fatal to him—but the time that has meanwhile passed in Underearth is of quite a different order. A human child, Sivesh, growing up in Underearth is visited by Azhrarn, "who would stay only for a second, glance smiling down at him and then be gone."

Lee explains: "The time of demons did not at all resemble human time. By comparison, a mortal life flashed by like the span of a dragonfly. Therefore while the Prince of Demons went about his midnight business in the world of men and out of it, the child glancing up, seemed to see the man in the inky cloak only once or twice a year, while Azhrarn had perhaps gone to the nursery, as it were, twice a day."

Uncoupled by this "as it were," the text breaks free of the lingering constraints of the time and space which normally organize reality. As even the present moment grows mercurial, longer-term time is open to speculation and reverie. Azhrarn can say to his dead lover's soul, "Many thousand mortal years have passed since I parted from you. Why do you seek me now?" And among the remote and supercilious gods, time has virtually disintegrated. They "had gone on in their timeless, inanimate contemplation of infinity.... At some hour in the Future, or in that timelessness of Upperearth, the Past, these ethereal beings would consign the whole of earth to death, ... once before (or in years to come) they had grown irritated and had opened the valves that held back the rain. They had drowned the earth in a flood...."

Whilst time in this disconnected and little visited heaven passes in unalterable calm, time in Underearth passes in animated chaos, punctuated by forays into the more brief and vulnerable but equally frenetic time of earth. Chronology is further unsettled by constant variation of pace.

Recurrence, however, has a stabilizing effect. Known by his black skin and white garments, Death's proximity is evoked before the catastrophe of Baybhelu by Nemdur's wife. "When Nemdur's dark wife came, walking with white gauze upon her fragrant somber skin ... the glimmer of the lamp made her lovely face into an ebony skull." The amber-haired Sivesh drifts in and out of the person of Simmu. The blurring becomes explicit when the text refers to "a beautiful boy, Sivesh, or as some say, Simmu."

Lesser persons and events also resonate through the texts. Zoryas, father-identified, daughter of a king, in love with power and her own beauty, prefigures the strident and masculine queen Narasen, the mother of Simmu, who supplants Death in his own kingdom and, later still, comes to be an object of worship in a city of ghouls ("It is maintained that some of them worshipped Naras, Queen Death...").

As characters become increasingly interchangeable, their recycled stories ambiguously suggest reincarnation. Sivesh, transported to the Underearth, pines for the sunlit world; Simmu, placed among humans, is in love with the demon world as if obscure memories of a past lived there draw him inexorably into the embraces of Azhrarn.

As the sequence progresses, time grows ever more densely overlaid with itself, and characters become more profoundly marked by their own (or others') pasts. Though this earth may be flat, the narrative moves in the round, constantly circling back to its own beginnings. In stories of demons and humans, identities and powers merge more thoroughly in each subsequent "incarnation." Humans, though always fallible and given to error ("They had got the story wrong again, and wrongly they would tell it for a number of years to come") are also empowered by the accretion of stories until they gradually become almost equal to the immortals who meddle with them. At first, immortal Death, Darkness, Fate and Madness were able to play, unscathed, with the lives of men; at last, they pay their respects to a prodigiously old and mortal woman.

Nature, Knowledge and the Demon

Azhrarn's ambivalent and unpredictable nature is balanced by his relations with nature, either human nature or Nature itself. When the immortal Lord of Darkness first dies and comes to life again, he conforms to seasonal cycles and passes through a vegetal episode as a tree, which an Eshva-woman replants in suitable conditions:

"At once the tree thrust its roots into the fruitful soil. Jaseve[4] became aware that they were in a forest ... the boughs knotted so intense and dark ... no speck of sunlight could get in, even at high noon."

After his second death, he also regenerates slowly in the quiet darkness of a cave.

On the only occasion when Azhrarn creates a person, he chooses to make her from a flower. His response to natural beauty is often a turning point in the narrative. Seven fair sisters[5] restore him to the living world with their midnight dances, and when Azhrarn perceives the reunion of a soul split into separate male and female parts, he offers his blessing, because, "They were beautiful as two things can only be beautiful which flawlessly make one whole thing...." In the androgyne, symbol of completeness, the true nature of the pair is restored. The ideal is neither male nor female but balance. "The imbalance of both, counterweighted by the other, had become the most exact of all balances. Negative aligned with positive.... Iron was silk; silk was iron." Structure is as important as appearance in this aesthetic of nature.

Even the little silver whistles with which Azhrarn's favorites can summon him have odd natural shapes, "the thigh bone of a hare" or "the head of a serpent." Lee, however, mildly informs us, "It was never wise to ask a boon of a demon." The outcomes of bargains made with Azhrarn correspond with his tricksterish nature, not with human hopes. When an old witch wants her youth restored, he says, "though I will not give you your youth, I will see to it you grow no older..." and strikes her dead. Even Zorayas, who cunningly tricks Azhrarn into outstaying the fatal moment of sunrise, is successfully bought off because Azhrarn senses her weakness: Underneath her armor she is badly disfigured. He transforms her into a woman so beautiful that even he is left "smiling still that what he had created seduced him."

Nor are the aloof, seemingly asexual gods immune to Azhrarn's nature. When he penetrates their heaven, he rouses the butterflies which "at some astonishing metaphysical revelation within themselves ... would flutter from their crystalline robes and dissolve like bubbles in the blue, blue air...." He also marks out their territory and its ultimate symbol as his own: "...he came to the Well of Immortality, and he spat in it. And such was the nature of Azhrarn, that the leaden water roiled, and for a moment grew clear and bright, before the greyness overcame it once again."

The prospect of human intrusion, which threatens, "Sweat and blood and shouting on the frigid blue pastures, horsedung about the harpstring palaces...," is worse still, and the tower of Baybhelu is toppled before it can touch heaven. But demon nature is never inert. A demon's deepest fear, his "cold dream," is boredom, and he seeks constant engagement. The poet sings, "We are your plaything, your amusement.... Without man on earth ... the time of the Demon Lord would hang heavy indeed." As for the Eshva, their lesser mischief is "merely the correct order of things."

However, when Azhrarn, to whom hate "had been a familiar, a beautiful harp which might be played, a skill, a jest," sees it is destroying the human world, a different aspect of his nature emerges and he offers himself as an object of sacrifice. He is always contradictory. His smile is "cruel and therefore full of a wonderful tenderness"; and "an artist in his vengeance...," he will later desire to be revenged upon the ungrateful world. When he asks Dunizel, "Tell me then my nature," her reply makes reference to nature, "Cruel, so cruel, so cruel.... Relentless, terrible. Your wish to cause pain like pain itself. Deeper than night, colder than winter, no more to be turned aside than the moon's rising."

Dunizel understands that pain will accompany Azhrarn's love.[6] All things need their opposite and counterbalance. As she inscribes on a wall of the holy city, "The bitterness of joy lies in the knowledge that it cannot last. Nor should joy last beyond a certain season...."

Bisuneh is shocked to discover the common identity of lover and tormentor when Azhrarn attempts to seduce her in the shape of the man she is to marry. Initially deceived, she suddenly sees "beyond the eyes, beneath them, surfacing as a black shark surfaces from the waters of an innocent sea, another pair of eyes looked down on her, invincible and wide."

But, startlingly, Dunizel, on first seeing Azhrarn, softly laughs.

> "Forgive me," said she. "I knew also your appearance would be godlike, and that you would be handsome. But now I see that your beauty is like the heartbeat of the earth."

Clearly, few people know Azhrarn as he "truly" is. Claims to knowledge of him appear with officious regularity: He is a hideous beast, a monster inhabiting the darkness.[7] He is the cause of all wickedness. Dunizel's instinctive insight into his nature so exceeds his own self-understanding that she risks angering him. Azhrarn, in fact, energetically resists self-awareness and thus is at the mercy of everyone's projections. Ordinary men and women are bedazzled and either misinterpret what they have experienced or tell deliberate lies. He shatters their illusions and, shape-shifter incarnate, disrupts their faith in their safely predictable gods.

Lee shrouds Azhrarn in a certain aura of mystery. His internal life is obscure, and the text makes comments such as, "what he thought no man knows...," or, "Who can guess his mood?" or, more expansively than usual of his rejection by mankind, "it must have hurt him very much." His unguarded moments are fleeting. When a goat follows him and is eaten by a lion, Azhrarn looks back over his shoulder "with a cruel pity, an ironic, sympathetic merciless regret." But humans bury his nature under a heap of theories concerning his motives and character. Even when his early deeds have become legend, indecision and speculation persist, and Oloru (a mortal form of Chuz) recounts stories of Azhrarn like theological debates. He doubts if his unbrother's little silver whistles "could summon him if truly he would not be summoned. Nor must he definitely grant wishes at the summons. Nor could such as he be made a fool of.... Unless he had desired the novelty, desired dangers and a snare to befall him."

The demon is further veiled by people's ritual avoidance of his name. He is referred to as "the Black Jackal, the Master of the Night." Moreover, "When they spoke this way they spat afterwards to clear the words from their mouths...." But no amount of avoidance can dispel his presence. When he is absent from the text, we continue to read it in his shadowy light.[8] Symbol of wickedness, he is an endless, unacknowledged undercurrent. When Azhrarn tells the story of his own life and death, many of the pilgrims feel "...a bizarre welling of guilt, of shame and fear."

Perhaps Azhrarn's most dangerous property is that he might be the serpent in the garden who provides knowledge of man's true nature. When he appears to Bisuneh in the form of a woman, he says to her, "I hear you fear men." She asks who he is, despite "knowing somewhere deep within herself and failing to comprehend her own knowledge." When he appears to a crowd in rapidly transmuting forms, each person sees him *according to their own nature*. At first he appears as the primal forces of nature. He is an "inky wind ... a pillar of smoke ... a stormcloud ... a tremendous lightning flash." Then, as if in an exotic evolution, "out of the lightning flew a black gull on blade-like wings...," which becomes in turn an eagle, a dragon, a wolf, a black dog, a panther, a jaguar, which "grew the slim waist and rounded hips of an amphora, the full breasts of a courtesan, a woman's face, lovely beyond reckoning, with smiling lips and an ocean of black hair.[9] And then she too transmuted, and each one who stood, or kneeled or cowered before the metamorphosing force, beheld someone familiar to himself, a wife, a brother, a neighbor or a child."

Some of these forms, such as lightning or a panther, are specially associated with Dionysos, who, like Azhrarn, transforms all those who come into contact with him. This demon lover is not specific to the female psyche.[10] "Mortals did not refuse Azhrarn. His voice, his eyes, his touch produced an alchemy that thrilled their nerves, infatuated them ... outlawed their wills...."

In the forbidden region of Underearth, nothing is forbidden. The rank and file of demons also "did not adhere only to a single road, a solitary room in a vast treasure store. The delightful door of one chamber led into another."

But such polymorphous pleasures can be dangerous to men. When Azhrarn finally displays himself without disguise to the pilgrims, appearing "as his own people saw him.... Each felt a terror then that was not exactly terror, a pleasure that was not at all pleasure."

Opposites Attract

Death's Master examines the childhood origins of eroticism and the later conflicts that arise from it. The opposing forces of Eros and Thanatos—otherwise Love and Death, or Pleasure and Pain—are personified in Simmu and Zhirem. The love between them has no ulterior motive and springs solely from their natural polarity as opposite aspects of a single thing. As they grow up, their closeness becomes an intense sexual attraction for Simmu, and intense opposition to it on the part of Zhirem.

Despite Simmu's habit of slipping from one gender into the other according to occasion, the two appear mainly as male. Fluid of gender and semi-androgynous, Simmu is at ease with the erotic; but Zhirem no longer remembers the hideously damaging torture that has turned into self-disgust and the desire for an abstract, disembodied purity. The flame of invulnerability makes him untouchable also, and he helplessly associates love with hate, pain and death.

But libidinal instincts persist, even after the repression of them has itself been repressed, and the repression of sexuality induces sadism and guilt. Viewed as the source of the Fall, sexuality is the original sin and introduces death into the world. A misogynistic linking of love and death is commonplace among erotically repressive religions. Though the link between love and death is also part of goddess religions, in this context it signifies the cyclical processes of nature and frequently suggests the possibility of renewal or reincarnation.

Lee's moral evaluations depend upon circumstance and are neither rigid nor polarized. "Evil" might be inseparable from "good," or a necessary stage in a larger scenario; wholeness probably means more than "evil." Her characters enact their own particular parts in an endless struggle to recognize and reconcile opposites. Heaven and Hell both require proper representation: "Without Contraries, is no progression. Attraction and Repulsion Reason and Energy, Love and Hate are all necessary to human existence."[11]

Lee, like Blake in this respect also, clearly sympathizes with the rebel individual. The "breaker of chains" may be of either sex; Dunizel's rebellion is made more extreme by the fact that she belongs to a celibate religious order and yet conceives Azhrarn's child.

The struggle for reconciliation also emerges in the construction of character. Zorayas, who takes up the practice of black magic to compensate for disfigurement, has much in common with the untouchable Zhirem. Both experience great pain and are persecuted for their difference. The situation of Zorayas is sympathetically explained: Lust for power and magic practice steps in because love is impossible.

> Even the bright bricks of success had not built a stronger house for her. Within, in the lowest region of her soul and mind, unknown to herself, she was still a small voice crying for another glory to salve her hurts....

The text can be read on another level: When Zorayas seeks to expose Darkness to the (fatal) light, she also exposes herself to Darkness, as Azhrarn puts "the seal of dark night upon her morning." (Her morning, however, like most of Azhrarn's gifts, is not long-lived; she soon falls in love with herself and vanishes in a resounding explosion of ecstasy.)

This trafficking between opposites goes both ways. Zhirem cannot face union with Simmu—Thanatos cannot embrace Eros—but nor can Simmu confront death. His extreme fear of "any creature that was dead" results in his quest for immortality and war on Death, and thus the destruction of his pleasure. Eros, like Thanatos, is drawn helplessly towards its opposite.

The children meet in the temple refectory where Zhirem, a newcomer, is being tormented. Simmu charms a bird from its sleeping place and, without a word of explanation, places it by Zhirem's plate. The moment poises (like childhood itself) between mundane and magical. The other children are baffled, and "No one spoke to Zhirem any more, for good or ill." The two are already set apart. "As two opposing poles exert magnetic influence between them, so these two opposites seemed held in a tension of unseen rope which bound one to the other." As they notice their *reflections* in a stream, they become "for the first time truly aware of another human who was as real as they."

Simmu's infancy is lived in nature. Nurtured by demon Eshva women, suckled by tigers and deer, he is outside any moral or social contract, with no duty even to speak or maintain a fixed gender. His graceful androgyny and whole, undamaged Eros endear him to demonfolk.

> ... the wicked innocence of the Eshva [was] still on him and in him.... To the Eshva everything was sensual, sexual: moonrise was an orgasm of the heart. A touch was love ... everything was ... part of the dream. Eshva lusted after the music of a look, and they never sought to analyze the sensations that poured over them, only to prolong and enjoy.

This Rousseauesque child is arrested in blissful, pre-verbal infancy where instinct and magic run free[12] Lee represents instinct—"the dream"— as the proper source of magic power. She treats magic less simply than in the *Birthgrave* sequence, where it was largely "good" or "evil," according to use. In Simmu, "Instinct, the father of all human sorcery, rose untrammeled to the surface of its soul like bubbles from a lake's floor." In his unnaturally natural context, "Before it could chatter out one word of human speech, the child could charm the bird from the cloud and the snake from under the stone. And though no mortal brain could ever quite fashion the sibilance of demon musings, yet this mortal baby had a knowledge of them...."

Among humans (though for the time fixed in the male sex) s/he is still an enigma. "His obliqueness, his actual unhumaness ... set him too far off to fit a role." He continues to make small use of speech and silently slips past the guardian monks and into the desert night to play with foxes.

Simmu's pre–Oedipal sexuality is the same as any other instinctual pleasure. Uncontaminated by the desire for power or domination, he is also indifferent to consummation—at least until stricken by jealousy. In the love triangle that forces Simmu to leave his magical, infant universe and shatters his unitary experience, Zhirem, the love-object, is the mirror opposite, not the mirror. It is not the entry of a third party, in this case a female prostitute, that arouses Simmu's jealousy, but the recognition that Zhirem is sexually aroused as a "normal" heterosexual male. Nor can he understand Zhirem's need for sublimation, or how blocking off pain also blocks off all possibility of pleasure or sexual congress. Simmu's ignorance of pain makes even his jealousy curiously directionless, just something to add to his rich repertoire of feeling:

> The soft flames which had always lapped him, unanalyzed, now gored and snapped. Eshva-like still, he ran to the fire rather than away. Envy was a green blade in his side; he twisted to enjoy the piercing of it ... twist the green blade in the wound, learn it all and more.

Jealousy does, however, stir the return of his sexual fluidity. For Simmu, gratification lies in *games* of flirtation, seduction and infantile (and therefore *goal-less*) pleasures. His pleasures have a large imaginary element—the baby Simmu, left for a moment beside the statue of a boy, becomes instantly female in order to complement its sex. When the adolescent Simmu disguises his feminine seduction of Zhirem in the appearance of a dream, he does it less to deceive than because, for him, carnal love belongs in dreams: "Eshva ... dreamed of dreaming and lived in a dream, and liked to walk the world by night in this dream, unspeaking, beautiful and oblique...."

Simmu has no desire to wake to the tyranny of daytime reality. After the seduction of Zhirem, when s/he absents her/himself "to revel in her joy alone," s/he is simply seeking the continuation of her dream. Only such a hopeless dreamer could expect to live outside the constricting demands of human society.

Simmu's seemingly endless capacity for delight fades when Azhrarn's gift of the city of Simmurad proves fatal to it. Once he is confined inside this great monument to immortality, his heedless fluidity comes to an end and his sex will change only when he is asleep.

Zhirem is unlucky from the start. Forced to forswear pleasure, even his aspirations to "goodness" are undermined by his desire for women. When he yields to Simmu and then fails as a healer, he tries to enter the service of demons. Once again he is rejected; "wickedness" is too erotic to redeem him. His only remaining desire is to serve Death.

His invulnerability is a "benefit" that has "a sister in misfortune." Disguised as a mad magician, in a scene with strong satirical undertones, Azhrarn is almost a caricature of a psychoanalyst as he explains that, "in burning off mortal weakness, mortal luck and happiness were also burned.... Ecstasy and vulnerability belonged in the same dish.... It was the fire's light had harmed Zhirem, not the darkness."

Magic that is an intellectual domination of nature is damagingly bright. Instinct operates in darker conditions.

Zhirem's repression of the memory also reads like a case history: "The unremembered pain and screaming.... He feared to remember. Someone haunted at his heels, must not catch up ... he wanted to be angry ... also sometimes ... to drop down like a stone into the dark pools of his own thought and to lie there drowned and at peace...."

Immersion in fire makes him long for immersion in water, but when he does eventually fall to the bottom of the ocean, his invulnerability prevents him from drowning.[13] Abandoned even by Death, his desire for cruelty becomes overwhelming. With his name changed to Zhirek, he embarks on a career of lust, sadism and destruction. Simmu, guilty of seducing and abandoning him, is its obsessive object.

But Simmu also has a repressed memory. As a newborn infant he had seen his mother carried away by Death. Narasen is "a warrior and a man who had been forced to play at motherhood," but she needs a child. After coupling with numberless living men, she pays Death to raise a dead one to father it, with the promise of spending a thousand years inside his kingdom.

In this narrative, sexual union is always more than simple pleasure, and often powerfully alters the participants, sometimes in ways one might not have anticipated. Simmu is able to *unseal* the heavenly cistern and drink the water of immortality by deflowering all of the nine virgins of the Garden of Veshum (or Death). Though Eros defeats Thanatos, Simmu's victory over death also brings about his ruin. But at the moment when Simmu is recreated as an Eshva, sexual union becomes purely regenerative: "...when Azhrarn possessed Simmu and yet once more destroyed and yet once more reincarnated him through the death-like throes of ecstasy, then Simmu became in every nerve and artery and muscle, in each inner mote and outer circumstance, animate, carnal and real ... even among mortals, then and now, love is a catalyst."

Death, like love, is a source of change, knowledge and the dissolution of consciousness. When Zhirek meets with Death, *pain* is represented as a form of love, and the meaning of both grows very complex. He describes his appalling cruelty to Simmu as "the only wound I am able to give myself." This is a deliberate descent into hell, but sexuality can also produce its own sort of hell. When Simmu and Zhirem are lost in the wilderness, they cling together with the desperate need of children:

> ... lust was new to them, and it was all they had. They began to lose purpose and fear and love and logic; they became two part-starved animals which endlessly coupled, which had been forever on the shore, forever would be....

During their time in the desert, Kassafeh and Simmu are also compared to children or animals. "So they wandered, subsisting and imperishable, these two children, for despite everything they were very young." At their first meeting, Kassafeh ironically addresses Simmu as "sister." She is referring to his impersonation of her, used in the Garden of Veshum to gain access to the sleeping quarters of the other eight virgins, but she is also stressing their non-adult roles. Simmu perceives Kassafeh as more animal than woman: "He would see in her the gazelle, the lynx, the serpent—his own psychic menagerie." The story of the child-god Amor and his girl-lover Psyche shines through his seduction of her. "She had come to love him almost in the moment the lamp shone upon him in the bed, but really she knew nothing of him. He had arrived as a stranger.... And a stranger he remained." He is less a specific person than the liberator she has been waiting for, and she exclaims childishly, "Why you are a hero."

Kassafeh wants to participate in the glory of Simmu's "hero-deed," but later, "starved of drama as much as of love," she takes Zhirek for her lover. She too has arrived at a confrontation with Thanatos, and moves on to seek her destiny in Death himself: "What hero is greater than Lord Death ... here was the impervious and imperishable name on which to tie her own."

Also seeking her destiny in Death—or perhaps just her fortune—is the self-styled "younger sister" to Narasen, the witch Lylas. This "lady of the pomegranates"[14] manages, as if in spite of herself, to be the girl-child Persephone. Separated from her mother Demeter, constructed as an object of male desire during her days as a child prostitute, and finally become a servant to Hades, her pomegranates turn poisonous. Perhaps uniquely, Lylas feels no attraction towards Azhrarn. Erotically, she is already dead, possessed by Thanatos. In the Underearth she allies herself with the masculine figure of the death-queen Narasen. Lylas is always attracted to unadulterated masculine power and becomes a student of a strictly masculine magic. Thanatos seems to have a masculine cast.

Eros, on the other hand, often seems barely aware of gender and is contradictorily portrayed as a wayward child, a winged creature of both earth and air, with potential to be angel or devil, an infant both naive and sexual, ambivalent, perverse and paradoxically innocent. Attempts to repress or control the erotic produce sadism and emptiness. Zhirek is little better off than his victims. "He was jealous of their death, or else he strove to drive himself to feel anything jealousy, pain, rage, for all emotion was smoldering out in him. Even cruelty became a habit."

But not even Zhirek can repress dreams of love completely. Washed up from the sea, "He dreamed of women, all the forbidden women he had been denied and warned from enjoying. Golden and pale and cinnamon and amber. They lay with him, but at the summit of his ecstasy a whisper would say to him: *Love is not enough....* But, being now wise and educated, he forgot."

Unfortunately, he always continues to remember pain. Simmu, conversely, remembers nothing, not even himself. There is nothing to keep him from returning to the absolute beginning, to his animal-angelic nature and the infantile bliss of the Eshva kingdom.

Lovers and Enemies of Death

Narasen, Queen of Merh, chooses death over sex when she murders a magician to avoid being violated by him. The scene is full of oppositions, not only of sex and death, but the reversed sexualities of man and woman. Issak, formerly an abused catamite, now helplessly attracted to a lesbian dominatrix, lurches absurdly between offence and apology. As Narasen penetrates him with knife and spear, his dying curse reflects her disregard for female nature: All Merh shall be barren, until such time as Narasan shall be fruitful. The "waters ... the milk of the herds ... the womb's richness in every female thing" will all dry up. Narasen eschews fertility, preferring the manly pleasures of leopard hunting. Despite her inventiveness and courage, finally she is sterile, an envoy of Death.

Lee promptly has Narasen on her back, being enjoyed by indiscriminate hordes of strangers, yet unable to conceive by any "living" man. As Merh succumbs to disaster, she enterprisingly seeks out Death to provide her with an unliving consort. Death is a courteous and impassive figure, who sheds "passionless, icy tears" merely because they are "a symbol of himself"; but, like Azhrarn, he suffers an immortal fear of boredom and strikes a bargain with her. In the ensuing union between a live woman and a dead youth, Narasen's love of Death is uppermost: "...she thought of Merh. And Merh was a leopard and ... Narasen arched her back with the pleasure of the slaughtering of this leopard, and she felt its death like her own." Simmu is born in understandable gender confusion, and directly after the birth Narasen is murdered and removed to Innerearth.

An often comic power struggle between Narasen and Lylas, the witch-handmaiden of Death and earthly poisoner of the queen, continues with undiminished energy in Innerearth, where far from serving Death, Narasen grows so shrewish that Death quits his own kingdom to escape her.

Death's origins are discussed in a curiously metaphorical style.

> Perhaps the gods had made Death. Perhaps men had made him, the shadow of their terror.... How long had he existed? Long enough to have come, in however strange and opaque a manner, to an awareness of himself. Or to an awareness of what himself must be.

Embodying an interesting paradox, Death, though unknowable to man, seems to want to perceive himself through human understanding. And yet, "Men looked in his desolate face, and could not afterwards remember it. It slipped from their minds like water through the fingers...."

Relations with Death range from tragic to absurd. When Lylas summons Death with her little drum and kisses the ground before him, she is hoping to be able to exploit him. Kassafeh, though part sky-elemental, at heart remains a merchant's daughter; she seeks to profit from Death's name, unaware that she has always served him—"for the black god of Veshum's garden had been none other than Uhlume." Simmu wrestles with the logical impasse of his proposed war on Death: It can never be fought because all casualties of such a war would be victories for Death. Even granted immortality, he cannot defeat the un-mortal enemy. Zhirek, meanwhile, only longs to be overcome by Death. "A release to some, a dread to most.... Zhirek sank against the white-robed knees of Death. In a way, Zhirek really was in love with this stranger."

In his dealings with mankind, Death can seem like a beleaguered adult amongst a swarm of demanding children. He is always polite and without human cruelty. When Zhirek asks to be given Simmu in reward for service, Death replies, "Cruelty is your food, not mine. Even now, not mine." He alters gradually—remaining gentle and impartial, but increasingly exhausted and despondent—as almost everyone, except for Zhirek, seeks to overcome him. By the time Narasen has finished with him, his only remaining feeling is an infinite weariness—a *mortal* weariness. Kassafeh offers him comfort, but together they engender a sense of passion spent. Of an evening he "lay down and rested his head in her lap. The fatigue of a thousand centuries had caught up with him." Only Narasen remains perfectly fresh. Equipped with apparently limitless energy, as Queen Death she grows more death-like than Death in his usurped kingdom.

As "the strange flat earth went on about its business through the night," the reader is aware that the cycle will continue: With his past burnt away from him, Simmu is returned, "pristine" and "amnesiac," to a new cycle of existence among the Eshva. Stripped to dry bone in the desert, Zhirek, who has lived on the thought of Simmu's endless agony, discovers that Simmu is wholly renewed; his "brain and senses worn nearly featureless," he still clings to the past and weeps at the impossibility of destroying love. But neither can love conquer death. The devotees of Thanatos, Narasen and Lylas, remain fully active after death. After his unhappy bid to overcome Death, Simmu must shed all memory so entirely that even his species memory is erased. It is, however, precisely this erasure that makes his re-creation in another species possible. In the end, Nature is given the final victory over both death and love.

3. The Flat Earth—Mortals and Immortals

From Sexual Energy to Love and Madness

Suggesting that demonic energy is poised to erupt into the human world, the entrance to Underearth is surrounded by a ring of volcanoes. These primeval features also hint at times predating the emergence of man, when sexuality and love were "probably invented" by demons. Azhrarn "had played games with humankind for eons, and before humankind, who knows but that he had not played games with the little creatures that crawled from the sea of chaos aboard the flat four-cornered earth, the minuscule sparks and atomies with which mortal life had begun."

Azhrarn's meddling has few limits. He can reshape human passion, derange human consciousness and claim carnal possession of anyone who arouses his desire, or even his curiosity. He may act magnanimously. With Sivesh the scene is stately: "The phallus of the Demon ... entered him as a king enters a kingdom conquered, adoring, his by right of surrender." But if his lordly rights are thwarted or he is treated as an enemy, he takes revenge with deliberate cruelty. His slightest touch, even indirect contact, is capable of awakening dark forces. A pilgrim who experiences his touch only through the handle of a whip is straightaway altered into a sadistic murderer. Speaking of Azhrarn, he says, "He is not a magician, but a god." "Such," Lee wryly tells us, "are the credentials of pleasure."

Authorial comment occurs more regularly at this stage, accompanying the increasing complexity of the material. Azhrarn's inconsistencies are also growing more frequent and beginning to develop a logic of their own. Despite himself, he too is beginning to be touched by feeling. He had once blithely pronounced, "Love? ... There is no such commodity. There is carnality ... worship ... obsession.... But no man sees love, and no demon sees it." Now he says, "I do not give my love lightly, but once given it is sure." Lee adds, "Which was not quite exact.... But love has many houses, many countries ... love is, too, a product of thought. While it seems to destroy reason, yet nothing that *cannot* in some mode reason can ever love."

Thought has been at work in both human and demon worlds. Experience replaces innocence. An "age of absolute Innocence," follows Azhrarn's death, but the world soon returns to "its old, honest, filthy and natural proportions," and as people change, so does Azhrarn. In *Delusion's Master*, love and madness both gain dominion over him. His mystery is breached as humans are able to spy on his "private universe of love's obsession."

The dialectic of reconciliation has shifted from the attraction and opposition of Eros and Thanatos to the equally endless struggle between love and madness. Less primal, less polarized, love and madness coexist in tense proximity. Their psychic territories merge. The "unbrothers" Chuz and Azhrarn generate sexual conflict and ambiguity. Azhrarn says, "In certain lands, your title and mine are mingled. I too am master of delusions." And Chuz, who is often discovered talking to himself, soliloquizes: "Be then yourself Delusion's Master. And Chuz shall be the Bringer of Anguish, the Jackal, the Evil One."

Though they share certain traits, their *personalities* are quite different. Azhrarn is astonishingly beautiful; Chuz is doubly aspected, his golden beauty at war with a hideousness sufficient to cause insanity in a beholder. Azhrarn is suave, sometimes heroic; Chuz is anti-heroic and often comic. Azhrarn's pride is unbending; Chuz is infinitely unstable. To hide himself from Azhrarn, he forgets who he is—or was. His "sanity" is a kind of madness, his "madness" a sort of sanity.[15]

> ... lunacy was like a psychic fuel, a flow of energy along his quite incorporeal nerves. Though fashioned as a kind of man, he did not reason like one. Nor is it necessary to assume that he, the master of madness, was xhimself positively mad.

They veer between repulsion and attraction, "wary, contemptuous, interested and enigmatic. So Lords of Darkness responded to one another. Somewhat attracted to, rather offended by, each other's existence." They have common interests. Like Azhrarn, Chuz is fascinated by humanity's hubris. He incites the building of the Tower of Baybhelu as the means to a raid upon heaven and immortality. When the tower is cast down, Azhrarn arrives quickly at the scene of the disaster, "intrigued and titillated, as ever, by the self-destructiveness of men." Chuz then begins, subtly, to tempt Azhrarn, playing on his pride. "In a century," said Chuz, "humanity may forget—many things." Azhrarn instantly becomes obsessed with whether humanity has indeed forgotten his act of self-immolation on its behalf. The madness has begun. As Chuz-Oloru will later remark, "Madness is no respecter of persons. We perceive even the mighty Prince Azhrarn has been its gull. But a short while since, he was mad of love, for love is simple madness."

Love is a madness to which not even Azhrarn, master and inventor of the erotic, is immune. Chuz too will be overcome by love. Among the varieties of love that congregate in *Delusion's Master*, some sort of madness is always present. Where opposites remained largely polarized in *Death's Master*, love may be recognized as pain or pleasure or a fusion of the two and is in all cases, precisely, quasi-scientifically detailed. A metaphysical cast tinges certain erotic episodes in this book.[16] Zharet's ecstasy, which is "of a specialized kind" as she couches with a demon, reads almost like some esoteric manual.

"The first moments of the ecstasy were searing green and sapphire, and in them she struggled, blinded and sobbing.... The second ecstasy within the first was the color of wine, and here all her senses became one, and that one shot through her like the spindle of some revolving star, so that all about herself she spun.... The third ecstasy was white, far whiter than any city. And here she was transfixed, and her frantic writhings, her gasps, her cries, even her breathing, stopped. Here on this summit she became a silent shriek. She could neither change further nor return to what she had been.... Her spasms were one single master spasm, frozen in molten whiteness, without beginning or end. And in this third ecstasy she was suspended for a thousand years."

We are once again in one of Lee's variable time-zones. She continues, "she fell back through a violet cloud and into her body ... as if her soul had known orgasmic rapture rather than her flesh."

But the residue of this rapture is not benevolent: Zharet absently fingers "a quite illusory and quite murderous pin" and later there will be seventeen murderesses. Zharet, who has become a pawn in the game between Chuz and Azhrarn, will suffer death by ecstasy.[17] The individual is powerless in the grip of the erotic, subject to extremes of violence and excess, open to sadism or masochism.

Delusion's Master wastes no time explaining that "There were several doors by which madness might enter any house. One was rage, one jealousy, one fear; there were others." When Queen Jasrin disposes of her small son so her husband will love her exclusively, Chuz materializes in her bedroom like a family physician, but when she begs for her sanity, Chuz truthfully replies, "sane you could not bear what you had done...."

Azhrarn is obliged to undergo the madness of love with more than human pain. Light and darkness can be seen coming together as he waits in the dark for her. "The deadly moon rested on her elbow overhead." Dunizel, lamp in hand and reflected in the lake, resembles an approaching moon, and, as a "daughter of the moon," she too is tinged with lunacy. Fate comments, "Doonis-Ezael, Moon's Soul ... had an allegiance ... to madness—it ran in the family, her own mother was an idiot until the comet cured her—to destiny, and to death. Only wickedness had nothing to do with Dunizel. So, of course, she became the mistress of Wickedness."

But she is also part-daughter of a comet, and thereby kin to the sun, which is death to Azhrarn. To love her is therefore an act of madness.

She instantly acknowledges his sadism ("Your wish to cause pain like pain itself"), then offers herself in undeniably masochistic terms: "I may easily be hurt. For a great while I might be tortured before death overcame me.... I offer myself as a sacrifice to you. Work out your rage on me, Lord of Darkness...."

She offers him "recompense" and unconditional love, and once again a Psyche discovers the god where she had been primed to expect the beast.

> And how can such beauty be the wickedness I comprehend you are, Lord of Lords? Oh you, who would lead us into evil, what a waste it is, for could you not lead the whole of mankind to joy and goodness by one look of your eyes? Yet, no matter. You are worth dying for, Lord. The world would die for you herself, I think, did she know you as you truly are.

When she adds, "do you mistake yourself?" he becomes angry. Taking on the form of a wolf he bites her savagely, then heals her wound with his own blood. This curious union of apparent irreconcilables swiftly mounts into another distinctly metaphysical erotic scene.[18]

"But though he lay with her, he did not do so in the carnal sense. He stared into her eyes with a demon's stare that never blinked, and her eyes, meeting his, chained by his, ceased also to blink, only reflecting his. And in this way they were throughout the night, unmoving, like stones laid on one another, in a bizarre ecstasy of utter stasis. And it seemed to the young priestess that his blood actually ran through both their bodies, and that their flesh came to be no longer separate, nor their minds, nor their souls—her soul, and what in him passed for a soul, his immortality."

Azhrarn then leaves. When he does eventually return, he sternly examines her mind for traces of himself, since "he would never have pardoned her for putting him aside more than a moment, even in her dreams." But he is satisfied.

> For though she saw the gods—each of them was Azhrarn. Some were female and some male, some exquisite children, some exotic animals, but each was Azhrarn, each and all. And if she saw a sky it, also, was Azhrarn. And the seas were Azhrarn, and the earth.

Drawn on by Dunizel, it is "as if he beheld his own influence for the first." Carnal pleasure is maturing into love. Sadism and masochism are growing up, changing from primitive fantasies into the recognition of coexisting opposites.

3. The Flat Earth—Mortals and Immortals

However, not all oppositions between Azhrarn and Dunizel can be so easily resolved. When a daughter is conceived, a triangle is created. Echoing Jasrin's jealousy, Azhrarn cannot bear to share Dunizel's love. The conflict is worsened when Azhrarn claims the child is his to dispose of as he wants. "She shall be my legacy to them. I will make her strong and terrible, and then I am done with her. And you are done with her also, Dunizel."

A battle of wills ensues. Azhrarn holds to his intentions. "I am the father of wickedness; do not think I will have regard for this creature I grew within your womb, not even for your sake." Dunizel is equally adamant. Despite Azhrarn's nightly entreaties to leave with him, she refuses to abandon the daughter whom she names Soveh—her own name at birth—and endures separation from Azhrarn.

> Knowing she had only to speak his name aloud in the darkness to bring him to her side, she knew, too, that to do so would be to acknowledge surrender to his wish…. No, Dunizel would not resign her child (hers, also, hers) to such an advent. She could not call to him.

The struggle for possession of the child bites deep.[19] Maternal love challenges carnal ecstasy. Dunizel is willing to sacrifice even the love of Azhrarn for it, and he is powerless against the primal nature of mother-love.

He inadvertently brings about her death as he and Chuz wantonly incite a mob of crazed pilgrims to extremes of madness. After Dunizel is dead, they come together carnally one last time, uniting love and death in yet another way, "Her body, that was more soul than flesh, meeting with his that was of supernatural atoms." Initially, Azhrarn rejects the possibility of such a disembodied act of love, but Dunizel knows better.

> "My body is composed of love. Love me, and you, even you, will tell no difference between illusion and reality, for in this case they are one." No human man could have possessed her as she was. But neither she, nor her love, nor her lover were human.

Dunizel has understood the continuity between flesh and spirit. Azhrarn is not yet ready to do so. He must endure the torment planned for him by Chuz: "It is his psychic heart which shall be chained and lashed and bound to a wheel and scalded, and his psychic heart which shall be ripped out." Claiming the specific human ability to die and thus be reincarnated, Dunizel says, "There is no parting…. I shall be with you, as now, once more in some other age."

She can submit gracefully to the pain of parting with loved ones. Azhrarn cannot even express his grief except through Nature. His horse dies of his "invisible, unexpressed agony," and the forest into which he enters "commenced to sing, because it could not weep, a melody ... like air, that if it might be reproduced, would kill life with sadness."

The pain he feels as he witnesses the death of Dunizel in his sorcerous mirror is unprecedented. "They said the glass shattered in a million fragments like grains of salt.... They said that true despair had not been created until that instant of the mirror's shattering."

Azhrarn still has a long way to go before he can accept the lessons of his existence. He is "like one that would scream but had no voice, or one who was wounded with some dreadful internal wound that no physician could come at to heal, so he was and so he suffered."

Splits and Syntheses

Even more clearly than *Delusion's Master*, *Delirium's Mistress* asserts the *divine*, Dionysian status of madness, and seeks its reinstatement, not its subordination. When Chuz engages in a genuine metamorphosis and takes on human form as *both* a disguise *and* a reality (forgetting who he is), it is a reminder that Dionysos is a hybrid, half human by right of his mother; contradiction is built into his nature.

In *Delirium's Mistress*, demon nature has lost much of its advantage and most of its integrity. Death shares his dominion with a mortal woman; Azhrarn, changed by the love of a woman, is now so complex even he is baffled—"some part of him he did not recognize, for even with human men, several persons may live together under one name and inside one skin." Madness, divided in itself and further split into the identities of Chuz and Oloru, goes mad for love of the Demon's part-human daughter, who as Soveh(az)-Azhriaz is also split.

When Azhrarn makes Sovaz into the contradiction of a "goddess on earth," even the torpid gods retaliate and she is obliged to undergo endless trials deriving from the accumulated history of the flat earth. But its history is also its psychology, and the adolescent Soveh-Azhriaz feels deeply uncertain about her existence and her essence. "Even if she was aware of it, she did not know what she was.... And so she was—or so she was not." Only when regressed to childhood and, like Simmu, scoured clean of memory is she ready for an integral existence. Balance is restored by the inclusion of death: Paradoxically, weakness is a key to strength and, paradoxically, in this renewed form *she is and she is not* the same.

In a scene that hovers between comedy and intense feeling, Oloru girlishly faints at the sight of his own Chuz aspect.

> She laughed a whole instant, did Sovaz. And then her laughter was done. Some other emotion rushed now over the first.... It filled her with inexplicable excitement and hurt.... She held him to her so her warmth should come between him and the skin of the world that was to all supernatural things, always a lure, a lover's embrace, the snare of an enemy. In that second of confusion she nearly understood her father.

Oloru faints again when threatened with the sword (a response that spares him from it) after a mischievously satirical song about an evil magician. Lak Hezoor, "intellectually obsessed by night and all dark things," is a sitting target both for Lee's humor and for Oloru (Chuz), who persuades him that he is "a match for the Vazdru in all things uncanny."

Fainting is a metaphor for death in both these stories. Azhrarn often demonstrates how the love of immortal demons is drawn towards creatures that die. Chuz-Oloru is helplessly attracted to the vacillating Sovaz, who "had been since her conception, his madman's goal." He is overcome by this Underearth Sleeping Beauty, posed as if enjoying a little death, and wakes her with a kiss; she is attracted to the fainting "Lord of Darkness, brought low by his own intrinsic terror. And who, indeed, has never but once looked deep within himself but once, and been afraid? ... Aggrieved at desertion by others, she warmed herself now at his *psychotic constancy*."

But when it is his turn to be awakened, he remembers nothing beyond a dream. When Sovaz gently questions him—is he not perhaps a liar?—Oloru shrinks from the very idea. And yet, even in the midst of this cloud of forgetting, the engagement of each with the other brings both roles, human and immortal, into play with eyes, and lies and kisses. "his eyes caught fire from an inner glare.... See, said these wicked molten eyes, how entertaining it will be to play this game together....' 'Most, beautiful of mortal women,' lied Oloru. 'Most beautiful of *mortal* men,' lied Sovaz."

Lee supplies some explanation here:

> Chuz, reborn Oloru, became Oloru. Chuz forgot he was Chuz ... each Lord of Darkness exuded the glamour of his ego from every unearthly pore.... But ... Oloru's essence cried loudly: Youth, maleness, self-conscious sexual ambiguity, charm, brinkmanship, neurasthenia. And such were the notices of mortals. And the demons, maybe briefly puzzled, withdrew again and left him alone.

Something seems odd at first glance, but the insertion of essentially modern wording into this description of Oloru predicts that Madness will live on into an era when demons will have become anachronisms unable to account for mental illness. Chuz's nature is expressed through dualities and divisions, but even as he deliberately lies, the truth emerges: "...presently in the stillness, she said to him, 'There too is death. One day I shall die. I know it now.' 'Our kind does not die,' said Oloru, forgetting an instant to forget."

There are many discussions about qualities of being in this volume. Fate (who appears only rarely) ponders the characters of the Lords of Darkness: Both he and Death are aware of their symbolic natures, but Chuz has "gone mad himself to prove he exists and is real." As Wickedness, Azhrarn "firstly existed, and then took on the role."

Jokes also accumulate. An extended joke centers on Azhriaz's undersea lover in a beguiling digression that burlesques a debate on the rebirth of the soul. Tavir is confronted by a petrified body he had once occupied in a former life when he was a formidably pompous philosopher-magician in the long-drowned city of Simmurad.[20] Still living but *soulless*, the body launches into an inflated diatribe on the benefits of immortality.[21]

> Pay attention. This is a mighty theosophic paradox.... All men possess souls which are immortal. But some men prefer longevity or eternality of the body, seeing that with each new life we are forced to undergo once more the idiocy of birth, childhood, and unknowledge, not to mention the discomfort of physical demise.

Ignoring the warnings of Azhriaz, Tavir agrees to return his soul into his former body, at which the magician, released from petrification, leaves Tavir's apparently lifeless body on the seabed. Tavir has abandoned Azhriaz (and his own body) in order to bond with another male, an event by now so frequent in her life it has become commonplace. But this time at least nobody pretends to be saving her: Chuz-Oloru has already "saved" Sovaz from her father's clutches; her father has 'saved' her back again. Chuz is also bonding with Azhrarn when he accepts his punishment of going mad but ignores the fact that Sovaz is being punished too.

However, Sovaz-Azhriaz is never passive in the face of salvation and struggles fiercely to escape the more painful of these rescues. Embarking on her Drin-built submarine (once more saved by Azhrarn), she protests bitterly. "And where is Chuz? ... And my mother? Where is she? And cold Dathanja, that priest from a womb-temple of rock—where? I am alone."

She has to endure interminable loneliness during her earthly ministry. At thirty-three she "stood alone in the bare room high in the sky. The womb of Azhriaz ... was now a closed dumb winter fruit of ice. She had taken to herself mage-craft, battles, an empire, but no lover, since Chuz.... Yet she was seventeen years still, as on the eve of their parting. And still a weeping child, within the sparkling jewel of sorcerous night."

This same "weeping child" flees from the avenging sun-angel right out into the chaos beyond the edge of the world and, "alone in blackness," hears, "miles off and eons under her, her own voice crying out, like the voice of the infant that she still was and yet had never been: 'Mother—O my mother help me!...'"

For a short time we lose sight of this double being; when she returns it will be as an absolute child. Though in the same apparent form, she will have become a true infant. And just as invisibly, just as absolutely, all creation will have changed along with her.

> The world arched its back, the sky leaned. For a second all matter heaved toward oblivion, or new life, which was the same.... And then the balance swung again. Smoothly, everything came to rest, like a gentle wheel which runs down.
>
> Shaken like a bag of salt, earth's substance settled. Like salt, every grain in a fresh place, yet salt still, thinking itself unaltered.

Zhirek, evolved into Dathanja, a wandering priest, discovers Azhriaz-Soveh beached on a mountaintop, asleep in the lap of Fate. Waking, the newly-infant Soveh turns to Dathanja, "like herself, half demon, half human, an immortal," as if to a parent. A "weeping rain" begins to fall, dissolving "the *figments* of men, angels, rocks, *allegorical* Lords of Darkness." Dathjana gives way to this gentler reality: "...as he comforted this daughter never born to him ... he comforted himself, held in his own arms with her. The one he had been. The one he was."

Dathanja goes about healing the sick, teaching and telling stories. The full-grown, infant Soveh follows along, with a "strange crew" of wanderers, including a dazed and baffled angel that, though it responds to the change in Soveh's being and no longer seeks to obliterate her, still feels bound to pursue her. There is also "a disgruntled magician" (the stealer of Tavir's soul) who rambles on, making absurd philosophical comments on every possible occasion. The joke continues. The body of Tavir turns up and coaxes his mortal soul back into itself; the philosopher fails to notice that his soul is gone; he sits in an overstuffed (like his brain) upper room where he argues loudly and endlessly with his mirror. A lighthearted death and comic reincarnation subtly prepare the way for the gentle emotional tone with which the sequence concludes.

The return of Zhirek-Dathanja into *Delirium's Mistress* is anything but random. Though long-dead, Dunizel intervenes with a dream that sends a young boy to release Zhirek from his pillar of rock and bring him to Azhriaz's city. Zhirek is an emblem of the desire for death, and death is necessary to reincarnation. His long stay in a pillar of rock causes a transformation equivalent to reincarnation. Azhriaz addresses him as "Unwilling Birth of Stone," and he replies, "I am a newborn infant. I am an unmarked stone sloughed by stone."[22]

His claim that he is "done with Zhirek" is proved false when Azhriaz immediately puts his invulnerability to the test, but he also is *not* still Zhirek. During a temptation in the wilderness, though he resists an apparition that promises him power, he gladly embraces an apparition of Simmu-Hhabaid in a highly erotic scene:

> Sometimes her hair was of a watery sheen, sometimes an apricot shade, she was a sea-princess, she was a girl who danced with unicorns. And sometimes she was a youth, her breasts flattened to hard pectorals.... And he held her fast, though now she struggled and was transformed—to beast, to sprite, to conflagration and to waterfall. He held her by her snake's waist ... riding the winged horse of lust, blinded, slain, born....

When this is termed "a sin," Dathanja *laughs*. "'That,' he said, 'is not a sin.'" Lee adds, "Zhirek, the invulnerable sorceror, was no more. It was Dathanja who soon strode away into the morning." But when he tells Azhriaz, "I am not priest or teacher or magician any longer," she replies, "All three you are ... and will ever be."

Her final conversation with Dathanja before her flight into the sea anticipates a coming freedom from the exercise of power and from fixation with the past. When she asks Dathjana to serve her and he refuses, she says, "'I can bewitch you.' 'You can,' he said, 'bewitch the world. Where then is the victory in bewitching me?' 'It is true,' she said. 'Go wherever you will.'"

In agreeing to his autonomy, she sets the process of her own release in motion. Dathanja's later teachings will draw in the outlines of this process. He is asked, "Do you say then that all men *must* first do evil that they may learn how to do good?" "There is no 'must,'" answered Dathanja. "I say only that, in most cases that is how it will fall out."

He speaks at length of knowledge gained through "experience" rather than through "ignorance and innocence." Blakean experience rather than innocence also inspires Azhriaz, now become Atmeh, when she meets in battle with Ebriel. She greets this third angel-automaton with flirtatious swordplay and seductive tricks that deflect his fixed purpose. "'Beloved,' said Atmeh, 'demons are not to be trusted. And mortals, neither. And I am both...' And she kissed his mouth, briefly, in the way a bird alights upon a bough where it knows it may not linger." Ebriel laughs "aloud and beautifully" and she explains her intentions to him.

> I shall seek to lose my immortality, that fabulous gift for which men have murdered one another.... My quest, Ebriel, is not to be a goddess or a demon. But to be a human thing which lives and dies and is reborn. To slough my immortality—will be to gain it. To search for true life ... to gain my soul.

However, she speaks more imperiously to the gods who despise all forms of experience: "Listen to me, you peerless, souless gods, I rule nothing and no one, and so, soon I will outshine you, for I will be a mortal. And one day, as you never can, I and mine shall inherit the earth."

This voice still has the ring of the demon-goddess in it. Like so many characters in the book, she retains what she was even when she becomes entirely new. As Sovaz dissolves into Azhriaz, so Azhriaz melts away into Atmeh. In her fight with Ebriel she is said to be "Atmeh become Sovaz again, or Azhriaz." One person does not excise or replace another; each dissolves into the next, leaving the first identity to merge into a new synthesis.

The Great Quarrel

After Dunizel's death Azhrarn continues to jealously reject his daughter. Her resentment matches up to his: "...he put me aside and forgot me. I was of such little worth." But when her elopement jogs his memory, she is swept away by father and lover's turbulent struggle to possess her. She hears Azhrarn tell Chuz, "You, I have pursued like a lover," and his madly literal reply, "it would not be politic, Azhrarn, for two Lords of Darkness to couple." Azhriaz comments, "Unbrothers each closer than ever either was to me." Azhrarn is nevertheless suspected of incest, and rumors rumble on when Azhriaz refuses all suitors. Azhrarn protests, "Let mortals err or philosophize as they wish. She that is born of me is not my lover. I am not the clay of humankind, and their muck does not stick to me"—which surely indicates that he must feel it does.

Still calling herself Sovaz, she wanders the earth in search of Chuz.[23] She only reaches a decision to serve her father during a strange interlude at the sealed-in city of Shudm, which swells like a pregnant belly on the landscape. As the inhabitants all devour each other, parents still sacrifice themselves helplessly for their ghoul-children. "So, even your people love their children. Apples of fire. O dearest Father, how is it you can deny me anything?" she cries out. However perverse she (or her father) may be, nature will force both her parents to love her anyway.

And so she takes on the name Azhriaz and summons Azhrarn. Neither is ready yet to confess to anything so human as emotion. "Azhrarn looked away ... she could not help but recall for him Dunizel. The first sight he had of her ... had gone through him like a sword." He also feels some revulsion towards her as "his own wickedness." "[H]ad Dunizel, maybe, caused him to *question* his wickedness, his character...?" If so, it has not brought him much self-knowledge. Azhriaz has made herself his feminine counterpart, yet he still fails to acknowledge her either as part of himself or as an independent force who is usually well ahead of him in matters of self-understanding. However, when she refuses to admit that she is weeping, he does at least note that, "Each word spoken was a tear."

Both father and daughter have suspended their sexuality in apparent depression at the loss of a lover, but there are larger, more buried reasons. When reproached by a former lover for contaminating Underearth with his misery, Azhrarn says, "You were the pleasure of dawn and first light. But the day has advanced."[24] He has moved beyond that "shadowy sunrise lacking a sun." Azhriaz reads the situation with a typical, thankless skepticism, "*And he is embattled with sun creatures? Not for my sake.... It is his game, of course, and he does not like to lose.*"

Azhrarn already encountered the sun at the time of his first death and through Dunizel, but when he battles with the sun-angel he has changed so much that the original laws of demon nature are inexplicably contradicted.

> The sun had come up.... In that gale of light, Azhrarn had blazed—but was not extinguished. This was impossible. It mocked the laws and the lore of demonkind.... Melqar released the enemy. Since the enemy, sable and shadow and night and black wickedness—*was also the sun*.... Truth is at the door, howling and stamping her foot. Truth is not always decorous.... Then best botch up an explanation.

Azhrarn absorbs contradictions extreme enough to cancel out the rules of existence. Demons who touch him are burned by his skin: "He had touched sunlight in a morning sky and fallen from heaven like a severed star." The sun, belonging to the worlds of humans and gods, changes his nature. He becomes "the black sun." As Soveh, after watching an eclipse, will wisely ask, "If the sun can be a darkness, cannot darkness be a sun?"

Essential to this so-called "Great Quarrel" is the irreducible fact that a *goddess* is usurping and perverting the position of the gods. One god remembers Azhrarn's kiss sharply, and insists, "this woman mankind call a goddess is none other than the offspring of that demon prince ... we, inescapably, must offer war to such." The gods prefer to be seen as asexual, but "affirmed that this one of their fraternity should take on for them the onus of retribution ... and it did seem that he was now *masculine* ... the rest of the gods punished him for the vestiges on him of outgrown things, not to mention for having been kissed by a demon."

But there is more here than a simple male on male embrace. The battle with the angel is ritualistic, "a gesture on all sides." The swords used are "phalluses of spiritual death, organs of ungeneration," and the "points of the swords touched each other, nearly delicate, as if they kissed."

In the "death" that precedes renewal, expectations are inverted in a comparison of demons and humans: "Demons did not die. At least they did not remain dead. (They were like mortals in that.)" Azhrarn will not be resuming his old existence in his city. His body is taken to a cave where a Drin (dwarf) changed into a worm for his former misbehavior, eventually awakens him. Emblem of death and burial, this little worm shyly lectures Azhrarn: "Love is love. She cannot be seen because she is everything. We fight her. We turn her away. But we can no more do it than throw off our own life. In the end love alone remains."

The only reward Bakvi asks is to become "king of the worms of the demon country," modestly prefiguring lessons that demons need to learn; and back in his sunless city Azhrarn once again achieves the impossible: He "stood there upon the streets of Night's own kingdom and was *day*."

He also does the psychologically impossible and releases Azhriaz. "She is an immortal and she lives ... let her live then." A decision to cease meddling with humans follows naturally. The desire for the triumph of wickedness on earth has grown stale. "I am done with mankind.... There are other games or I will invent them."

Though dead, Dunizel has not "done with mankind" and quietly guides her daughter towards mortality. She answers her daughter's calls for help, both with dream-sendings and a winged lion born in a reverie during her pregnancy. Expressing Azhriaz's relations with Dunizel, the lion first appears when the girl nears the city where her mother died. Throughout her long odyssey as Sovaz, Azhriaz, Soveh and the wisewoman Atmeh, it is

Azhriaz's traveling companion and transport in most major journeys.[26] It carries her when she goes to find her father. It descends into Death's kingdom as she seeks a cure for immortality. It takes her to the deathbed of Oloru. It accompanies her on her journey to rejoin Chuz.

Dunizel never claims to be more than a mortal woman, but her creation of the winged lion, with its "silent thinking face," belies her claims. The winged lion is a Sphinx, emblem of matriarchal power with a riddle about man. Atmeh parts with her beast just before she gives up immortality. She is seated in a "meadow curded with flowers.... The lion purrs as Atmeh sings in its ear. Then Atmeh claps her hands, and with a flaunt of great pinions, the lion tips itself up into the ether, becomes a tiny daylight star, and is gone. Atmeh sits down upon the earth to plait a garland of yellow flowers."[27] She has relinquished an immortal's power of flight and adopted earth as her proper domain.

Even when purportedly serving Azhrarn, Azhriaz is as anxious about the destruction of her city as her mother was for Belsheved. "'A vast quantity of lives,' said Azhriaz. Her face was very white indeed. The Drin, puzzled, gobbled politely at the bank. What should she care for human lives, the Demon's daughter?" But only as a simple child, using the name her mother gave her, is Soveh fully able to reconcile the contradiction of her parents. After a solar eclipse—the embrace of sun and moon, and end of their "Great Quarrel"—Soveh says to Dathanja, "...when the shadow left the earth, the shadow that was on me, this too drew away. Here I am. No longer Sovaz or Azhriaz. No longer Soveh, your child ... each grows up.... But the moon, changing her shape, is still the moon, and just so with love."

Reconciliation with the double-aspected Chuz soon follows.

> "Chuz," she said, "are you not the symbol of everything, the fair and the vile together? And you, the dealer in lunacy, a pitying father, a rescuer, the kind physician who binds the bruises of life. The spirit of poets, and prophets, the lord of frenzies, religions, music, magic, love and wine. You are the master of the key to the inner mystery. You are the breaker of chains."

This powerful resemblance to Dionysos, the half-human, half divine Liberator and "breaker of chains," also associates Chuz with women's mysteries. The union of the lovers is the interplay of mortality and immortality. At their first parting, Chuz says, "Time is endless and ours. Love and death are only the games we play in it." Now she says, "Our love rocks the world. Yet what a little event is our love."

When Atmeh swallows the adamantine drops of Azhrarn's blood embedded in the amethyst die which Chuz gives to her, she is swallowing her own future death.[28] The die, presented to her in a damson lotus, represents the union of god and goddess.[29] When Soveh lives out the childhood originally denied to her, "Along the margin of the shore, the lotuses had turned to twilight mauve ... they did not die. But Soveh the child, playing among them and swimming between their stems, only took them for another aspect of all life.... They did not therefore cause her hurt or aggravation, as to Sovaz or Azhriaz they would have done, being recollections of Chuz."

The woman-goddess, reduced to childhood, forgets her lover as surely as the mad Chuz once forgot her. But when her memory is restored—"Do we not always remember through all our several lives, old friends and former kindred, however we or they are altered"—it is of a special order:

> She had, the girl, the woman, all her memory.... It seemed to her that her soul had itself lived bodily, often, before it had been summoned to the child in Dunizel's womb ... was there not more to be learned through a diversity of lives, through the confusion of genders, temperaments, creeds, wishes...?

Reunited with Atmeh, Madness becomes sane. "How could anything be ugly in your company?" he asks. "That one, half hideous, half deformed, when he approaches you, he grows handsome." But sane is not the same as reasonable. Though "the world was growing skeptical, and sensible, and sound, and blind," Atmeh and Chuz are beyond "this dark of experience and reason." Lovers are "least reasonable of all." When Atmeh swallows the die and puts a limit to her time with Chuz, "He ... held in his arms now a mortal woman ... that was like clasping the tides of the sea.... How massively the mountains stand, while low to the ground the sand blows.... And then there are no mountains, none at all, the sand has kissed and whispered them away. And still the sand blows on."[30]

When the Lords of Darkness visit the bent and aged Atmeh, who sits with her goddess's emblematic snake upon her knees, Azhrarn initially still threatens her and argues. She offers him her unconditional love and speaks of love's undivided, all-encompassing nature. At this, Azhrarn's pride finally collapses and "though he was the dark incarnate, yet darkness fell away from him." He finally admits to her, "you are *her* child ... Dunizel that was the moon and sun together. Your mother's daughter."

The thousand and one meetings of light and darkness, the great quarrels and reconciliations, the deaths and reincarnations are only visible moments in a vast flux. When Atmeh, the ancient wisewoman, seeks out death, Death describes her as "hungry for endings." She, however, describes her wishes differently: "...to inhabit many lives and be lessoned in these ... metamorphosis is necessary."

Night's Sorceries

These stories slot into different positions in the sequence. A boy, abandoned to the care of corrupt monks, stumbles upon Oloru and Sovaz who are hiding from Azhrarn in a forest. The couple reward the boy for refusing to betray them. When he thereafter worships only the goddess, Lee playfully adds, "when Beetle ... put offerings and incense at the feet of her, Night's Daughter, Fate never told him he was ahead of his time."

The second story also takes place in an enchanted forest, where Eshva, with an uncanny resemblance to fairies, evoke A *Midsummer Night's Dream*:

> ... between and above the grass, there moved three or four or five flickering or glowing fires.... Around and about they danced, mingling and eluding, until all at once they brightened and faded—and there instead were some beautiful and human-like beings, still moving in a graceful and flickering dance across the grass.

Moonlight revels spill across the pages. Searching for the beloved who has rejected her, Marsineh finds a demon lover. The beloved is transformed into an ass and a Vazdru, "a being ... that was partly of flesh, partly of fire, and partly and mostly of the dark," who remarks, "Of all the fools there are, there are no better fools than mortals."

But all is eventually put right. Even the ass, left behind in the wild, is unmolested by lynx or wolf because of his strangely human gaze. The ass, though dedicated to Isis, is also a beast of Dionysos, who gave this animal the gift of speech. In the earlier books, Chuz is often seen clutching an ass's jawbones. Now, "with the ghost of a damson-colored mantle, and in one hand two jaw-bones—which clacked open suddenly and pointlessly exclaimed: '*Love is love*'," he restores the lover-ass to his original shape.

The theme of *apples of fire* returns in the story of a prodigal son who finds true happiness in a sumptuous palace peopled by talking pigs and other animals. The pigs, sacred in the Eleusinian rites, once more suggest the shadowy presence of Dionysos, as they explain the principles of animal reincarnation and the philosophy of the animal kingdom: "...animals did not possess each an individual spirit, as in the case of humankind, but were all part of one collective spirit." Though the son longs to "be a cat, a hound, a horse or a shining milk-white Boar," he is sent to visit his dead father's tomb. Queen Death is there, but the panther king who identifies Narasen as the "Leopard Queen" rescues him. Sovaz, meanwhile, enlivens the subplot of this story.

The marriage of sun and moon is rewoven in *Dooniveh, The Moon*, a story that describes a demon's attempt to court Azhriaz with a flying horse, got from mating an eagle with a black mare. She scornfully rejects it, and the twin product, a wingless bird with a horse's body, is thrown hastily away. A blind goose-girl adopts Birdy as her house pet, and when a thief and rapist arrives, Birdy saves her by assuming a terrifying size and aspect. Birdy reappears in the last story.

In a story rife with resonances, Azhrarn returns to meddle in a very familiar desert. The green eyes of Jalasil are also very familiar. Long gone identities are resurrected as Zhoreb, a member of a cult derived from the now garbled teachings of Dathanja, spurns Jalasil's love, and Azhrarn, wearing the form of a woman, arranges for her to have revenge through the love of Zhoreb and his death. Azhrarn "beckoned to Jalasil across all the hills of oblivion. 'Return to the earth,' said Azhrarn.... Then the essence of Jalasil seemed to fill her like water. It brimmed up to her eyes, and she opened them ... not knowing where she had been ... and hardly recollecting, for that matter, who she herself was."

In a version of Atmeh's death, a poor and unfortunate woman, known in her village as "Unluck," takes in a pair of failing, old wanderers—Atmeh and Oloru are making their last journey together. As they sit by the fire a lotus grows on the hearth and a nightingale comes indoors, which "chimed and chirred and rang, and filled the room with bells and stars." Of the plain but vocally exquisite nightingale, Oloru explains, "Beauty can never be destroyed, merely transposed." After the death of Atmeh, the woman feels "all empty, not as if she had been robbed of anything, but rather as if she had been rinsed clean." The next morning she is young again.

A story, tellingly titled *The Daughter of the Magician*, is also about beauty transposed, and the reincarnation of a mortal soul. A young girl is wedded to an evil magician and impregnated among a cloud of butterflies. She dreams of butterflies, emblems of the soul. One, attached to her waist and thus the body of her infant by a wire, is the soul of Atmeh, caught by her old demon suitor. Late in the pregnancy he shows himself to the girl as he truly is. A deformed child is born prematurely and exiled to the cellars. After an escape and various painful adventures, she is left for dead, but discovered and adopted by a kindly merchant. And so the story of Ezail of the marigold hair begins. A friend of the merchant remarks, "the soul of that one you found beside the causeway shines through her skin like flame through a broken lamp."

Elsewhere, a queen, seeking to become pregnant, is advised by a witch to swallow a crushed die. Her son, Chavir, is "blue-eyed and black of hair, and sufficiently elusive in his behavior some said he was touched in the mind ... he was a cultured lynx in human form." Chavir "sang in his sleep.... He sang he loved the girl-child of a magician.... He sang of one he called Night's Daughter."

He follows his dreams to a holy festival where intoxicated women are celebrating Dionysian rites in the city streets. "I have heard tabors beating and sistrum clinking ... the lovely virgins of Jhardamorjh dance through the avenues ... and their eyes are wide and wild, like the eyes of mad dreamers. There is surely something they drink or eat here...." Ezail, there with the merchant, is chosen, despite her deformities, to be the Exalted. Sent into a sacred precinct round a hill that recalls Mount Citherea, she finds the skeletons of other Exalted who have apparently died of fright at the sight of the inappropriately worshipped Birdy. As Ezail sits peacefully on the lawn with her fellow deformity, Chavir breaks out of prison (the breaker of chains) and joins them. He begs Ezail, "allow me to free you, for this one life only. To be with me," while the immortal Chuz explains his human form. "It seems that once I was some other, but in order that this moment might be ... I grew and was Chavir, who wears your colors of blue and black, as you wear mine, my marigold girl."

We are given one last panoramic view of a world that appears to have grown larger since the days of its magical childhood.

> The vast world of the Flat Earth lay between its mountains and its seas, robed in panther black, and jeweled with the lights of mankind. And from however many thousands of towers did the dreamers and the scholars scan the heavens for a trace of gods and fortune, and in how many millions of hearts did the forgotten knowledge of all things see the and sleep.

4

IN THE STEPS OF THE GODDESS

A Heroine of the World

Origins in the Tarot and Mythology

Painted across a huge canvas, *A Heroine of the World* is a progression through both seasonal and life cycles. Amongst numerous quasi-historical and cultural sources, it refers consistently to material from the Tarot or "Devil's Picture Book." Recurring card games and fortune-telling are always significant, and Aradia is twice given cards picturing her symbolic or meta-identity.[1] The narrative follows the "Way" of the Tarot that lays cards in a figure eight, the symbol of eternity, to represent the passage of life through the outer and inner worlds.[2] The Wheel of Fortune at the figure's center portrays the cycle of death and reincarnation. Suits of Wands, Swords, Cups and Pentacles signify the elements of Fire, Air, Water and Earth, as well as the progression of the seasons, which is given great prominence here. Seasonal changes reflect both Aradia's internal states and the cyclical character of life.

Full of pagan meanings and symbols, the Tarot became linked with witches, to whom this novel makes intermittent references. The Medieval Queen of the Witches is sometimes called Herodias or Aradia, whose name also contains resonances of Ariadne and Diana. Bypassing the need for literacy as it traveled with the Gypsy population, the Tarot was available to the common people, and in drawing from Indian, Oriental, Egyptian,

Greek and near-Eastern religion and myth, and alchemichal, Gnostic and other arcane and heretical beliefs, it took away elitist control of the keys to ancient lore. It also reflects a bond with Goddess religions, which focus on the rotation of the seasons. Insertion into continuous natural process rather than linear progress towards reward or punishment leads infallibly to death and reincarnation. Jane Harrison describes the Orphic Wheel:

> The notion of existence as a Wheel, a cycle of life upon life ceaselessly revolving, in which the soul is caught ... was borrowed from the Egyptians by the Greeks ... Rebirth, reincarnation became ... *new* birth ... new souls are old souls reborn in endless succession ... man has not severed completely his brotherhood with plants and animals....[3]

She also laments the loss of "Year-daimones." Olympian "personality" gods no longer serve either man or nature.

> The Year-daimon lived his year-long life that he might die, and died that he might live again ... that which is life and reality—Change and Movement—the Olympian renounces. Instead he chooses Deathlessness and Immutability—a seeming Immortality which is really a denial of life, for life is change.[4]

Aradia personifies the variable goddess. At first she stands between aunt and mother. On the threshold of puberty, half-way between the transcendental and actual worlds, she is the maiden aspect of the triple goddess. Myth blends seamlessly with narrative as she passes through seasons of nature and the soul, descending into the realms of the goddess of death and gradually absorbing all the elements of which the goddess is composed. Her many "irrational" choices, her curious, undenying acceptance of shattering events, make her journey into "a way" or initiation. Aradia has a markedly feminine character. Unlike most of her precursors in Lee's work, she makes no attempt to incorporate traditional male functions, though she does not refuse what is thrust upon her. She kills in self-defence or "accidentally," and accepts power only as part of her destiny. But her loyalty to her feelings is undeviating.

As in other works, names are significant. Pellucidly identified with nature, fertility and love, Aradia's mother needs no personal name. She is "like some busy flower ... a hyacinth or sweetpea," spilling over with the color and generosity of the Tarot Empress or the mother-goddess, Aphrodite-Demeter. Aradia, a child with "sunny hair," is the Fool of the deck, setting out on the path of life. At the same time, Aradia is Kore-Persephone and the story of Ariadne, whose name hers echoes, appears in her relations with Thenser, beginning as she saves him from the death sentence of Minos-Gurz. Aradia is Dia to her beloved mother but her aunt uses her proper name.[5] Stammering with fright, she calls herself Ara after Elaieva's death and inadvertently disguises herself.

Name indications can be very small. The mother's affectionate expression "little stoat," makes a hidden reference to witchcraft. The stoat or "weasel, like the mouse, hare and other little animals is a witch animal ... always connected with death and inheritance."[6] And when two little servant girls invade Aradia's room, wear her clothes and force a precocious sexuality upon her, one is called Mouse. They complete a childish version of the Three Graces, who appear in the Tarot as the Three of Cups. Reversed, this card indicates "exploitation of the affections of others."[7] Mouse and Loy exploit Aradia's loneliness and lead her into exploiting the affections of the aging Colonel Gurz.

The name of the goddess, Vulmartis, and her features also alter according to region. Aradia's mother and Aunt Elaieva embody different aspects of the goddess. "Virgin," "nun" and "priestess," the cold, unapproachable Elaieva is the Tarot Priestess, Isis or Hathor, so extreme in her non-carnality that when she comes upon Aradia clinging desperately to her departing mother, "Like guilty lovers my mother and I sprang apart."

Lee pays very close attention to detail. The two pillars depicted beside the Priestess to mark the entrance to the land of the dead appear outside Elaieva's house. Elaieva will shortly die by her own hand. Tiny observations constantly foreshadow things to come. As Aradia parts with her mother, her foreboding is expressed in exactly the sort of detail which a child might notice: "My tears had stained her silk bodice dark as blood."

The many iconic forms of the Goddess (cards, statues, rituals) have both anagogical and dynamic natures. Their narrative importance may rival that of human characters as both human and transcendental content flows through them. Aradia addresses a statue of Vulmartis much as she would her mother, but though this goddess (who, incidentally, wears "an Eastern headdress") is unambiguously kind, like a human mother she may not respond: "I knelt at her small feet, which had golden hearts painted on them.... Her sweet face was compassionate. And yet I knew she did not hear me. Like a moth, I dashed myself helplessly against her gleaming stone."

The statue in Elaieva's private chapel is "very white and hygienic," an aseptic goddess well-suited to a woman whom Thenser calls "Ice bitch." Before her suicide, when Elaieva at last speaks to her niece, she is equally aseptic. "I apologize, Aradia ... that I couldn't love you. That was not in me. Go down now. Look after the key. You will need it later." Aradia's response—"I might spit at her, at her feet or in her face. Not possible.

When I had been with her I had been my mother's daughter"—has a significance going far beyond immediate circumstances. Spitting wards off the evil eye. Loy teaches Aradia to spit as they watch the enemy army entering the city. But now, as her "mother's daughter," she makes no attempt to ward off the evil eye of her aunt or to turn her fate aside. Her mother's death, her aunt's suicide, are a necessary introduction to the destiny of one who belongs so entirely to the mother-goddess. Several levels of reality—the child's reality, the psychological reality, the symbolical reality—all work together. Aradia, prepared by her love for her mother, will give unconditional love to Thenser in a feminine destiny of suffering and endurance:

> ... ideas circled in my brain, but under all, the enormous vat of nothingness, and I, a tiny speck, floating at the brim.... I had brushed against Fate, Death and Truth, giants towering in a child's stumbling dark.

But, as she wisely comments on her mother's death, "The greatest untruth of all was a fact." The mother is dead but the Mother-Goddess is immortal and lives on in other forms, especially the forms of nature. Visiting the palace gardens, Aradia experiences a bliss she believes is sent by "Vulmartis the Maiden."

> Such sweetness ... bubbled through my blood. I came alive.... Butterflies exploded from the wild lawns, petals showered me from a low and perfumed branch.... It was very strange, as if sadness itself had been the prison, and it had taken only the unlocking of its door to release me, back into the true, real world.

However, it is not only her mother, rediscovered in Nature, that Aradia internalizes. She also takes on qualities belonging to her aunt. When she inherits the house, Mouse calls her, "bitch ... like *her*—like madam." Her likeness to her aunt continues to be remarked on, especially by Thenser, who clearly loves the Goddess in her entirety.

The card of the Lovers enters the story along with a game of cards that Aradia plays with her aunt and Thenser. A young man flanked by two women turns his face towards the dark, older woman but stands closest to a fair-haired girl. The man is Thenser, at first enthralled by Elaieva but destined to love Aradia. But, more importantly, Thenser must be identified with the card of the Magician, first card of the Tarot deck, in whom the mingling of Hermes, Dionysos and Theseus[8] creates an almost opaque complexity. Hermes, the trickster, is virtually interchangeable with Dionysos, Eros and the World Serpent, mate of the Mother Goddess, making a natural connection with the apple tree that is so important to Aradia and the book. Hermes's union with the Goddess is shown in the last card, The World Soul, or Anima Mercury/Hermaphrodite, a dancing figure holding two wands. But the Magician's magic wand also represents skills in trickery. Hermes is the patron of thieves.[9] Thenser is a traitor who boasts, "I stole my money by deception of the Emperor."

A symmetrical system of exchange is embedded in the narrative. Each figure or card gives something specific which must be reciprocated. To Aradia, Elaieva is a negative emblem of death who takes away her mother, but the key she leaves will be crucial and will open the desk containing Gurz's death-list. And although Elaieva rejects Thenser's love, she places the key to it in Aradia's hand. Thenser reflects Hermes the psychopomp as he brings Aradia news of her parents's death, and as she scratches his name from the death-list and reinserts him in life, she reflects the life-giving Goddess. But she is also linked to death and must pay for the life saved. She pays by accepting Gurz's love—though she views his transports with utter incomprehension. "When he took me to bed.... Whatever was it that happened to him? He must be mad."

Although the key gives her ownership of the house, Aradia never puts it to rational use. Frequent irrational choices produce a psychological reality that stresses interiority and feeling. Objects are also symbols: The key unlocks the door out of childhood and into a journey that begins in a semi-conscious commitment to Thenser.

The Tarot Hierophant, who is linked with The Priestess, holds two keys. Gurz, as the possessor of one of these keys, immediately identifies himself. With authorial attention to curiously minute detail, when Aradia finally reaches the Gurz estate she finds that, like The Hierophant—one who "likes his world to be neat, tidy and carefully labelled"—every object in his rooms has been labelled.[10] The Hierophant is also a bridge between mundane and spiritual, and Gurz forms the link between Aradia and his mother, The Lady, another goddess-figure and reader of cards. Fussy, scholarly and rather pompous, at night, alongside the statue of Wiparvet, Gurz resembles an underworld god: "The somber glim underlit his face, as the god's face was underlit ... light spangled in the Kronian's beard.... I saw the black mask of the wolf-jackal, stippled with gold...."[11] It is the key-holding Hierophant who takes her into the arena of war (King of Swords) and death and on towards the Emperor.

The quasi-historical card of The Emperor, referring to the Byzantine or Carolingian Empires or Emperor Frederic II, appears in Kristen Kahrulan. Though necessary to the plot, he has little personal meaning, except insofar as Thenser steals his money and his bride. Warring factions and changing allegiances suggest historical upheaval, and the occasional practice of exclusively female rites or the fact that only males have family names suggest a period of cultural change.

The Magician's obviously phallic wand connects him with fire, lightning, the thunderbolt, the dorje-caduceus, but on the table in front of him lie emblems of all four suits, meaning that Thenser will be obliged to pass through all the seasons of world and soul. Like the god of boundaries and strangers, he has the same peculiar fluency in languages as Aradia and is always on the move. And like the god of the crossroads—the place of necromancy, witches and the gallows (The Hanged Man)[12]—as the Dionysian lover of Persephone-Hecate-Aphrodite, Thenser wins back Aradia-Ariadne, the bride of death, by sheer, brazen trickery.

Kahrulan solicitously warns Aradia, "'From what I hear, he's a creature of the water and the fire.'

"'So am I,' I said. 'Oh, so am I.'"

War and Some Degree of Peace

As characters and cards are superimposed, cards also overlap each other. During the retreat Gurz appears with his head "wrapped ... in an Eastern turban of cloth." He has developed a passing resemblance to the King of Swords, with his Eastern headdress and crescent moon horns. The Queen of Swords is a card meaning suffering and widowhood, an identity Ara-Aradia accretes when she becomes Gurtz's wife.

Swords signify death, suffering and Winter, but the element of Air also means intelligence. Young, inexperienced, plunged into war, Ara manages to survive by instinct and wit. When a soldier swears to violate her, she is unable to turn to Gurz: "I must juggle with the adult code again, whose rules I did not really follow.... In order to retain his protection, I must shield him from Drahis." The camp-following fortune-teller, Jilza, also typifies this instinctive cleverness—"Her face was stern and pure, but I knew, through everything, she was a trickster, too. By which, I do not mean a charlatan." Ara has learned to read the marks of Hermes, but Jilza declares her credentials anyway. She keeps a "key to the lore of the lands of Taras Ind, the secrets of the Serpent Kings. I can tell you this and that. You, in exchange, might give me what you believe I earned."

Jilza is several times referred to as a witch. Though of clearly Northern origins, her headdress is "an Eastern thing." She radiates a shaman's animal power. "She was a mountain of shining black bear-pelt.... It was like touching the living bear. The fur itself crackled and purred with life and heat." As they look up at the moon together, "It was like gazing through a rim into some vast cauldron."

Jilza gives Ara the card of the "Heroine, or World's Girl," to whom "Lightning is attracted." This key phrase will be several times repeated.

> Hyacinths spilled from one hand and changed to papers, then to smoke, blood, pearls, and drops of transparent water as they fell. At her feet the stream became a woven carpet, the design complex but abstract. Her other hand, the right, held up a wand, which lightning was striking. She smiled, but tears were on her cheeks. She had a diamond tiara, though her feet were bare and half the edge of her garment was tattered.

Visible in this are Aradia's flower-like mother, house deeds and death warrants, the smoke of war, the blood of death and miscarriage, the wealth she inherits, the poverty she embraces.... Jilza sees something trans-human in Aradia. And again Lee seems to be issuing instructions for proper interpretation, this time through the cards: She said that ... I had another self, a shadow or reflection, of whom in turn I was also the mirror and shadow, and thus my way had already been influenced, plaited and incised...."

Ara does not know that the coral bracelet she gives Jilza is a Gurz family heirloom, nor, presumably, that, coral gives children magical protection. Nor that the amulet Jilza gives her will dispatch Drahris.

Drahris recognizes a goddess of death in Ara. With the "bauble" of a human head hanging from his stirrup, he says, "I might have known you'd be here lapping the blood." And when he finally contrives to rape her, she recognizes "the culmination of all dreads. I had known it was unavoidable. Even the witch had foretold it." But, unaware it conceals a knife, she does not intend to commit murder as she strikes out with Jilza's amulet.

> The Murderess. Now she was myself.... Jilza said at my inner ear: "*Lightning is attracted.*"
> Once, I had saved the life of a man. For that I had known a sacrifice was due. But what sacrifice for a sacrifice?
> I dreamed Urtka the Bear sat grinning and laughing in the forest, strung with severed heads....

Both Jilza and Urtka have tricked her.[13] She recites the "charm of my childhood," invoking the kindly mother as the apple tree: "The apple tree, the apple tree,/ Her apples green, her apples sweet."

Around her the landscape of death and desolation becomes an abyss, "devoid of living beings.... The armies were blown away, all men and women ghosted into other regions, of the sky or the earth's entrails." In this Hour of the Wolf, the Kronian god, Wiparvet, prowls through the text, signifying death with "all the stars garnered in his eyes."[14]

> Bereft of the anchor of humanity, as in suffering and hate and war and love we are, peculiar phenomena become easy to credit; what is always in us, conceal it as we may, causes them to be.

Wiparvet also presides at marriages, but, immediately after Ara has signed the marriage contract, the howl of the wolf predicts the death of Gurz. At this marriage of death, Ara makes the familiar exchange—in this case with a lie set into a complex web of feeling and internal paradox:

> I had loved my mother so very, very much. How I had loved her....
> "I love you," I said. I wept ... I gave him that. It was all I had, that lie. That good and special lie. That deep perverted truth.

Gurz has played the soldier uneasily. Early in the retreat, she observes his character correctly: "He was the pedant of the party. They tolerated him. He had never fought a single engagement." The skirted robes of the Hierophant recall the era of goddess worship; behind these skirts Ara will discover the figure of The Lady, his grandmother, a woman of great age and power. Beneath his pedantic exterior, Gurz has many posthumous secrets to reveal. Sexual initiator, bridge between worlds, Gurz also mediates between Swords and Pentacles, Air and Earth, the desolation of war and the bucolic loveliness of his estate, Krase Holn.

While her legal rights are being established, Ara has to wait in the city. She is taken on by Vollus, a woman who initiates her into the protocol of the adult world and arranges her legal representation and her personal presentation. Groomed almost out of recognition, Ara sees herself transformed into a white goddess with bleached hair and elegant and often symbolic garments. Vollus is "the mistress-magician ... behind the mirror...." For Ara it is, "the moment of my rebirth, the first time I saw myself as she remade me."

Vollus's house is in essence a seraglio, "a house of women, where only the fey shoemaker and his girlish assistant got in." Surrounded by Indian carpets, an Eastern "god of joy," and an outsized cat that resembles the Egyptian goddess Bast, Vollus is both pleasure-loving and staunch. To Ara's remark that her birthday falls on the festival of Vulmartis, she replies, "Who's Vulmartis? Vulmardra is your goddess now." Vollus is Strength, a card showing a woman grasping the jaws of a lion, which signifies control over instinct.[15]

When Thenser arrives at a party Vollus is giving to introduce Ara to society, he fails to recognize her. Ara comments, "It was I who recreated him, that man in black," though, as if to avert any taint of hubris, she quickly adds, "If I had remade him, she had remade me from scraps."

Meanwhile, Thenser's arrogant gambling borders on vulgarity, though he casually pays a friend's debts with his winnings. Both Thenser and Ara can exhibit a worldliness that anchors their more mythical aspects. When Thenser is forced to accept a challenge to a duel, he is explicit that it should not be a fight to the death. Though a soldier, he shares Ara's revulsion for killing—but not apparently for humiliating an opponent to whom he refuses the death-thrust, in spite of his pleas to die. As Thenser plays the trickster, Ara wonders, "...was it something intrinsic, to begin by deceiving, working up to *this*?"

After the duel, she falls ill. Feverish, she also begs,

> Let me die. Oblivion was beautiful and precious. The black lid. Oh, yes.... There was an apple tree with enormous branches that spread across the heavens, but severed heads hung among the fruit, and golden candeliers.... I sank a million miles, into blackness beyond all black, and suddenly I was cool, and the pains left me.... There on the floor of night I touched another.... The comfort was so profound, so comforting ... let me not lose this holy and unreasonable moment.

Death is not only the frozen killing fields, it is also a release from pain. With a convalescent weltschmertz, Aradia departs for her estates.

> I descended the auburn stair of autumn ... as if my feet, in fashionable sandals, met only the thin pavement of existence, and below churned the sea. But I was not afraid. Not of the way before me. Not of the shadow behind me. Not of my debt to Vollus.... I was only sad.

Entering along the "wolf-emerald artery of the estate," Ara finds the presence of the goddess in nature everywhere. The staff twined with flowers above the gate, the wheat and honeycomb set before the shrine to Wiparvet, the orchards and wheatfields, the topaz wine, the utter abundance of it all make her a returning mistress of Arcadia. She gradually succumbs to its beauty: "In a peculiar fashion, I had begun to be happy." But this is no longer the happiness of the child in the palace gardens. The shadow of death has passed over her, revealing that bodily life is a prison. "I was not truly in a cage. Or not in any cage but that I had already suspected, the physical box that shuts up every one of us."

Aradia, in her purely human aspect, reflects and reflects upon all that she passes through. But she is also "the mirror and shadow" of "another self," and all that she passes through reflects some aspect of the goddess. Generally, Aradia does not perceive this transcendental being as innate in herself, but in this halcyon spot, dedicated to Nature, she catches glimpses of the goddess incarnate in herself: "I go about ... for all the world as if I were some icon of Vulmardra, the harvest-mother, and in this landscape, perhaps I am."

The goddess is powerful in Krase Holn. A little shrine hidden in a stand of birch trees conjures up Aphrodite with its "dove pale stone ... the roof like the upper third of an eggshell." As she steps into it, Aradia is swept up by an otherworldly force. "Two giant hands seemed to hold me cupped in them, off the earth, two unseen eyes seemed to stare at me." At dawn on the day of the goddess's winter festival, she wakes to see the women and The Lady assembled in the shrine:

> ... they had killed something. It was a little black water-hen ... knowing the dominion of Death, neither would I have killed you, little bird....

At first she feels only horror and revulsion:

> ... by the altar was the grandmother Lady ... her hair unloosed, thin as grey smoke, yet long to her knees.... She was crazy and the rite was filthy and barbarous. I would be rent and ripped apart....

But horror gives way to participation as Ara steps into the temple "The *pressure*. The *power*. I was in a globe like that of a pale golden tulip.... My sex, my breasts, engorged. But it was not sensual. It was a cup of lightning and it held me."

The Lady gives her a yellow rose. It transforms in her hand into coins, blood, tears, a carpet. It steadies as "a field of golden grain." It has become the landscape at the feet of The World's Girl. Ara joins in the singing of the women: "I could not decipher the words. So I sang to her softly, in its mother tongue, the rhyme of the apple tree, which they had said was once a hymn of Vulmartis."

The many forms of the goddess are all one. Though Ara may loathe the spilling of blood, the death aspect of the goddess cannot be excluded.

In the midst of all this the Emperor arrives. He is careful not to intrude on female rites. His relations with Aradia tell the story of male gods who displace the goddess of the south and east: "...in these men was the North, that spirit of iron and brass which had destroyed the one I was, made me the one I had become. This invasion, though only now of an embrace, a mouth, the truth made *actual*."

Krase Holn appears to have a charmed ability to embrace both cultures. Though the domain of women, "the clockwork house continued to run. Granny, Vulmadra and I presided redundantly." Granny adds, "there's sometimes a black wolf seen, the god's wolf." In winter, beside the lake, Ara sees the Wolf-God approaching "like a low black wave along the earth.... He might kill me if he desired."[16]

In this garden of earthly delights, death conceals itself in innumerable small and seemingly innocent details, such as the red of a dress or jewelry, "from the mausoleums of the Serpent Kings—snakes and crocodiles, biting their tails, or one's throat." Death sits at Ara's dinner table and, instead of her guests, occupies her thoughts. "Were they all now, all those moving breathing men and women, *bones?*" Thenser's friend, Vils, is "a living shadow between me and the shadow-army of darker truer things." Elaieva also seems to return, eerily speaking out of Ara's mouth. "'Betrayed,' I said. Or she said it, that woman who spoke with my Aunt Elaieva's voice." And when she talks to Kahrulan, she comments: "Aradia would have burst into tears. But Elaieva rose slowly to her feet." Elaieva casts a shadow over all of Thenser's visits to Krase Holn, pointing to him as the one who inflicts pain. But he also feels pain. "Suddenly looking up at me, he went very white.... He did not know me ... he was seeing Elaieva.... 'You are twice a traitor,' I said. *She* said, Elaieva, the doll, the demon."

More sadly, she says, "For three seconds I was the one you loved, when you were a boy of twenty in a ravaged city. But then I was again a stranger." Thenser is more Theseus than Hermes here, described in ancient cadences. "Traitor twice-over. Worse than any corpse your name will stink." This is the abandonment of Ariadne-Ara, who sacrifices family and country to save her lover from the Minotaur. But Thenser has not forgotten from mere indifference. "'I see the dead everywhere,' he said.... Behind his beauty, and his eyes, was a whirlpool of rage and pain...." And Aradia matches her "brother in race and treachery, deceit and anger," in suffering and awareness of death. She muses, "Thenser, tomorrow it is the Vulmartia.... But mostly it is my birthday. Aradia's last. For in autumn, Aradia truly will be no more." Aradia is about to become the consort of the Emperor and at sixteen to pass officially out of childhood, but her comment also foreshadows the descent into sexual passion and death.

The autumn fertility rites of Vulmardra correspond with the largely rural rite, dedicated to Hermes, of bride seizure.[17] Aradia tells us, "In the legend, the god in his wandering was brought to the goddess in a glade," and when she comes on Thenser in the woods, he is "unknown" and a "god."

"The god leaned on the tree, but sensing me, lifted his head.... He was clad as a man, for travelling. The disguise could not deceive ... though he was in the spell he had not known it. Then he knew."

Bringing together a whole spectrum of signifiers, Thenser tells Aradia, "I was drawn off the road by a shadow like a black dog."[18] He holds her with ominous foreknowing, "as if I had indeed come back from death with him," but even so he lies, and she weeps with a "Love too strong now for pleasure or happiness. *Pain*, welcomed now like any lover. Fleeting, dissolving." This is not the same Aradia who recently remarked, "Not to be touched had brought a kind of happiness, as if each month of chastity washed off some staleness, healed some bruise. Kahrulan intruded ... the terrible display Gurz had made of himself, could I too be capable of it? I was afraid of that. Afraid that this man ... would take me to the brink and fling me down. Then I resisted the sensual gratification he might have given me."

Now she willingly gives up peace in exchange for passion.

"That night of weeping all the tears I had said were spent, the waters of my soul I had not known existed. Heart's blood."

Then, abruptly reentering the immediate world, she adds, a little wryly, "And it was the only blood I gave the goddess. My monthly female time had failed me."

This, at the moment when she is about to secure her future in marriage to an Emperor, is a disaster. She persuades herself she doesn't want the child. But still her feelings are in conflict. "I saw it plain for one whole golden second, the golden miracle within me."

And it is a time of miracles. Sleepless, she visits the shrine in the night and seems to see the goddess in a preternatural white owl, which flies up in her face, carrying a dead mouse in its claws. The Lady is already here, playing with the three cards "of the She"—"the Priestess, the Heroine, the Hag." Realities fuse. "How could she transmogrify into a bird. Or was she the goddess? Had Jilza been the goddess...?" The mere mention of Jilza indicates trickery afoot. Showing Aradia the three cards, The Lady recites their subtitlings: '*Lightning Is Attracted ... The World's Girl, Of the Maiden; The Moon, Of the Crone, and Calling the Sea; Of the Mother ... Dispatches from the Towers.*"

She designates the cards: Aradia is, of course The World's Girl, she herself is the Crone. Of the Mother, she says, "Neither of us can claim this card. I am old, but young beside this one."

And then, with her usual idiosyncratic abruptness: "'Lightning,' The Lady said, her owl's claws scrabbling on her lap. '*Seize* it.'"

Immediately Ara begins to bleed. She finds herself glad and angry, relieved and cheated: "The goddess took the shackles from me. She gave me liberty. She *stole* from me. She *robbed* me of his seed—"

But one scenario is already giving way to another. They start to overlap. The marriage goes ahead, but is not consummated. Ara, who has lingered through an entire rotation of the seasons in her Kronian estate, gives it to the Emperor in exchange for her freedom. Now she will go to search for Thenser. Krase Holn is already receding into the distance. As, for the last time, she watches Kahrulan "at the window.... Gurz he became, looking away from me into the night, looking away and away."

Then he is gone. In a moment she will be gone—"Rush chariot, fly..."—on her way to cross the water, leaving everything behind.

The Left-Hand Path

Opening with a sea voyage, Part Two of *Heroine* moves from Earth to Water and to the suit of Cups, symbolizing love, pleasure, the feminine as womb or heart.[19] The tone grows lighter. The ship's "black wolf" dog performs captivating tricks and dines at the captain's table. This more fluid environment gives Ara freedom and independence. Her moment of flirtation at Krase Holn was heavy and anxious, but here a young, Mediterranean romantic bursts into tears as he declares his love for her. "Suddenly laughter won. He was a compendium of it all, Thenser upon Elaieva's stair, myself upon this foolish journey." Aradia's laughter has barely been heard before. It is a turning point.

She has also grown politically astute. Too poor for bribes when she risks a visit to the "devil" slave ship, she buys her information with the Emperor's name. Failing to find Thenser at the port, a temple to the goddess draws Aradia inland to the old town. She earns a living by executing small drawings. With a pot of camellias for company, she describes herself as happy, but the text has a hollow note: "I need want for nothing./ Nothing./ Nothing."

This region's goddess comes from "Sibris," the Cyprus of Aphrodite. Surrounded by white pigeons, her statue represents a naked woman holding "a shell before her loins, not coyly, but with divine occultism." Dolphins decorate the temple. Aradia attends a festival of Vulmartis. Reunited with the goddess of her childhood, she weeps and prays for reunion with Thenser. A woman persuades her to overcome her embarrassment and, using a pink candle, work a spell to bring her lover back.

The apple appears again. Ara notices a painting in the window of a studio, "hardly in the way of an apple at all.... It rested in pale mysterious space, and was so beautiful one wished to drink it or drown in it at once." Its painter, "a gray, grave boy of about fourteen ... who sees another earth..." wants to paint Ara as the goddess. His apple painting lures Thenser's companion, Irmenck, into the shop where Ara now works, and leads her back to Thenser. The boy also alerts Aradia when Thenser is betrayed to the slave ship's captain.[20]

Again Thenser fails to recognize Aradia, or even to associate her certainly with the Ara of Krase Holn. She does not reveal her name: Convention dictates that he must make the connection himself.

"You're the Princess Aara Gurz.... You're an adventuress.... But what is the plot of this drama?" he asks. Aradia speaks to him in their mother tongue, and suddenly he has an urgent need to know her. "You begin to seem like every woman I ever met with, lay on, saw on a street.... Save me from madness. Reveal yourself."

She begins her story like a riddle: "Like you, I played both sides. Like you, twice a traitor, and a lost child." She then watches "his face change, its mask come unraveled, and the beauty of his realness and his hurt cut through me." Eventually stumbling upon her identity, Thenser says, "You were Aradia." He uses the past tense, as if she has died and been reborn. Her reply, "I too was a thing of dust," also acknowledges death at the heart of life. But any admission of love must be wrung from Thenser—"It's a fantasy, beautiful and idiotic.... Aradia, don't make me say these things."

She next meets him as she preempts an ambush. There is no space for emotional scruples. Swept away with Thenser, Aradia joins battle and kills a man. It seems to compound the bond between them, and she says, "My life was damned when yours was. Everything I did, in some way, a bleak echo."

They are at last united, but when she moves with Thenser to a little island, Aradia silently wonders, "Who are you, this unknown stranger, this fellow-human of another gender, another race of the world, this pleasure-giver, this burning warmth that holds me, rocks me through the seas of night?"

The theme of her sojourn in Cups is the stranger-enchanter who kindles sexual passion. Aradia retains "an unconscious belief in fairy tales" and grows fretful like Psyche in the palace of Amor. As Thenser spends his days away from her, she is left imprisoned in a cage of desire.

> He would guide me weak and moaning, mindless with the need for him, away into the heaven of ecstasy from which I fell back delivered of all hope. Thereafter I was never at peace with his visit.

The beauty of nature increases her pain.

> Wild mint and lavender and saffron smoked on the hills. I heard the running streams. An eagle went over the sky like a god. The beauty

of these things made my hurt more poignant. At each start of my spirit towards delight, the reminder came, like a pang of loss or foreboding.

Thenser at this point is withdrawn, secretive and sometimes cruel. He says, "You live in a dream, Aradia ... do any of us exist for you?" and later, "You love too much, or think you do." In "a rapid self-questioning," where "all the underpinnings of my emotions seemed endangered," Aradia doubts her own observations.

> The village was very poor.... I saw ... the thin bodies of the children.... But I saw too the flowers growing in the broken walls, and the cats sunning themselves, the colors of washing as well as the darns and patches. It was again my naivety, or I was wrong.

She struggles valiantly to appreciate Thenser's "social and political commitment. But I could not grasp the fire.... Gradually, by listening, suspending self, I became Thenser." Sometimes "the Shadow left him." And sometimes he comes closer to her: "Work your magic. You may save me yet."

But Aradia's pleasure is becoming tainted. She finds herself sleeping through her days. At a ball, she meets Retka, the man to whom Thenser has pledged his allegiance. The meeting is full of omens: "A shadow fell across me, covered me.... He wore blood red...."

Back on the island the festival of the goddess evokes loneliness, with "the women singing in the hour before dawn, a strange echoing lament." A Prince Firius, who had forced himself on her at the ball, traces her to the village. Appearing to equate himself with Thenser, "two heroes in his [Retka's] chariot," he attempts to rape her.[21] Though she repels him with a kitchen knife, Aradia panics and sets out to join Thenser. She arrives late and unannounced and cannot find the street where Thenser is living. She escapes from a group of ruffians by demanding to be taken to Retka's headquarters but instantly regrets her mistake. "I wanted to get away from him.... The power that streamed from him, eating up or forming objects in the room, was indescribable." Worse still, she discovers that she has lost her dolphin wedding ring.[22] Retka sends her to the house of his mistress, the "moon goddess," known as Sydo, meaning silver cup.

Aradia has entered another cage. Thenser is bitter when he at last arrives at Sydo's house.

> The old familiar outcry, Aradia. Because I abandon you, you suffer these terrible calamities ... the village was safer than this town is likely to be ... society here now supposes ... that I loan you to Retka....

In spite of his callousness, Aradia still tries to understand him.

> His eyes were the hungry hunted eyes of something which hides, cannot sleep, is starving. I recalled them from the enclosure of a dusty room, a glade of a king's garden. My misdeed had not caused this in him. It was only the tickling of a feather on an open wound.

As he leaves, she comments, "We had come to the pass of speaking to each other, both, in a *language the other one did not know*'" (emphasis added). The paradoxes of separation and unity, death and life, symbolic and real worlds, and the estrangement of genders continues into the interminable drought-stricken summer. The water in the cup has run dry.

A sentence, read aloud from a novel, produces ominous reverberations:

"And thus they entered, *separately yet hand in hand*, the House of Night."

War again threatens. Retka's visits are disturbing. He describes Sydo as "a gleaming serpent on a warm wall. When winter comes Sydo glides away." Sydo grows increasingly sinister. As they dine together for the last time, she refers again to The House of Night, a prison from which only the dead emerge: "...she laughed.... There was a mindless evil to her, just that of the snake before it lunges.... I whispered the name of Vulmartis."

Aradia is moved into Retka's headquarters. On his own ground, Retka's power is overwhelming. "From the jungle-forest of his black locks, that face ... [was] a thing twisted brand new out of primeval chaos ... one could not look away."[23] About to depart the city for safety's sake, Aradia dines with Retka: "...you trample us in your gallop to hell," she tells him. She has slipped back into otherworldly spaces: "It is all a pretence ... in the vast auditorium of space and time, a theatre that may end in death, but is also meaningless, a *lie*."

In a return of the exchange motif, he rapes her. She is paying The Devil his dues. The Tarot Devil is an underworld god, a chthonic Pan who has a naked man and a woman chained to his throne. His "mystery" is the absolute center of impersonal carnality, in which sex becomes a sacred rite. Escape is out of the question: "...it was a rape to which I had consented. For it was power, it was destiny bearing me down ... this overthrow of self, liberating as the conquest by death.... I was no more anything, was obliterated...."

With papers and funds, she sets out in a carriage with two horses. But "The *chariot* had a slovenly look" (emphasis added) and soon Aradia is robbed of both money and transport. She continues on foot, "in a kind of delirious resignation," and reaches a village that seems like "the doorway of night." Unhappily, the treacherous Firius is here and accuses her of treason. She is taken to a fortress known as The House of Night.

This prison has already appeared in *Dispatches from the Towers*, the card of the Mother, too ancient for even Gurz's grandmother to claim. The Tarot Tower shows two tiny figures falling from a vast lightning-struck tower.[24] The lightning represents divine illumination and recalls the phrase '*Lightning is Attracted.*" The subterranean Devil has made way for the light-bringing Lucifer. Unbearably immense space meshes with tight imprisonment.

> You courted vertigo whichever way you gazed—down to the bay below, the miniature sea-fans pleated with foam, the fishbone of the boat—or upward to the tapering of the eyeless towers with the gulls swarming about their tops like flies.... It was an underworld, somehow positioned in the air.[25]

Aradia knows where she has come. "The entry to the mansion of death, surely, will be like this. The vaulted darkness, composed more of shadow than stone." Even before she has reached her cell she comes upon a statue of the black goddess of death, "a gaunt old woman of black marble.... I thought she must be a Vulmartis—the goddess as crone.... What other deity would consent to brood there in that wall, as in a hall of cold hell?"

This hell is isolation: "There seemed no other living thing within its caves of stone." Living reality has been internalized, and in this dark space she realizes that, like Psyche descending into the underworld, she is carrying a child. At first she supposes it must be Retka's, but the wardress tells her she is four months gone. Her compulsive sleeping, her heaviness and inertia are explained. The run of Cups is almost complete. This time she desires the child intensely: "...alone and in darkness—this fragment of a light, I hugged it close."

The warden has already shown her the death masks of four women hanged there for witchcraft. (This prison seems exclusively dedicated to the deaths of women.) But it is not legal to hang pregnant women, and he punishes her in "retribution." She is abruptly wakened from a dream of her mother and her daughter, and moved to a tiny underground cell. There are no windows. The darkness is absolute, unbearable, belonging equally to womb and tomb.

"The air was heavy, like liquid.... The silence was even louder here."

In this cell, reduced to nothing, with nothing to give the goddess but her dreams, she at last learns to put herself unconditionally into the hands of a goddess who is "Celibate as obsidian. Priestess and crone together." Stripped of everything, she finds the needed prayer.

> The black eggs of her eyes look down.... What can I ask of one who will not give?.. in my hands an offering. In the dream I brought you nettles, all I could discover. But this too is a dream, and I have white poppies and chrysanthemums, the flowers of sleep and death.
> These I lay across your palms.

The goddess in the shrine at Krase Holn is recalled.

> The statue is alive. The pressure has begun, pushing outward from the stone. And I am caught in the pressure, like an insect in rushing water. Round and round, until I fall across the feet of the hag, and clasp them. And the stone of her feet is warm as the stone of a hill in sunshine. Help me.'

In the intolerable darkness Aradia makes pictures in her mind, "igniting before her a yellow candle, and the rays of it ran off like golden twine and filled the corridors and stairs." This is Ariadne's ball of twine that will lead her out of the labyrinth. Almost immediately, light begins to trickle under the door, and she is taken upstairs to yet another cell. She is offered a choice: "To have miscarried, or to be given up."

Back in the light, she clings to her vision of the goddess: "My only chance was to remain a little mad.... Sanity meant I must accept defeat." The exchange of cells also has its price. Her hanging is now imminent.[26] She is given a bath and a dress for the event, but she holds to hope: "I bathed for an appointment with survival." The dress "of a gossamer blueness ... augured well."[27]

Out on the rooftop where she is to be hanged, Aradia is reborn in a burst of light so dazzling the darker purpose of the moment is obscured. With the noose round her neck, she says, "My eyes are full of blue infinity ... I see the sun is like a diamond." The Tarot Sun is almost the end of the Way. Two naked children dance in a magic ring under a huge bright sun in the card of new life and safe haven after the perils of descent into the underworld. Suddenly, from nowhere, "A man with yellow hair is thrusting a cup in my face.... I found I was seated on the platform of the gallows."

Thenser, disguised in enemy uniform, and Aradia descend the cliff and escape in a waiting boat. Aradia displays little curiosity about her rescue, but Thenser's destiny interests her. "But what," I said, "for you?"

"There's the world," he said. "There's you, if you still care for me." Then, for a second, he placed his hand on my waist, where the swelling of the child began. It was like the touch of a flame. The life inside me seemed to spring, as if it knew him. "And who's this?" he said. He held me fast; he did not mean to let me go.

The *world* that Thenser speaks of is the Tarot World, the last card of the Way. It portrays a naked hermaphrodite, dancing in the center of a wreath against a blue background with a wand in either hand. The figure symbolizes the cosmic egg, rebirth and completion of the cycle. Amor has returned to wipe away the Stygian sleep and transport his divine bride up to heaven.[28] Aradia has grown from a little girl into a woman.

The farewell glimpse of the lovers reiterates the symbolic nucleus of the story. Theseus and Hermes are once more indicated. "Around the headland in a while I should see a ship with two white sails."[29] The last note is one of pure pleasure. "A moment before, out of ocean into heaven, a dolphin leaped like silver." In a small boat on the sea, with no fixed destination, Aradia is entering a new beginning.

—5—

REALITY, LOVE AND OPPOSITION —SCIENCE FICTION

Drinking Sapphire Wine, The Silver Metal Lover, Electric Forest, Day by Night

---

Drinking Sapphire Wine[1]

Lee's science fiction is often thematically similar to other works, and here death and renewal become both mechanical and comical in an advanced society run by robots. Determined that humans should feel only pleasure, they eliminate work, birth and death, and provide replacement bodies, with form and gender according to taste. A caustic, rebellious and sex-changing protagonist struggles to become autonomous, and reaches the conclusion that real life requires real death. The book is playful and inventive, especially of teenage slang.

Sexual experience as a means to self-knowledge is pushed aside by a need to distinguish between unexamined sexual pleasure and a personal understanding of love. Where adolescent sexual experiment is almost obligatory, the heroine's (she tells us she is "predominantly female") first real love is for her pet, which, like herself, is captive and dispossessed. Her first properly considered action is for its benefit. "I'll drown again, I thought ... but before I did anything I thought of the pet. It would probably go *varadann*

5. Reality, Love and Opposition—Science Fiction

with panic.... It wouldn't like the asthmatic drowsiness of dying, and I couldn't explain. Oh well, I could always drown tomorrow."

With their suicides and sexual promiscuity, the *Jang* (adolescents) of Four Bee are encouraged to imagine that they are living dangerously. In fact they are only living mindlessly—thinking runs contrary to the interests of robots who are caricatures of social and psychological control. The narrator constantly fights to wake from the unreality of this futuristic world. Her efforts to reach reality continue even in dreams, but her pro-human leanings and inexperience of nature combine to make the real world into a romantic, fictional object: "The average Jang dream ecstasy is to be a mote of pulsing light ... a kind of cosmic all-over comprehension of having love ... I could turn a seven-dimensional geometric exercise into an epic adventure."[2]

The narrating I is deliberately difficult, especially over political issues such as the economy and work. She resists paying for goods with the effusive expressions of gratitude that supply the system's energy. And the currency of emotion (what robots lack) is subject to their unwritten belief that faking is as good as feeling—or probably better, since it is less potentially dangerous—"Dream Rooms and Adventure Palaces have diverted the emotions along harmless channels."

The protagonist shop lifts to avoid the humiliations of purchase and giving genuine value to what she acquires—"I always attach importance to the things I steal..." and "I never pay for anything if I can help it. I just enthuse ever so unexcitedly, and drive all the robot assistants *zaradann*." Naturally, her beloved pet is stolen.

After a visit to the Dream Rooms, a law-abiding friend insists on paying with *thank-yous* and *groshings* and *derisans*.

> "Thank you," I droned urbanely.
> Machines registered protests.... All right, I thought, I'll show you.
> "Oh, thank you," I screamed. I took an ecstasy pill and soared and soared. I ranted. I screeched until my throat gave out. I hugged the machinery with unbridled passion, and tears of love ran down my face ... outside.... Perfect sunlight hit me in the face and threw the husk of my visions at my feet.

Synthetic, chemically-induced displays drain off real emotion.

Lightness and humor often camouflage the text's studious opposition of man-(or robot)-made scientific control, and uncontrollable nature and robots do not always prevail. When the narrator fails to procure a father for the baby she wants (robots condone teenage pregnancy), and by contriving a few clandestine sex-changes stands in as both father and mother, the baby literally explodes as the robots are assembling it. Robots are also emotionally deficient. Though the heroine greets Moddik's sarcastic humor and pragmatism in her desert commune as an antidote to complaining, drug-saturated Jang, when the truth emerges—that he is a robot sent to destroy "very, very dangerous anarchists,"—the narrator says, "it was finally out, the bare facts of their rivalry, what I had always instinctively felt. Programmed they might be to serve human needs, but in some hidden dark of their personae, they hated and despised us."[3]

Beyond the hectic sex, drugs and seemingly limitless sense gratifications that the technology supplies, the greatest corrupting influence is the promise of one instant replacement body per month and the knowledge that no one is actually going to die. As in Lee's Flat Earth, immortality is the thief of souls.

Whether motivated by suicide, fashion or a whim for altered gender, unrecognizable bodies are casually assumed. Reality is thrown into disarray and the plot often hinges on confused identity. Though name is the only sure indicator of identity, the narrator has none. When she visits her friend Hergal, adapting to a new body after his fortieth suicide, and says she is going to *cut him out of her circle*, she is piqued by his apparent unconcern; but as she is leaving, he enquires politely, "who are you exactly?" "He just didn't try," she comments. Her parents (*makers*) now both male, also fail to recognize her but interrupt an orgy in order to store her new image for reference. The narrator cuts them short. "Don't bother ... I'm changing again in sixty units or so." Only the pet reacts naturally to what she looks like, or, as she remarks, *smells* like, and runs away in terror when she unthinkingly appears in a new body. With unusual thoughtfulness, she reverts to her former body and, after its death, miserably contemplating another body change, she confesses, 'I carefully never admitted no one would be bothered that I'd changed, no one would run away honking and hide its white fur and orange eyes among the silk grass."

The theme of recognition—coming to recognize others, and thereby oneself, beyond mere appearances—can be played out in full in a world in which physical form is so readily alterable. Essence and identity are humorously discussed when the nameless narrator dreams of the dead pet.

> "You're dead," I said to the pet. "True death. Obliteration."
> "Certainly my body's dead," said the pet casually, "but ... what about that thing they use at Limbo, the thing the androids don't have, the life spark, the soul? ... [H]ave you forgotten *everything*?"
> "How else could I get by, without making myself forget?" I said, and didn't at first know what I meant.
> "Finally you can only get by letting yourself remember."

While the narrator learns with effort, the pet is a natural philosopher who knows precisely what needs to be remembered.

> "Pet," I said, "I've forgotten your name."
> "Names," said the pet. "Is that the only thing you care about?"
> And it bit me hard, so hard I woke up with a shout.

Questions of appearance and recognition constantly shape the narrative. When her friend Danor returns from the city of BAA with a new body, the narrator still recognizes her. She (or he, as she is at this point) misdirects a group of Jang towards a "nice little thing in pink," and quietly makes off with her friend. A muscle-bound bully is killed in an ensuing duel but attends the trial, resuscitated as a dainty, tittering blonde, "balancing precariously on her weeny silver-slippered feet," and it is instantly obvious that the narrator will be found guilty.[4]

The faithful Hatta, in love with her from the beginning, remains often unrequited because of his preoccupation with the deception of appearances. He inhabits ugly and even non-human bodies, hoping he will be loved for himself. A running refrain is provided by his proposals and her responses: 'Not with you looking like that we couldn't,' I said. Well, I mean. Outraged pimples and a couple of tons descending on you with three yellow pupil-less eyes to watch the effect." On the one occasion when Hatta appears in a pleasing body—to cheer her up after the death of her pet—the proposal comes from her, but when they have love, an event which she finds unusually *groshing*, Hatta is acutely depressed.

> "Can't you see," he said softly, "how useless it all is?" ...
> "But I loved every minute," I said. "Didn't you?"
> "Oh yes," he said, "I loved having you, my *ooma*, and you loved having my body, my new, unreal joke of a body. I loved you and *you* loved the shell of me."

The heroine's first experience of true emotion is with the pet. In a classic Lee juxtaposition of opposites, the vivifying rain that makes the desert bloom is also a prelude to the death of the pet. Where real life is to be found, there also real death will appear:

> ... all around the little animals were rushing, bouncing and orgying in the growth.... Suddenly I was part of it, with my brand of mankind, my Jangness, my cityness ... my hair was scarlet fur, and I danced and ran and laughed and sang with the mad small animals among the glory of the woken green.... Then I found the pet....

> Oh, we ran, side by side the pet and I, and never have I known such closeness with any of my race, my mankind, as I knew with that white animal I stole in casual and neurotic need, from a store in Four BEE.

She becomes a real human by recognizing herself as part of nature, but she still faces the task of learning to love another person. The motif of theft reappears when, riding on a stolen mechanical dragon, Esten (in whom she does *not* recognize the re-embodied Hatta) joins her in the desert. He is wearing the same "poet's" body that she had before the prospect of life in the desert had persuaded her to adopt a more practical female body: "Only the tan was different, designed to take the sun. Dying of consumption the poet might be, but he didn't fancy sunburn on top of it."

Lee plays with the idea of love as something stolen rather than given or exchanged, and with the paradox, which has appeared previously in the book, "that most of us only want to make love to ourselves..."—"Here's your chance *ooma*. A never-to-be-repeated offer," Esten tells her.

> I knew the theory fine. Another thing he'd stolen from me. Something in it too, if my reactions were anything to go by.

As he seduces her in a body that was originally her own,

> He didn't caress me or speak to me, simply held me there, letting my flesh find him out, even if my brain refused to do so.
> But my brain, submerged, overwhelmed by my flesh, remembered and remembering, conjured him from itself until we seemed one thing, indivisible.

Later, laughing, he asks, "Well now ... was I as good as you were when you were me?"

But Lee is not going to allow the story to end on such a light note. Hatta is not killed, but he is horribly disfigured as he dismantles the bombs Moddik has planted. This time it is the narrator who steals Hatta-Esten's old arguments. "You're still you—still *me*, you body-thieving bastard.... Oh yes the body turned on me, looking like me and everything, but it's you who got through to me, you fool."

She concludes: "I've learned your new name, Esten, and I've learned that if I love anybody, yours is the name he gave himself."

As the narrator and Danor, now fertile on a diet of "home-grown" food, loll gravidly in the sun, awaiting the natural birth of their babies, they have reached a new threshold, arrived at through false realities and painful truths. Once, trying out suicide by plane crash with Hergal, the narrator asked, "why do you always do it like that? It *hurts*." "Pain is a reality," he replied. She learns about loss when her pet dies, she finds her will to live in a duel, and in choosing nature she chooses eventual death in a desert that echoes the desert of the Flat Earth. "Don't be afraid of human death and age.... It's just dust blown over the rocks."

The Silver Metal Lover

Silver (an acronym for Silver Ionized Locomotive Versimulated Electronic Robot) resembles neither the robots of Four Bee nor the abused Magdala of *Electric Forest*. Silver is more than a kinetic work of art. He is art able to (re)produce art in the form of music. Providing pleasure according to personal desires, even unconscious ones, he becomes humanly unpredictable when love enters the equation. Built only to *respond*, he does not seek his own satisfaction until Jane, wanting him to love in the same way she does, refuses to accept his *difference* and thus undermines the logical premises on which robot-nature is constructed. Her premonition just before she meets Silver matches him, being both mechanical, "like a key turning," and extra-sensory. "It seemed as if I knew something very important, and only had to wait a moment and I would recall what it was. It was like being in love." But when Silver is charming and polite, her own emotions humiliate her.

> "You horrible thing," I whispered, "How dare you stand there and talk to me?"
> The reactions were astounding. His eyes went flat and wicked. He gave me the coldest smile I ever saw, and bowed to me. He really did turn on his heel, and he walked directly away from me.

Soon, however, angry with her friend Clovis, she also turns on her heel, "just like the robot."

Lee concentrates throughout on resolving differences: between human and machine, male and female, carnal pleasure and love. These sometimes overlap or blur—especially for Jane, whose acute lack of autonomy makes her almost as constructed as a robot. Her mother redesigns her body, down to details of hair color and weight, and appoints six friends because she has read it is the statistically ideal number. The twins, Jason and Medea, are loathsome; Egyptia is selfish and hysterical and eventually betrays her; only the flawed Clovis can claim to be a friend. Demeta regulates her daughter's opinions and emotions, though as Jane remarks, "I do what she says, but somehow my life—my true response to life—goes on quite differently." Her "true responses" are written down covertly in a book.

Demeta's intrusive attempts to control Jane's sexuality recall robot pressures on Jang. After a night with Silver, Jane remarks ironically, "she had always told me to get to know my body. To be at ease with it. She now seemed to think it faintly unnecessary that I had, I was."

Demeta's name is more pretentious than mythological, but Jane recounts her response when a troop of monkeys are killed by helicopter blades: "I cried. Mother then told me nothing dies ever, animal or human. A psychic force inside us survives physical death, and continues on both in the spiritual and in other bodies.... What was the connection between them and the red-haired robot outside the Theatra?"

The transmigration of souls has been tailored to the psychology and technology of the future, and the cyclical motif is apparent in the reference to Silver's singing "as if time were playing in a circle inside the notes." Lovers are again reunited over space and time, though at a tactful distance, as Lee ends the book with an epilogue that confirms that the robot is more than a machine. At first Jane is skeptical when Silver's posthumous message reaches her in a seance, but when the oiuja board spells her name as Jain (the spelling had been a code between the lovers) the message is proved authentic. The spelling also aligns the twenty-four sophisticated-format robots with the twenty-four *Jina* of the Jain religion who gained release from the bondage of physical existence. Silver's incarnation in the body of a robot reflects an ancient religious theme and fuses several apparently irreducible cultural elements.

In addition to cultural, sexual and racial reconciliations, Lee's texts also militate against speciesism and failure to give proper value to members of nonhuman species.[5] The pet in *Drinking Sapphire Wine* is important both as itself and as interactive character, and the final premise of that book—that in matters of love the physical body is of secondary importance—applies to both the pet and to Silver before he acquires his human personality or soul.

Because of Jane's unswerving refusal to read Silver as only a robot, despite the evidence of her senses and the well-meant reasoning of Clovis, they both begin to change and grow into extensions of each other. The process begins almost at first sight. He is hired to sing at a party; she is wearing a green dress; he sings an adaptation of Greensleeves: "Alas my love, you do me wrong,/ to cast me off discourteously./ If passion's limit is a song,/ the lack will work hell with my circuitry." She catches up with him in the street, but he does not seem to recognize her from their earlier meeting. She angrily insists that he sang Greensleeves purely to embarrass her, but he denies it. She says,

"I don't believe you."
"I can't lie," he said.
Something jerked inside me, *like a piece of machinery disengaging.*

Silver explains that when he meets responses he has not been programmed to expect, his "thought process switches over," making him "appear distant and blank." Although his logic is impeccable, we still retain the impression that his choice of song was not random, and that perhaps we must believe he possesses some faculty resembling the human unconscious. It seems that lack has already worked some kind of hell with his circuitry—or is it Jane's inappropriate responses? His lyric pleads to be loved beyond "the limit of a song," and even before she sees his face she falls in love with his singing.

Music plays a central part in the story. "If only I could sing," Jane thinks, shedding the tears of an aesthetic emotion she does not recognize as the prelude to a duet. When he sings, she feels that, "He sang into my veins where blood had been and where instead the notes and throbbing of the guitar now flowed," and when he kisses her she feels, "as if a singing tide washed through me." Jane grows more like Silver as her talent for singing surfaces and enables her to earn a living and find independence. As she finds her latent self reflected in a (Silver) mirror, she ceases to accept the self-definition implanted by her mother and no longer needs to hate the false self she has been.

The robot, who needs to negotiate the crossing of an entire species barrier, has a larger task, especially as his manufacturers perceive his unrobotic stirrings as a mysterious malfunction. Bravely confronting the seedy P.R. man at the robot workshops, at first Jane is deeply relieved to see a confirmation of Silver's individuality. His "brother" and "sister" are demonstrated to her and, in a febrile and breathless passage, she sees that they are, "Alike, but not alike. The same hair, but different. The same amber eyes; different, different. The movements, the voice, the same, the same, yet different.... I was so glad I could have wept...."

Yet when she sees Silver in a vulnerable, disassembled state, her first reaction is to perceive him only as a robot. "*It's* a mess," she says, congratulating herself on being cured of her "adolescent dreams." The regressiveness of this moment is underlined as she comments, "My mother's training was at last paying off...." But the lapse only reinforces her feelings: "How could I have left him in their testing cubicle..? Eyeless, machinery exposed, dying and knowing it?"

Silver does not consider himself capable of suffering, and Jane often attributes to him feelings he cannot logically accept. "You're trying again,

Jane, to get me to do something I'm not geared to do, which is analyze myself emotionally," he says. He counters her "unconscious" with "switched off," and turns aside her pointed comment that he speaks of himself as "I" with, "Rather ridiculous if I spoke any other way." "Do you like me?" she asks. "I don't know you," he replies. Then comes the central question:

> "But you think, as a robot, you can still get to know me?"
> "Better than most of the humans you spend time with if you'll let me."
> "Do you want to make love to me?" I cried, my heart a hurt, myself angry and in pain and in sorrow, and in fear—all those things he was spared.
> "I want to do whatever you need me to do.... With a feeling of great pleasure if you're happy...."
> "You're pre-programmed to be pleased that way."
> "So are humans, actually, to a certain extent."

When she first asks him to make love to her, to her astonishment, since she believes him incapable of saying no, he refuses, telling her, "My vocabulary is less limited than you seem to think."

He reads her feelings of estrangement and self-disgust correctly. Jane is in search of emotional discovery, not disengaged sex, and describes her feelings with an ardor for truth that equals his robotic inability to lie. The moment expresses an interdependence that Jane does not yet grasp: "He could give me pleasure of the emotions.... I'd trusted him with the truth.... I didn't know him. He was unknowable. But I trusted him."

And Silver replies, "To my knowledge, you're the first human who ever did love me.... Magnetized, yes. Obsessed. Not love."

Yet when he does make love to her, he makes her an offer stereotyped as feminine, which contradictorily suggests that he *can* lie: "I can fake it if you want."

She makes him promise that he never will. It is a promise that he will be himself. He keeps his promise, but his self alters as he and Jane live penniless and happy in the slums and sing songs about love, which "is like the sea, which changes constantly, and yet is still the same."

Jane transcends her "natural" abilities by singing. "You've got through some barrier in yourself," Silver tells her. Silver also breaks through a barrier in nature and experiences real human love. It is a tremulous moment because, as he reminds Jane, "I'm only three years old.... I have a lot of ground to make up."

> [H]e ... stared down at me in a kind of bewilderment. In the veiled, multicolored light, his face was almost agonized, closing in on itself.

Easy with emotional oxymorons, Lee takes the unusual opportunity of splicing human behavior and robotic logic. When the lovers accidentally meet the malignant Jason and Medea, Silver deliberately frightens them. Jane tries to point out that hatred of humans is a contradiction of his programming, but he is disturbed and refuses to speak about it. They walk home "Like two lovers who'd quarreled." His struggle to realize his evolving identity forces him to set aside his makers' original programme, just as Jane has to abandon her mother's conception of herself in order to become herself. Neither has much confidence in their right to self-generated being. But when Jane anxiously speculates that her mother may drag her back home by force, Silver points out, "your mother would never do that. She doesn't want to publicize the fact that she hasn't got the totally balanced, perfect, well-adjusted, enamored, brainwashed mindless child she intended."

However, it is loving and being loved as part of loving that are the central focus here. Various books, including *Volkhavaar* and *Birthgrave*, resolve themselves in loving that is not necessarily reciprocated. But this time the pleasure or happiness of the other becomes the pivot. As Jane says:

"My joy was his joy. I'd been crazy to say what I had, that he couldn't love. He can love all of us. He *is* love."

Illusion and Disillusion: Electric Forest and Day by Night

With protagonists confused about where, who or what they are, *Electric Forest* and *Day by Night* recall *Birthgrave*. But, as the angle of observation shifts from subjective psychological process to objective experimental study, the hand manipulating its laboratory specimens becomes obscured. Uneasily ascribing real conspiracies to fate or circumstance, at best these victims catch only fleeting glimpses of reality. Wired with intense theatrical tension as the dynamics of power are unmasked, both books demand careful reading.[6]

Though *Day by Night* has a surface appearance of fantasy, the theme of conflict between science and nature is the same in both books. In *Electric Forest* science overtly dominates nature. Master-slave and male-female relations are examined when a female worker is placed in meticulously staged laboratory conditions. A guarded introduction and an epilogue bracket a text that emerges only retrospectively as the record of an experiment. *Day by Night* employs the conventions of fantasy to examine fantasy itself. Initially, its soap operas or "fabulisms" seem to serve anodyne purposes; they grow sinister as it emerges that they are shaping real lives on the far side of the planet. Though no sun ever rises, the chapters of *Day by Night* alternate between dissociated darkness and light. In both texts, the impossibility of telling what is "real" produces fear of madness and absence of meaning. The split severing mind from body and day from night exposes the gap between perception and reality.

The deformed Magda of *Electric Forest* is an "accident," handicapped by natural conception in a future where genetic technology ensures beauty. She is easily bought with the promise of beauty by a scientist engaged in clandestine experiments, supposedly on consciousness transferal. The baroque atmosphere of his research center echoes *Frankenstein* and the gothic novel ("A grim aura of an archaic lunatic asylum overhung these scenes"). Alone and deprived of everything familiar, Magda is constantly spied upon. "His pale face through the glazium glared in at her…. (He was mad. She would die … the consenting victim mesmerized by his madness.)"[7] But she continues to struggle—"She was not a machine, not a robot."[8]

When she asks why the lovely body into which her consciousness has been transferred feels so real, Claudio brutally represses any sense of autonomy: "machine parts inside a machine … tick-tock inside…." At every opportunity he asserts his dominance. "You are my marionette. Dance for me and keep your mouth shut."

He expresses his power in the language of gothic science, terming the "glazium mummy-case" containing her dwarf body and her mind a "coffin," and herself the "Vampire." "I can reduce you to a mindless stupor…. I can also kill you," he tells her and boasts of controlling her through sexual attraction. Shunned in her former body, Magda is vulnerable to the power of his sexuality, and suffers "terrifyingly unavoidable responses, as if she were some pre-programmed machine set going at the pressure of a key."

But she is not mechanical in the sense she imagines. Neither is she what she assumes herself to be. Magda is a decoy, a delusion installed in the genuinely human Christophine—the one "Magda" believes is a simulation or mechanical receptacle for her consciousness. The second Christophine, whom Magda thinks is a woman, is actually a simulation. "Reality" is an elusive quarry in this book.

Believing that she is Magda, the protagonist does not recognize that she is attracted to Claudio as the loved husband from a life she has been made to forget. But the fraud spirals on: Claudio, who appears to be conducting the experiment, is an actor performing a deranged scientist. As he teaches her "what to wear, what to do, and now and then in what to say.... He did not teach her how to stave off madness," irony reaches a high note: An *actor* impersonating the husband of a woman who believes she is a machine teaches her human comportment.

Lee's fascination with twins reemerges in the theme of confrontation by a double and she refers explicitly to the identical twins of *A Comedy of Errors*.[9] In the body of Christophine, "Magda" is primed to kill her double merely to discover if she will. Biological reality and identity are both sacrificed to scientific "objectivity," while the somewhat parallel structure of the plot also manipulates the reader.

Mirrors are central to the hypothesis of helpless attraction to a double. When "Magda" enters the body of Christophine,

> She turned on the mirrors and sat in the middle of them, glancing from each to each. And the mirrors seemed to exclaim: *Here you are. See! You exist.*
> This phase lasted a long time.[10]

Her meeting with the supposedly real Christophine stuns her: "Magdala felt her awareness of identity pass. Everything passed. The world passed. All that was left was Christophine.... To copy was inevitable. It was a mirror. It was herself.

A popular version of the myth of Narcissus—"Generally interpreted as an allegory of homosexual love, or a vulgar illustration of ego-mania"— is expressed by Christophine, who breaks the spell of the mirror by pushing Magda into a sitting position; "...a fundamental difference in posture between them ... offset their *hypnotic sameness*" (emphasis added). In fact, Magda only manages to kill her double in self-defense, while Christophine, relieved of her delusory alter-ego, rather chillingly writes up the experiment on herself in the epilogue: "...should there be a meeting between absolute doubles ... a psycho-physical link will evolve. Self-love is neither fantasy nor vulgar joke ... pre-programmed to put ourselves first. To kill that way is a suicide committed while staring in a mirror."

The same mirror phenomena, and especially its inversions, appear in *Day by Night*. Experiments here are no longer clinical, but are executed by unseen forces in an atmosphere of superstition, betrayal and fear of exposure to nature. As Vitra "invents" her fabulisms, and robots transmit them to the exploited workers underground, she believes the light side of the non-rotating planet is uninhabited.[11] She is, however, recounting events that actually occur among its people, and hubris on the dark side appears to incur nemesis on the light side. On a smaller scale, Ceedres uses facial mimicry to gain love and control.

Vitra's characters are obvious inversions of herself and others. Commenting on their feelings and morals, she says of her heroine (who mirrors her exactly), "She's intelligent enough, but emotionally an idiot. I suppose she has to be to fulfill any sort of story." Vitra's brother is skeptical about her creative talents. "There have been theories that the machinery of the Fabulism chamber makes the story itself. That the Fabulist merely receives, transmits and translates."

Translation is an important theme in this book, bridging the space between darkness and light, but, as polar opposites invert one another, neither is the other's shadow. "Vel Thaidis, the innocent, Vitra, the serpent. Interchangeable."

Although mistrustful and "allergic to his ambitions and his whims," Vel Thaidis unwillingly loves Ceedres. Moral and emotional splits are not merely personal. Truth becomes paramount as it founders in both worlds, but information concerning the light side reaches the dark side, especially its subterrain, only through the medium of fabulisms (dreams?). These are paralleled by light side myths (irrational beliefs?) of hell and heaven, and a religion based on the infallibility of computers (faith in reason?). Though Vitra derides their belief that the "gods gave them their science" and their "myth about a garden paradise," her own fabulism is irrationally infecting her life.

> All at once it seemed to Vitra that, rather than invent a story to entrance the rabble of the Subterior, she had woven her own self into it. She had created a situation which was in turn creating her, coercing her. She had become the slave of a mirage.

Soon Vitra and her brother, Vyen (Vel Thaidis also has a brother) are copying her malicious fictions into darkside lives. As the "fictional" Ceedres plots against Vel Thaidis, they fake a crime, falsely implicating Casrus. Reality is overpowered as this self-reflexive text questions the distinction between fiction and fact. As Lee apparently proposes that objective perceptions may not exist, she scrutinizes the very foundations of storytelling.

Deep in the subterranean hell of the workers, a fabulism shows Casrus a true account of the conspiracy against him. Psychologically speaking, he has gained access to the unconscious. Though there to produce energy, this hell is also a source of truth and home to collective dreams. "I see a box within a box," he says; and "his world, palace or Subterior seemed to have grown phantasmal."

Vel Thaidis, exiled to Slumopolis, suffers the extreme isolation that sometimes afflicts Lee's women, and is greatly saddened by the parental deprivation of the children there. "Children ... were the property of the slum ... sent out to power the city with their working capacity. They replaced the dead, nothing more." These children are "matrixed," reared, educated, even named by robots. Robots may not occupy the foreground, but their effects are constantly felt, most of all as, by replacing human parents, they cause brothers and sisters to become unusually close. But when the plot against Vel Thaidis succeeds, her brother fails her and turns to Ceedres, who addresses him as *"brother"*—"His blood tie with his sister hurt him like a bruised nerve, yet Ceedres had come first.... The brotherhood of gender staking its claims before the shout of blood." On the dark side, incestuous undercurrents precipitate a duel between Vitra's suitor and her brother, who kills her in the confusion.

Vel Thaidis and Casrus both pass beyond the boundaries of their worlds. Both dead by official definition, since removal to the zone between dark and light constitutes "death," they arrive in the mythical garden of paradise where robots are plentiful. Perhaps the light-side legends of god-given science are true after all. She retains only "shreds of her identity" and becomes "a pebble spun through chaos, no firm ground anywhere for sanity to take a stand."[12]

But inside the myth, boredom quickly follows. Vel Thaidis needs "fresh agony, fresh conflict to reassure herself she lived.... Where was the world? ... Where were the characters of her story? Where tragedy, terror and vengeance? ... Peace murdered her slowly." This heaven is no more luminous than the heaven of Flat Earth. Vel Thaidis snatches up a harp (what else?) and, as if music summons him into being, Casrus appears. At first his resemblance to Ceedres alarms her, but when he does not copy her facial expressions, "Suddenly she knew him to be another."

Lee finally seems to be putting aside her disorienting mirrors. Tentatively, certainty appears to be returning. Vel Thaidis is not asking a question when she says to Casrus, "You understand this place, and what has happened." Her conflict is resolved in "a Ceedres from whom she need not withdraw in shame.... That the processes of Kaneka had surely mated them was no more than a pale shadow in the recesses of her awareness."

But Casrus continues to search for explanations in a library that stores "The history and science of a million planets...." He discovers that Kaneka is only one of myriad gates leading out of the world of illusion. And illusion persists; this paradise contains its serpent. Casrus comes upon two huge fabulist's screens with chairs that have only recently been vacated. He tells Vel Thaidis, "Two persons have been watching every moment of our lives and the lives of those about us ... we're to take its place."

Their lives have always only been transmissions. Two controlling parents/gods/robots have been spying on every thought and movement. Heaven is only one more step towards the eternally receding horizon of meaning. But Casrus, though now the transmitter, continues to search. "Now, *now*, he saw, amorphous and untranslatable, a mystic answer.... *Untranslatable? Maybe not forever*" (emphasis added).

Casrus and Vel Thaidis never meet the former occupants of the chairs, but the reader finally overhears them discussing the motivation of "their characters," like colleagues in a psychiatric hospital, and preparing for the moment when, from the distant dome to which they have removed, they can begin to "play" against their new opponents.

The "reality" of the myth is that the powers behind the scenes are hybrids—semi-human, part divine. It is a shock to find that one is a variant of Ceedres, perhaps more sinister than ever as he comments, "I am enthralled with what I am. I intend to discover every facet, brain and spirit."

He will have time for it. "They were long-lived in their own essence.... There were eons before them, and behind ... beyond the opulence, and the tyranny, was not their situation worse than any other's?"

However, it is in a return to the "real" world that we are given a long view of events: "Fantasy, fabulism, whatever it was, the mood in hell was not quite as it had been.... Before they had foregone hope, lain down in brutalized quiescence.... Now they were waking up from the frozen centuries."

—6—

THE FATAL OBJECT —THE SECRET BOOKS OF PARADYS

*The Book of the Damned,
The Book of the Beast,
The Book of the Dead,
The Book of the Mad*

The Book of the Damned

The Book of the Damned, first of *The Secret Books of Paradys*, is composed of three novellas set in a *parallel* (Lee's word) Paris. All three portray physical and spiritual alterations, changes of sex, either through impersonation, transformation or androgyny, and breaches of the moral codes particular to a text's historical setting.

Each novella centers visually on a stained glass window. Possibly this refers to the tradition of stained glass windows as meditational devices. The window colors are reflected in three pieces of ancient jewelry: a ruby scarab ring, a topaz crucifix plundered during the Crusades and an Egyptian sapphire earring shaped like a spider. Each jewel is fateful for its possessor.

The novellas are also linked through recurring locations in Paradys/ Par Dis: St. Jean, a poet of the Decadence, drinks in The Cockatrice, which is a focal point in the medieval text; his name, given to the street in which the twentieth century narrator of the last novella lives, is adopted by her as a nom de plume; a modern house in the Observatory quarter is imbued with traces of the past and lies at the same location as a house often visited by the poet. The Obelisk "where they had burned the dead in millions during a plague named 'the Death'..." is referred to repeatedly in the story of the poet, and is used again in the third story to introduce elements from an Egyptian past which at the same time prepare the way for *The Book of the Beast*.

Strewn with plague pits and burial grounds, the city is also a necropolis, its stones alive with bloody memories that lead to surreal crossings of time lines. In *Empires of Azure*, using photographic terms appropriate to the 1910s/20s, murder is termed a *fixative* that records itself in a specific place, but the motive originates in a time before the building of Paradys, as myth continues to ferment at the roots of reality.

Writing is the main theme here, either inscribed on paper, charcoaled on stone or consisting only of images that replace it in a largely illiterate era. Two central characters are professional writers.

Stained with Crimson is a story of vampires, immortality and sexual transformations. The scarab ring passing into the hands of St. Jean seals a pact with the devil. Traditional desires for everlasting life are swiftly replaced by longings for literary immortality—apparently achieved, to judge by the later street naming.

When a dying man presses a ring upon him, the debauched poet, St. Jean, recognizes neither the Faustian transaction nor its price. He intends to be ironical when he gives a book to a friend, remarking, "If I die it may be worth something, for if I die they will know I was a genius." But when he meets Antonina, apparently the owner of the ring, his true desires take shape. She becomes his muse and obsession. He tells her he doesn't "hanker for fame," only for her attention. He intends to penetrate her with the "pin of the pen" and demolish her in a Sadean orgy of the imagination. "I had bludgeoned and possessed her body a hundred times, eaten her alive, licked up the juices of her flesh, gnawed her bones, and hanged myself in her hair." Of the books already written, he believes: "Each had shortened my life, killed me with its own especial little death." Clearly enamored with death, possessed by the Romantic imagination, he says, "There was some sickness on me, some plague, something. Gladly I welcomed it.... And all the books unwritten. Well, let them go."

Metaphor becomes reality on every side. A Romantic's muse requires total self-abnegation: When she rejects his book, he burns it and gives her its ashes. He discovers that she is a vampire, and death and rebirth take fresh shape in Decadence imagery as, weak with loss of blood, St. Jean suffers a "soft and tender illness" in a neurasthenic fever of writing. The "borders between unconsciousness and waking, between dream and reality" vanish as he experiences "dreams, glowing with enjoyment and color." He is writing again, gone beyond "sleep or sexuality ... with bright banners of words starting from the pen ... for that other world inside, beside, beneath, above, wherever it was, the heaven of my invention, liberty."

He enters a "blissful whirlpool of adoring, death-wishing delirium" but his blood turns *ink-black* and poisons Antonina—at which her almost identical brother, Anthony, kills him with a pointedly silver bullet.

The second phase of the story begins with resurrection: St. Jean erupts from the grave as his own female counterpart. Anna is also preoccupied with death, but complete in her sexual duality. At times inside a coffin—supposedly Antonina's—she pursues Anthony through increasingly dreamlike, underworld landscapes. A goat with "the pagan beast-face of Satan" assists her, but when a huge winged monster swoops as she makes her way along a "Hadean stream," her autonomy drifts away along with her pole. "Only the current drew me on."

In a ruined tower, the wine she drinks with Anthony is "blacker ... than ink." To this new muse she offers "nothing at all any more, not a book, not a line of prose." The skivvy cleans away the letters she writes in charcoal on the hearth stones, forcing her further into internality: "I had nothing to write with.... Write with my voice then on air, or with my nails in the plank table." Now she must use "air, magic or a dream."

"Like Psyche who had searched for her love in hell," Anna makes love with Anthony, then wryly adds, "But the onus of the myth had been to dash aside unconsciousness. I was not Psyche...." She seems to lose all power except as an observer of scenes that grow increasingly disconnected and dreamlike, punctuated by apparitions and sudden evaporations: "I found us then to be in a sort of kitchen.... By the hearth sat a girl with a snow-blonde chrysanthemum of hair." A malignant baby appears. With another dreamlike motif dispersed quite widely through Lee's texts, she notes how all the characters are running together. "Vampires, shape-changers, incubus-succuba—such vacant names.... We are one thing and all things. And nothing. We are nothing."

Anna mounts a transparent, metaphysical staircase; "Since reality and the physical world were only chaos, illusorily subdued.... Ascending, what did I climb but the heights of meaning?" She passes a window bleeding with every nuance of red, and out of its midst plucks the scarab ring.

Next morning Anthony is dead. Anna's remarks are detached: "A few drops of blood had spilled on the sheet. Under the left wrist, the blood had left an odd mark, but try as I would, I could not make it seem to resemble or suggest anything." Anthony's blood remains indecipherable, but the *writer* anticipates her own resurrection when Antonina returns and slips a knife into her heart.[1]

> One day, or dark, I will slide the ruby scarab from my finger.... I will find some other like myself, one who comprehends the real nature of reality. Shape-changer ... But not now. I am *on the wheel* with both of them and both of myselves ... [emphasis added].

The promise is fulfilled. The writer returns repeatedly in the *Book of the Damned*, each time in a different body and characterized by the features of the era, but always with the same essential doubleness of sex and being that confirm an alchemical nature.[2]

*Malice in Saffro*n is set in the less literate Middle Ages. Though distanced by third person narration, its medieval realities are observed minutely. Ghostly presences still appear, but hallucinations are now defined as visible spiritual experiences or visions. The adoption of clothing of the opposite sex becomes as radical as bodily sex-change from a medieval perspective. Manifesting the Dark Ages literally, Paradys, overwhelmed by the Black Death, is illuminated only by plague fires.[3]

Illegitimate, unlettered, daughter of a peasant farmer's wife, Jehanine is only valued for her labor. Her stepfather rapes her and she flees to the city disguised in boy's clothing, hoping her apprentice brother will protect her. But when he rejects her story and accuses her of false witness against his father, she accepts his inevitable prejudice against her sex. "Ah Pierre. Fair hero, but a man. How could it have been otherwise?" The debasement of women is again emphasized when a mysterious dwarf, Fero,[4] materializes out of the night and shepherds her to a nunnery, where she is told, "You're safe at last. Our Lord has brought you here." Familiar with orthodox Christianity, Jehanine laughs. "God was a male, Jesus a man."

But these nuns are Cathars with heretical beliefs in a dual creation[5]:

> ... the "children of darkness" addressed their prayers to the evil God, to Jehovah, Baal, Jupiter and the God of the Roman Church.... Mankind could be redeemed ... through recognition of the true and good god.[6]

The Gnostic affiliations of the Convent of the Angel appear in the Great Light, a stained glass image of the angel Lucefiel, and in reversed renderings of the gospels, such as: "God so hated His Son, that He gave him to the world that the world might have him." Fero too expresses Gnostic/Cathar doctrine: "the world isn't God's, it's the Devil's."

6. The Fatal Object—The Secret Books of Paradys

Cathars gave women spiritual equality, and Lee makes it clear that their persecution was intended as much to repress women as to resolve any theological disagreement. But medieval diabolizing of women is not a male monopoly; some women may be ultra orthodox.[7] The zealous Osanne, who always contrives to hear conventional gospel readings, pronounces platitudes about "The Pit of raging Hell" as she enters Jehanine's cell, sexually assaults her and then accuses her of being "one of the Devil's minions." But later Osanne is struck by lightning—i.e., by the Devil, whose lightning so often destroyed church spires.

These traumas change Jehanine, and her name becomes "Jehan by night, and Jhane by day, which two names were one, only a letter differently set, if he-she had been able to read or write and had known it." Illiteracy is a crucial issue. Uncontaminated by education, dependent on her immediate senses, Jhane's religious visions occupy an unmediated mental space. The pure mental activity St. Jean strains so hard to reach is precipitated. A transcendental experience that in the nineteenth century arrives only through extreme debauchery and self-abuse visits a simple woman spontaneously in the mental context of the Middle Ages.

In company with Fero, Jhane makes nightly excursions dressed in male attire and is soon leading a band of thieves and cutthroats on a rampage of crime. The text here has an oddly playful character. In boy's clothing Jhane dances, jokes, flirts, enchants the thieves at *The Imago*, or "Inn of the Apparition," and at first seems to herself to be inhabiting a dream.[8] But "dreams make their own laws," and Jhane steps outside the law from the moment she dresses as a man, her offence become criminal in the indissoluble medieval unity of church and state. Free speech is also a grave fault in women, but Jhane revels in transgression. "Her male attire, freeing her tongue, pleased her."

Out with the thieves, she takes the fatal jewel from her brother. The topaz—yellow like the window and the nun's saffron habits—is Saracen. These heathens "reject the Christ.... They worship a man. And an angel also ... the yellow stone, the topaz, he cut it from some breast-plate of a fallen pagan priest, in a shrine there." Imbued with Eastern significance like Catharism, the topaz is set like a crucified Christ upon a cross, suggesting the martyrdom of Cathars in the coming Albigensian Crusade: "...the sign of the cross ... for Cathars was the symbol of Satan's victory over Christ."[9] Jhane is stealing more than Pierre's privilege; in the opposing topaz, or "spark of fire," she is taking on a double identity on several levels.

Fire illuminates the narrative, cleansing, destroying, good, evil. Death by fire is cruelly appropriate to a heresy descended from Eastern solar religions, and identifying Lucifer, the morning and evening star, as the promethean bringer of true enlightenment. The window of The Great Light portraying the blazing Lord Lucefiel is central to the text, but other references to fire proliferate. Fero calls himself "Ferofax ... Fire Bringer." Jehan burns down the house of Pierre's master. Jhane, in her fever, screams out that she is burning. Plague fires are indistinguishable from the fires of hell.

In a passage evoking other texts that also contain motifs of stars, fires and demons seeking proximity to humans, the convent gospel states:

> God made darkness and it hung on the face of the earth. But the Lord, our Saviour, said again, Let there be light. He stole then one flame of the seven divine fires of Heaven. And with this he fell, burning, like the morning star. The sun was lit from his flambeau, and all the stars, and the moon, and all the lights of the firmament. And when he had cleaved through the earth and fallen to the deepest depth of it, that pit too became fire, a furnace that warms the earth's heart—a cleansing flame, the light of knowledge....

Jehan too assumes supernatural proportions among the thieves who suspect her of witchcraft when she drugs victims with narcotics from the convent infirmary. "[H]e put on animal shape, or wings and flew behind the stars as they went out. He sprang from the ground at the sun's setting. Winter, the time of dark day and long night, that was Jehan's country."[10] Crowned king of the carnival, Fero chooses Jehan as his "bride," but, with bride's clothing thrown over her male attire—a woman, disguised as a man, disguised as a woman—Jehan apparently prefers the ass, perhaps in tribute to *The Golden Ass* whose hero is transmuted into a beast until a vision of Isis restores and enlightens him.

And it is through a vision that Jhane wakes from her evil dream. A young nun she attempts to abduct becomes an ambiguous vision, dressed in Eastern silks and nailed to a cross, representing either orthodox Christianity's persecution of women or masochistic collusion with it. The figure swiftly transforms into a Beast-woman," surrounded by a horde of devils, leaving Jhane to wonder if Marie-Lis had "been the tempter, the evil one, the shadow mimicking the light...." But the vision of an angel replaces Marie-Lis and sweeps Jhane up into Heaven. There is no doubt about meaning here.

"The caress seemed to find her forehead, but her whole body was laved in it, even to the tips of her nails and hair.... Then Heaven shattered. She fell. She fell and the stars were made and in the pit of earth a light, to last until the last of the world."

6. The Fatal Object—The Secret Books of Paradys

This is the Cathar *consolamentum*, or the conferring of Gnosis. Jhane is radically changed. Jehan becomes "the symbol of all the evil of the masculine species," but Jhane discards her sins, which, "being insupportable, gushed ... from her." As she makes her way back to the convent, she finds the city ravaged by plague. The nuns have all gone to care for the sick; Jhane too dons her nun's habit and goes about the city laying her hands on the dying in the consolamentum. She begins an endless journey through death and dying, amongst a people driven to perversity and madness. In true Cathar spirit, "Jhane paid little heed ... the earth and all things in it, had never seemed familiar or sane to her."

When she has herself bricked up inside a plague house with the sick, she finds and tends a delirious Pierre. He recovers but is starving and she cuts off her own hand to feed him. The consolamentum is stretched to its extreme—"Part of her own self had become a part of him." This sequence also refers to the *endura*, or suicide, usually by self-starvation, which was common among the Cathar Perfect seeking release from an evil world. Jhane's "cruel malice had turned her towards kindness and deep pity. Compared to her own wickedness, Pierre's was of a slight order, and probably he had learnt nothing from it." She hopes he may use his life to learn and returns the crucifix-topaz that symbolizes a choice of destiny.

In cutting off her hand Jhane is losing what, for a literate person, would be the organ of writing. Vision here becomes the left hand of writing. "She could not read or write, and so she could not set down her vision of the apocalypse ... it did not matter in any case."

When the plague is over Jhane lives on alone in the convent. Pierre adheres to orthodox Christianity, is granted a vision of the Devil and lives to become famous for his images of a Hell that "would leap with rending flames ... would display Satan in all his might, eating souls alive, while the earth burned."

Pierre inscribes the age in the accessible and enduring form of church art. Jhane experiences solitary visions. "Her dreams were not fears or even questionings. Merely rehearsals of different chance." And Lee returns once more to the theme of multiple lives as Jhane's visions gather together different identities: "She was an angel herself. She was not indeed, *herself*. There was no gender, neither male nor female."

Once again, everyone seems to be fusing together.

> The dwarf ... became, Belnard her stepfather, he became the apothecary of her journey, and then he became—spreading and billowing—the fat woman with the keys—and then stretching thin and bearded he was Master Motius, and, getting fleshy and smooth again,

the mason, and losing flesh, Conrad, the thief, and folding inwards and out, in a quick succession, pious Osanne, the Mother, the young nun Marie-Lis. And then he was Jhane herself ... then he rose up and opened up into fire and wings and was an angel....

Jhane understands that the material world is only an illusion. "Life is a dream, said the angel who had been Jhane."

In *Empires of Azure*, Lee moves forward to Paradys in the 1920s, with its "neons of theaters and nightclubs" and its restless hunger for novelty. There are no poetic hallucinations or mystical visions in this temporal climate. A voyeuristic demi-monde accommodates special preferences and redefines sexual ambiguities and transformations as mildly intriguing gender perversities.[11] Even the journalist narrator engages in the mystifications of performance by shrouding herself in a masculine nom-de-plume. The exclusive use of this professional name invests her with an impenetrably aloof sexual duality.

She seems to have little private life. She produces articles for her paper; she reads other newspapers. Louis de Jenier, the transvestite performer she investigates, also uses newspapers to research the archives. Journalism is the preferred form of writing in an age of factual information that looks outwards for validation and meaning.

Mlle. St. Jean plays the role of recorder with no autonomous function beyond her ability to reproduce the story of Louis. She believes that noninvolvement breeds reliability. This stance drains off much of the animation of events, while the events being processed by her supposedly objective intelligence are made even more distant by the fact that they have already been transcribed, if incompletely, by another writer with a certain competence of his own. She remarks, "he was, obviously, used to and adept at writing things down."

Poetic transports leading to death have been replaced with literal reportage. Mademoiselle St. Jean will "rewrite or copy" from the account already produced by de Jenier. As she works from his diary, she tells her anonymous readers, "I invent nothing.... No. I invent nothing."

When something impossible ruptures the normal progression of events, it doesn't engender enlightenment, only a desire for rational explanation—except in de Jenier, whose perverse curiosity produces a need to *merge* with alien personalities. Transvestism, his only form of sexual pleasure, becomes an art form.

Three time streams mingle. The present occupies only a few weeks. In a restaurant, a man with the blank blue eyes of "a doll" presses a card upon Mlle St. Jean before two pursuers sweep him away. Louis de Jenier's name and address accompany a message reading, "In a week, or less, I shall be dead."

Mlle. St. Jean restrains her unhealthily close interest and waits a week before going to his house. One of de Jenier's pursuers admits her. Passing great cobalt-blue windows, he takes her into a study containing photographic portraits of two beautiful women, "Louis's two most admired animas," and records of his past impersonations. She finds a diary containing a message that reads, "For you, Mademoiselle St. Jean, to do with as you think fit."

One of the cobalt windows abruptly explodes and she sees the body of Louis, hanged with a rope. Thinking the agents may be murderers, she flees. Later, she follows a lead to a photographic portrait of Louis, dressed in the female role of Timonie. Timonie's story forms the second time layer of the narrative.

In addition to reporting that Louis died of a simple fall downstairs, the newspaper describes the murder and dismemberment of a young woman in the same house a decade earlier. At first Mlle. St. Jean's investigations are contemporary, trying to connect the murders of Timonie and Louis. But a sapphire earring that belonged to Timonie appears in the photograph of Louis-Timonie, and like everything else in the story it has a well documented history. Coming from a museum collection, it was once the property of Tiy-Amonet, an Egyptian sorceress and mistress of a Roman commander, evoking the location of *The Book of the Beast*. The garrison at Par Dis lies buried under Paradys, and the story of Tiy-Amonet lies buried under those of Louis and Timonie in a descending spiral of impersonations that forms the main theme of this novella.

Nominally, Mlle. St. Jean impersonates the poet: Perhaps journalism is an impersonation of literature. When Louis discovers the young woman concealed behind the poet's name, he exclaims, "I've found you out." Like is recognizing like. Attraction to likeness (a theme already discussed at length) as the secret of impersonation appears on a number of occasions: "Are you like me?" the ghost of Timonie asks Louis, believing he is Tiy-Amonet. The imaginary woman hidden in Louis's maleness is very real and only waiting to be unveiled. "His minutes and hours as a woman ... afforded him a transcendent excitement, not merely sensual, or if it was, then also a sensuality of the mind. He swam strongly in the sweetness of it."

Timonie only dresses up in accordance with a fashion for Egyptian things, and her botched impersonation of the original Tiy-Amonet offends the long-dead sorceress. Her insultingly *flippant impersonation* is avenged with "a ritual butchering."

At first Louis believes that the supernatural forces flow from "the afterimage of Timonie, but it was the spider-witch who worked on him ... easing him on in stages." In a series of references to photography, he says, meaning Timonie, "she was ... a recording, a photograph on the room." He understands that, though "self-obsessed' as he is, Timonie is "unable to clarify, externalize, and so center." She is only motivated by narcissism; his performances are professional: "...accustomed to being under the sway of another persona," he is drawn to Tiy-Amonet. "The supernatural wooed him; it had got endemically close to him as live human things never did." The "passion so strong it forms the print of an astral photograph on that room" comes from Tiy-Amonet. Louis concludes that "the earring ... acts like the photographer's silver fixative."

Even Louis's death is an impersonation, and an agent—a *nobody*—is buried in his stead.[12] But Louis is effectively dead anyway, occupied by Tiy-Amonet, a shell for something not himself. "any slightest iota of Louis as we knew him ceased."

When Louis's agent calls, accompanied by "a fashionable woman," Mlle. St. Jean believes she is Louis, supposedly dead and buried. Her shock increases as she realizes that it is a double creature calling itself Tiy-Amonet and Tuamon that is occupying his corporeal form. Tuamon is a truly androgynous creature; Tiy-Amonet had existed, "To smooth the sensibilities of a Roman commander." But the creature is not concerned about the sensibilities of Mlle. St. Jean, who is horrified to see it "undressing itself in front of me, with no sensitivity."

With this unwanted intimacy, the hidden is revealed, both the androgynous body of Tuamon and the inner feelings of Mlle. St. Jean. Like her namesake, the journalist is transported by hallucinations, initially of Egypt, and then:

> An azure sphere, flashing and dazzling with movement and with integral life. In the heart of it the monster basked, its eyes like portholes on a sea of sky....
> And I did not want it to end.
> I did not want the safe drab darkness to come back.

In a sense it does not. Although the journalist changes nothing as she records the story of Louis and Tuamon, her fact-fixated existence is illuminated by a past that regards writing as a magical activity. "An old tavern, the *Imago—the Apparition*—... was built it was said near the site" where Tuamon reanimated the dead, and Imago, as Lee points out, has a secondary meaning: "the thing which emerges from the chrysalis." As Mlle. St. Jean writes down the story, it emerges from its chrysalis in the form of writing appropriate to her own century. The writer-recorder is practicing a "special branch of magic." Louis, as actor-impersonator, was capable only of "coherence in patches," fragments, "phases of speech like the moon." Though her sexual duality is only nominal, it still fits Mlle. St. Jean for her role. In any case, her connection with the dead poet is more than nominal. They are linked together by a line that also appears in the first novella: "Fire is Will, Water is Grief, Earth is thought, Air a Vision."[13] This vision, the *Caerulei mundi regna*, or *Empires of Azure*, surrounds her in the sapphire earring, the stained glass and the blue eyes of Louis, Timonie and Tuamon.

The two St. Jeans also connect with Jhane (her name another version of Jean). She is evoked by one of Louis's dreams: A jinn shows a traveler the face of the Devil, then that of God, and both faces are the traveller's own. The content of Jhane's visions still lingers on, though the openings into the past that remain in the fabric of the city are not predictable. Timonie has been dead for only a decade, when Louis dresses himself in imitation of her, yet "The house seemed to have become timeless, nearly dimensionless, and he went across to the window-room in the dark, half-thinking the doors might open on a desert, the river of Par Dis, the past, space itself splattered with cracked stars."

The Book of the Beast

Stretching from the Roman Empire to the Renaissance, *The Book of the Beast* relates also to a prehistoric past. An amethyst amulet colors the text, and the eyes of Vusca's contaminated wife become "like lotuses in a marsh." The beast and men changed into beasts during the sexual act have emerald eyes. Heraldic colors and patrician purple indicate genealogical pride, whilst an antique "sigil" portraying "a cruel preying bird, perhaps a falcon," mistakenly celebrates a prehistoric demon that can only be subdued by ancient rituals. Its animal dissociation from *human* consciousness, makes it inaccessible to civilized minds. Lee bridges this gulf by introducing body magic of the most primitive sort.[14]

The strands of narrative are fully integrated in the amulet. Initially, the beast affects only the amulet's possessor, but when the amulet is ground down and swallowed in an attempt to destroy it, the beast develops sexually transmissible, genetically heritable properties, and the d'Uscarets acquire a curse as obdurate as any in Greek drama.

The amethyst is passed by a foreign prostitute to an unwary Roman soldier stationed in provincial Par Dis.[15] Though at first Vusca experiences good luck, the amulet begins to drain him. As always, a price must be paid for magical or demonic assistance. In the Renaissance strand of the story, Helise comments, "*I prayed to the Devil. He granted my desire and now collects his fee.*"

Vusca ingenuously assumes that the bird-headed figure engraved on the amethyst must represent "Thot, the Mercurius of the Aegyptians,"[16] but its presentation in a smoking bear's skull indicates its prehistoric origin,[17] and Vusca dreams uneasily of primitive religious rituals at the prehistoric site of Par Dis where the warm climate is (pre)historically correct but no longer contemporaneous. A "wild man" of the hills advises swallowing the amulet, saying, "Eats you. You eat."

Lililla, the prostitute, is entirely primordial—the serpent/woman/goddess/demon who has appeared in several texts already. As she gives him the amulet she starts "to sway like a serpent. He thought of the sybils, inhaling volcanic vapors, prophesying, reading riddles." She has "the liquid boneless movements of a snake." Even a rainy evening is reptilian:—"the stones and plaster, the tiled roofs, had a mauve, wet, lizardskin sheen." A woman pokes out her tongue "like a lizard's," and a peasant gives birth to a "baby which was scaled."

Lililla appears to be a lamia.[18] Of Greek/Egyptian nationality, she is known as "the lily whore," and like Lilith assumes the superior position and employs "a wicked, subservient mastery."[19] Vusca "had seldom if ever known a climax so intense. He found, astonished, when she removed herself from him, that she had also penetrated him." This double-gendered sex unravels the bluff, unerotic army commander who kills his bestialized son and commits suicide. Later, amethyst-eyed twins are born.

Reptile references continue, indicating ancient origins. When Heros is killed, Helise lies "flailing and lurching on the bed like a broken snake." Raoulin, a student lodger in the d'Uscaret house, visits a brothel and notices "weird shadows ... flung up on the low uneven ceiling, tangles of writhing knots, like serpents." A woman kisses him with "a little snake's flicker of the tongue."

The name d'Uscaret is an obvious corruption of Vuscarii, and the name Heros is a version of Eros. Lee's Eros is no winged cherub. Both Satan and Eros of the Amor and Psyche legend, which is central in this text, are given the title of dragon, which, with other magical, winged creatures, traditionally represents both creation and destruction. The first-born of the gods, the Orphic Eros, creates the world, but springs from the egg of Darkness and Night. Love is entwined with death. "The Renaissance identified him with death itself ... Roman sarcophagi ... represent the agonies inflicted on Psyche by Eros."[20]

6. The Fatal Object—The Secret Books of Paradys

References to Apuleius's story of Amor and Psyche are frequent. In the garden of the d'Uscaret mansion, Raoulin finds a statue of Psyche and, close by, the tomb of Helise, who still haunts the house. She describes a painting found in Heros's "Bird Tower" portraying Psyche as she flees, screaming, from a beast: "All the rest of the small canvas conveyed pitchy nothingness—but for one curious whorling hint of motion, seeming to come on behind her, somewhat like a flock of birds."

Eros may be shown as "a winged phallus" or "a small boy with a divine snake." Sometimes he holds "a torch downwards, the symbol of death" or torments a butterfly representing Psyche or the soul, though he is also "its great purifier." He is "a dragon or a snake ... something ... which is inhuman ... either divine or demonic."[11] Apuleius describes him as "fierce and wild and born of dragon breed."[22] Like Psyche, Helise is an innocent victim, ignorant of the fertile wilderness. The bridegroom is "a dreamlike icon," but the wedding church is saturated with omens. "The roof was ribbed—the inner belly of some apocryphal beast which had swallowed the procession whole.... Beyond the Angel Chapel was an underwater cave where she would drown in marriage."

However, Heros resembles "Jehanus, the beautiful, harrowed martyr from off the very wall. Only his eyes were altered. Their beauty had been brought to life with a green and stellar fire." She perceives only the god in her Saint John of the forbidden wilderness and becomes a Psyche searching for darkness: "...the monster of the myth made love to her in the blind dark, as in the blind dark the Unseen had made love to Psyche.... Helise ... clung to darkness ... was thrown into the Hell of ecstasy."

Heros's mother, dutiful as her Roman ancestors, brings lights, kills her son, poisons Helise and then hangs herself, but the curious mixture of magic and deceit lingers. While Heros occupies her garden tomb, Helise returns with emerald eyes. She administers an Alexandrian aphrodisiac that had worked upon Heros to Raoulin and, after "that dance of death called procreation," turns to dust.

But "trained to be something of a thinker, Raoulin was not properly a dreamer." Writing gets mentioned briefly as Raoulin, more scholar than sensualist, hesitates to visit the brothel, saying, "I have a treatise on the fifth humour"; and while Helise sips "a vintage like ink," and whispers tales about "M'sire No One," his paralysis is only physical. "His mind was alert, to be instructed."

He becomes a "madman," roaming the streets, impelled to rape and murder, but some conscious residue chooses death over possession. He stabs himself on the doorstep of a Jewish scholar. Haninuh has studied an ancient text that identifies the beast as an "utuk," or demon, of early

Assyrian origin, "scaled not feathered, from the fifth day of the earth."[23] "We're ancient foes," he says, but adds, "God made all things. Even the creatures of his servant, the Devil. We are instructed to note the lesson their existence teaches." This approach more or less corresponds with Lee's own attitudes.

Raoulin's exorcism demonstrates Lee's syncretist habits admirably. She collapses diverse religious ideas into a single context. Previously tending towards psychology, here she focuses directly on magic ritual. Fasting, drugs, and the like produce a vision of an ancient, pre-Hebraic creation, invoking the oldest deities. "there was nothing. Only the void." The primal goddess is present as sensually provocative rain. A dance of Salome, or "of a snake," is performed by Haninuh's daughter Ruquel, who has, unconventionally, "been educated like a boy" and knows about ritual and alchemy. Like all Lee's wise magicians, Haninuh combines learning with independent thought.

Ruquel strips herself away until her skeleton is exposed—the seven veils of Salome's dance signify the seven layers of illusion. The worship of Ishtar and the original Tiamat, of Isis (to whom Vusca's wife converts), and of John the Baptist in place of Christ, are telescoped into a religious evolution.[24]

There is also the personal content of the narrative. Ruquel has fallen in love—"It happened the moment I saw him there." Her scholarly father distinguishes between varieties of love and explains that precisely because she has conscious control of her emotions, she can perform the "dishonorable task" of regressing by sexual magic into a barely conscious time. Haninuh is seeking to reverse the consequences of failing to acknowledge the beast. Heros, horrified by "The body's urge ... that makes him one with the beast," was overwhelmed by it. Helise confronted the urge but was sensually in thrall to it. After his shamanistic journey, Raoulin marries.

The utuk is imprisoned in magical spells and buried in the river along with the warning that it may return. Though civilized man's efforts to bury his "beast" may obscure it, its shadow continues, stirring below the threshold of a desacralized world. "[P]rofane man is the descendant of homo religious and he cannot wipe out his own history."[25]

The Book of the Dead

Most of these separate stories are linked together and to the preceding books, using motifs that are both familiar and novel. Death and location in Paradys are constants, but the fatal objects are more heterogenous, not necessarily valuable, and have a new socio-political diversity.[26] The theme of cryptic or symbolic writing from *The Book of the Damned* reappears and the colors used in the subtitle—*Le Livre Blanc et Noir*—also evoke print.

Lost in the World has an early twentieth-century flavor as it pays tribute to both Conan Doyle and Rider Haggard. It reengages the theme of symbolic alternatives to writing, starting from Oberand's longstanding obsession with a manuscript written by "an explorer out of the countries of landscape ... (doubtless) a liar and romancer." This dubious manuscript describes a valley in Africa in terrain Lee titles The Mountains of the White Moon. Dating back to "the prehistoric dawn," full of "huge beasts, and flying things" that recall the monster of *The Book of the Beast*, this valley houses "a god said to be white, and of abnormal size." As Oberand pursues the legend, like "a mighty philanderer," Lee constructs him as an almost comically stereotypical white colonist. His superstitious bearers desert, and only one man, whose name, André, connects him with *Stained with Crimson*, remains. André calls the legend of the valley "a white man's myth of the darkness."

Accidentally finding his valley, complete with supposedly extinct creatures and a colossal, white temple with fallen pillars perhaps half a mile in length, Oberand survives in primitive style. 'He missed nothing of civilization ... not even his books ... the valley had become his book at last, open and to be read." His manuscript is deciphered when a huge flying predator snatches him up and he sees that the temple is a human skeleton—his white god—too vast to be identified from the ground.

Another myth of darkness, *The Nightmare's Tale*, uses the name St. Jean again, this time for an orphan of the Revolution with a burning desire to avenge his father. Leaving Paradys, he sails to a Caribbean island where the man who signed his parents' execution order has become a plantation owner. The landscape is of sun and shadow, the skins and clothes have the black and white contrast of the written page, but writing is only referred to in relation to letters *not* written or *not* sent by de St. Jean to his aunt. "It is possible that they were mislaid or unsent. One senses she did not receive any." Dargue's signature on a death warrant, with its wine stain "like a drop of thin blood," and a note from the woman de St. Jean loves are the only other traces of the deadly business of writing. Both are summonses to death.

Experiencing hallucinations even before disembarking, Jean de St. Jean's plan to murder Dargue is "a shadow act, performed in a dream." It recalls André St. Jean's hallucinatory entry into a dream world. When de St. Jean finds Dargue already dead, voodoo cultists offer to call him up from the grave to become a murder victim. This intense desire for revenge creates a fusion of passion, death and imagination, like that in the story of André St. Jean.

In *The Marble Web*, a conjurer entertaining at a party falls in love with Jausande and creates illusions, referring openly to other parts of the sequence. The story also stretches outside into an independent short story, *Elle Est Trois (la Mort)*.[27] The illusions juxtapose dreamlike images from the previous books: a girl with "the columns and cistern of a Roman atrium" visible behind her; a man in "hose and tunic, and the rounded, color-slashed sleeves of an alchemic century"; Helise "in a high-waisted gown and cap." A "great glowing cloud" discloses "an exquisite angelic face." Lines describing a "spider moon" spinning "a marble web," which accompany Jausande's dream, are by "the other Pliny," a writer already cited in *Empires of Azure*.[28] The thief, another Pierre, steals the ring that "had not yet adhered to her flesh"—as her betrothal also will not—and glimpses her "walking in a forest of gigantic trees ... the world of a million years before" as she sleepwalks through the night sky into the prehistoric Paradys. The conjurer never returns, and though the police look for him, when they find Jausande's body in the river his flat is empty except for the dust of decades.

Some of the more humorous stories are less integrated. Relatives brick a woman's corpse into her room because they fail to understand the commonplace nature of a curse stating: "*All you that dare to enter here will die.*" Julie d'Is, in whose vicinity people regularly die, is given the placatory title "*Beautiful Lady.*" After a cake-shop assistant who has served her dies, Julie is shot, and a flea-sized twin, half woman, half scorpion, is discovered on the corpse. A flea-sized monster must mark the absurd extreme in fatal objects, but it also recalls the Black Death of *Malice in Saffron*. In another story, a man who insists on marrying a white weasel in church is fatally bitten on his wedding night, but only generations later is the castratory nature of the nuptial bite revealed. Elsa pays for a feathered mask that nightly transforms her into an owl with a bottle of brandy stolen from a house she cleans and joins a long line of Lee's women—poor, abused, but independent, and with a fiercely guarded, private love of beauty which transports them into another world.

As Dionysos presides from under a dust sheet in *The Glass Dagger*, an antique assassin's weapon is given by her lover to the painter Valmé. The mirror is centered as Valmé passionlessly creates images, or mirror-images, of what she sees. Real and reflected merge; images trap souls.[29] Examining her portrait of Yshtar, Valmé reflects, "Surely, surely she had captured the soul of Yshtar ... a butterfly on a pin."

But her lover pretends to love Yshtar, and "Through the truth of Yshtar, Valmé had found the way, by night, onto the shining terrible path of actual feeling."[30] In a tangle of reflections, "Through the mirror of Yshtar, she saw what she had lost ... how sharp as broken glass the intervals of sun.

The knives of the rain entered the mirror of the canal...." But when Valmé discovers that her "real" pain of jealousy is unfounded, she loses the one thing that has escaped from the prison of image; "...all her days would be dust." Valmé impulsively hurls the dagger at Yshtar's mirrored reflection as she passes along the canal outside; Yshtar is killed instantly. Reflection and reality meet at last.

Finally, Lee inserts curious anecdotes, like items from a surreal newspaper, between the stories: A raccoon, escaped from the zoo, helps prisoners of the Revolution to escape the guillotine; at his own funeral a clown jumps out of his coffin; a giant silver man is seen striding across the sky. This mixture of explicable and utterly inexplicable seems to look forward to *The Book of the Mad*.

The Book of the Mad

In all three eras of the *Book of the Mad*, stretching from the nineteenth century to an indeterminate twenty-first or twenty-second century, landmarks remain: the Temple-Church is sporadically visible in Paradise; the Cockcrow Inn is still a rendezvous for thieves in Paradys; in Paradis a woman goes "walking under the Roman wall." Orange predominates. A girl's marmalade hair recalls Chuz; "...marigolds, flowers of the eternal, deathless soul" grow in the madhouse gardens, and oranges bleed from a wrecked ship.

In a Paradise devastated by pollution and perpetually shrouded by physical and mental fog, "rooted insanity" is endemic. Incest is so "normal," the twins, Felion and Smara, are isolated by their distaste for it— "not mad, at least not in the accepted manner. They had, therefore, no friends, no lovers." The city is depopulated anyway. Figures loom out of solipsistic mists, then vanish. No one follows up disappearances, and Felion and Smara gratify deprived libidos with random, motiveless murders that suggest a perverse programme of mental hygiene. Realizing Felion has killed twice that week, Smara says, "So I must ... I'll kill someone with rings, and bring you one, Felion."

The fatal ring(s) sink in amongst a welter of portentous objects, all full of subjective, inappropriate significances. Lacking a standard, meaning is patched together in a constantly mutating mental topography. A simple curse becomes "an awkward obscenity, for Paradise no longer had a God, a religion, or any regularized views of sexuality to form the substance of oaths." Only a labyrinth, a frozen and thus temporarily stable model of its maker's brain, connects the time streams. "Maybe it goes nowhere. Why should it go anywhere? He was mad too," Smara says. "Suppose you and I are insane, like all of them, but we haven't realized." Felion's reply expresses their alienation: "We've done our best to act out madness." Both cultural and personal sanity are questioned as the artist, scientist (Michelot is certainly a scientist) or poet doubles as shaman.

Each time-stream has its own interpretation of madness. In Paradys and Paradis, "madness" can dispose of inconvenient persons, especially women. When Leocadia inherits her uncle's fortune, her cousin, Nanice, gets her committed; and in Paradys, when the adolescent Hilde pursues her infatuation for an actor, her bourgeois parents declare her dead and install her in an asylum. In Paradise, where "madness" has become an anachronism, the twins still endlessly discuss the state of their sanity. According to her uncle, Leocadia is "not insane in the manner of Paradise" but her "madness attracted me to her." Leocadia observes that, "Since she was not ill, not mad, not a murderess or anything else they said ... they ... would change her into the Leocadia of their invention, Nanice's Leocadia, who killed and was insane."

Lee's Leocadia is inspired by the surrealist painter Leonora Carrington. Her enforced stay in The Residence recalls Carrington's *Down Below*, a detailed account of an enforced stay in a Spanish mental hospital.[31] Madness, according to Lee, has many styles and values. Little meaning emerges from the madness of the twins, but Leocadia's madness—like Carrington's—becomes a Laingian journey into an alternative consciousness that is integrating and redemptive.

The twins regard their absent uncle's labyrinth as a means of escape from a murky city with a river of toxic "Lethe water."[32] They overlook the potential of sanity encoded in the model mind. Michelot explains, "The exit from the labyrinth is always subjective," but Leocadia creates a release both for herself and others. When she paints a mural in her hospital room, "the wall of the painting opened, and became actual, like the gateway into a garden."

Michelot takes on triple form: as himself; in Paradys as the mad poet Citalbo; in Paradis as Thomas, a "warrior," driven mad by involvement in environmentally ruinous war technologies. Leocadia notes how "Thomas ... had begun to look so like Michelot," and Smara, glimpsing him, experiences an "infantile memory of her uncle...." Perversely seeking out insanity and seeing "potential" in a nineteenth century asylum that brutalizes its inmates, he takes capricious pleasure in provocation.[33] His perceptions of personalities go beyond the individual into the deeper layers of fate. A church in Paradis records: "*the names of the three who are jointly this demon are OBLATIC, SAMOHT, and TOLEHCIM.*"[34] Inserted into post-millennial technology rather than religious belief or drug-inspired decadence, he remains a "demon,"' like those in other texts in the Paradys sequence.

6. The Fatal Object—The Secret Books of Paradys 123

Michelot refers to Felion and Smara's "karma-collecting activities of murder" and hints that they might claim an inheritance in Paradis if Leocadia were dead. His motives are inscrutable—though like many of Lee's demons he has didactic leanings and perhaps considers murder instructive in a plot he often seems to have devised. On visits to Paradis, each twin murders a woman, supposing it to be Leocadia. When her former lover is murdered, Leocadia is blamed. As Nanice occupies Leocadia's studio with hard drinking and bad painting, Smara substitutes white spirit for Nanice's vodka. Nanice falls headlong into her own painting, and with pleasing irony, the canvas recording her death throes is bought by an art museum.

Felion finds the "heart" of the labyrinth "empty" and Leocadia's house "chock-full of nothing."[35] Though armed with torch and knife, he meets no Minotaur or Beast.[36] He founders on emptiness, but Smara comes closer to the saving possibilities of madness. She meets inmates of the parallel Salpetriere who tell her, "we search for other countries. Of the mind, the heart, and the soul. And sometimes we even search for hell on earth."

Paradis briefly becomes "heaven on earth" as, at a wedding party, the twins eat "food without stones in it or serpents—and wine, not hemlock." They find they know the dances of Paradis "as if taught in childhood," and they recognize their love for each other. But Paradise pulls them back: "...they knew hell. They had got used to hell."

Objects move from one time into another, carrying meaning with them, but Smara does not grasp the significance of a ring set with a human eye which matches the grey eye of Hilde's seducer, Johanos. Felion, finding "two dolls of Smara's, a necklace, and half a brown glass bottle with a shattered neck" at the entrance to the labyrinth, knows nothing of the doll, emblem of innocence in Hilde's story, or the necklace Leocadia finds in the grounds of The Residence, or the bottles of "Great Penguin" gin consumed in quantity by the nineteenth century madhouse staff, nor of Johanos' death in Paradys from anal rape with a gin bottle. The penguin depicted on the label of this proletarian brew is one of the book's most pervasive objects and inspires Leocadia when she paints her gateway mural.[37] As the gateway leads her back to sanity, it leads the other patients into a warm, snowy kingdom called Penguinia, an image belonging collectively to the asylum inmates of both time streams.

Other images also link the strands. Johanos is led to his death "through places very old, built over again and again, like some slow, terrible painting that could never be finished."[38] Water, symbolizing the unfixed state of madness, appears in all three streams. Lee is again meditating on the cycle of dissolution and regeneration, its Great Wheel now turned by water. As Hilde gives birth to an "orange child," the defining image is of the sea. "Behind her eyes the sea was drawing away. She lay aground upon the beach. Hollow, adrift, yet fixed, immutable and flowing." The moment records itself in Leocadia's first hospital painting. "The wrecked ship lay on the beach.... From the ship's side spilled her cargo of smashed glass and oranges, like blood from a wound ... the ship was feminine. And the sea had split her, and she ... bled." Legends of a sea shell found by the Temple-Church resurface as Felion kills a man "painting shells on the ground in the porch of the church." Leocadia discovers that the warders of The Salpetriere were all drowned in a flood (in fact, of gin): "Gone in a night. A great wave. Shells left behind...." The fogs of Paradise recall the sea: "...anything might have been below, a cliffside, even some sluggish, silent sea." Hilde is subdued by the "Waterfall," a device in which patients were all but drowned. Her body is thrown down a well, and Smara dreams that "someone dropped our mother in a well."

Smara's brief life is shaped like Hilde's by a malign—or sacrificial—destiny. When Smara anonymously adds a small snowball to the shipwreck painting as she passes through Leocadia's hospital room, its influence on the gateway mural is indisputable. Leocadia is aware of "unseen sounds and unheard lights" in a synaesthesia of multiple realities. Though her doctors believe that "something in the painting of the penguin had released her.... They spoke to her of projection, of unknown country being the cipher for death and so of rebirth," their psychiatric metaphors are a Great Wheel of mental existence for Leocadia. "[P]ossibly she had had to go mad, in order that she enter The Residence, and there perform the magical spell upon the wall."

She will spend most of her life painting "huge canvasses of a land of ice ... and as she picked her way across this snowy id, she painted the meeting of a black-haired queen with a young girl who carried a child in her arms." When asked in old age who this girl is, she replies, "God knows," but thinks, "*I know her really. She is the young virgin at the Sabbat.... Through her the power comes to remake things.... Something I did. I made a world.*"

Leocadia's last recorded desire, before she dies at the fairytale age of "one hundred and five and a half," is that she will "find her way into *Penguin*, which she had earned, and which was, presumably, only the afterlife." She dies sensing a warm snowball touching her shoulder.

Felion and Smara also achieve their desire for death and physical union. As the labyrinth begins to melt, a huge stone penguin falls from the roof "crushing their bodies together, so that the bones of each broke through the other's skin and mingled." And their uncle's lifelong desire to become an *oblation* is realized as his melting "mind" releases him into a fluid state.

7

FOLK, CLASSIC AND FAIRYTALE

Kill the Dead, Cyrion, Sung in Shadow, Volkhavaar

Kill the Dead and Cyrion

Kill the Dead and *Cyrion* share an irrepressible, teasing humor. Out of the legends of the dark magician and the golden knight, Lee brews an ironic antidote to overindulgence in conventional fantasy, using the forms of folk ballad and story cycle, as in *The Canterbury Tales*, for models.

Kill the Dead puts a lightminded, lightfingered, minstrel harpist together with his stern father, a professional ghost-slayer.[1] Though Myal initially has no idea of their consanguinity, an Oedipal urge to murder his father is instantly aroused. But Myal is incompetent, incoherent and sick. "I want to kill you. I came all this way to kill you...." Myal began to cry. "I can't do anything right, I never could." Seconds later, he is deliriously calling Dro *Daddy* and begging him not to beat him.

Parl Dro, an exaggerated lord of death and the underworld, with a "concert of strong features" and eyes of "impenetrable blackness," is, however, flawed—he is lame (ergo he is human) and faulty also in his compulsive bad jokes.[2] These belie his severity and establish his generally non-sexual relations with women, although to his Oedipal son's amazement he does have romantic attachments.³ In this father-son story, women tend to be shadowy, dabblers in witchcraft and the paranormal.

Lee uses folk and fairy lore exuberantly. Tarot cards once again extend identities, as a Maid of Vessels, a Queen of Fire and an aging Queen of Swords complete a mysterious triptych. We learn how a ghost-killer conducts his trade. When Parl Dro's childhood love, Silky,⁴ is struck by lightning whilst sitting in a tree, a keepsake lock of her hair enables her ghost to lure him to his death. He acts on instinct and sets fire to the lock of hair that links her to the living world.⁵

As the killer limps through the silent dusk past a house where two sisters, one living, one dead, shrink in fear, we learn that Dro "in his swathing of black, had been mistaken for Death.⁶ Card-casting and similar divination generally foretold his arrival in the shape of the ominous King of Swords." Tongue-in-cheek descriptions interweave with Dro's irrepressible comments. To the live sister Ciddey's⁷ threat to call the dogs on him, he answers sardonically, "You mean those dogs I've heard snarling and barking ever since I came through the gate."

He also enjoys an exhibitionistic entry: "Dro let the door reel shut behind him. He stood a few extra seconds, allowing the more determined gawpers to satisfy themselves." But he is not too self-absorbed to notice snatches of "perfect music, sheer and fine as a shining fish," or the young minstrel who quickly picks his pocket. Though Myal acquires only a decoy purse filled with pebbles, and his musical skills, being above ordinary, do not receive their due from the common man, Dro recognizes his talent and, all tricks and teasing, declares himself glad "that your music isn't as trite as your dialogue."

When he later "kills" Ciddey's ghost sister, Ciddey drowns herself in the river and becomes Myal's pretext for parricide. Or perhaps, Lee suggests, he is pursuing his father to obtain material for a ballad. But motive sinks into obscurity as Myal pursues Dro, who is pursuing ghosts, whilst Ciddey, empowered by an unseen baby tooth embedded in Myal's harp, pursues Myal, hoping to exact revenge on Dro.

The characters finally disperse in an eruption of confessions. When Ciddey confesses to drowning her sister in a well, her ghost is laid to rest. Dro then confesses to a night once spent with Myal's mother. However, he has repressed the memory of being murdered the following morning by an angry husband. The Ghost Killer is a ghost; his son is "the link [that] must be metamorphosed—burnt, crushed, dissolved.... In order to be free of his own imitation life, Dro would have to take Myal's life." His other option is to disappear, and he promptly vanishes.

But Lee refuses to allow him to escape so easily. The book ends with an alternative Chapter One in which Myal has built a new instrument, had a little luck, and found himself a girl. He tracks down his elusive father to an apparently empty wood and hauls him back into existence. When this is done, he merely laughs. "'Well, drawled Myal ... knowing now what to say. '*Fancy* meeting you.'" In the oral tradition according to Lee, it is clearly even more satisfying to have the last word than to murder your father.

Cyrion, a conglomeration of stories, and thus not strictly within this book's remit, is an outstanding illustration of Lee's pleasure in narrative. In multiple images and an elaborate series of interlocking puzzles it pays homage to the oral tradition and a hero of popular legend. The mock-heroic tone is again playful and irreverent, with the reader a frequent recipient of the teasing.

Upright and "plump," Roilant—"Cousin Pudding"—is scouring the city of Heruzala, desperately seeking the mercurial Cyrion, who may or may not be among the company assembled at the inn.[8] As Roilant offers money for information and clutches at straws, endless stories of Cyrion's exploits accompany endless flagons of wine, and the cast grows larger, drunker and increasingly eccentric.

The first story, *Cyrion in Wax*, refers to a wax doll of Cyrion, stuck full of pins by a malevolent sorceror: Cyrion is, in fact, wax in the hands of his unsilenceable narrators, a blank with no lack of contesting authors in search of him.[9] Everyone knows some story about him and each carries traces of its narrator. The mason's story features bitumen; the scholar tells a story about scholars, pedantically prefaced: "know him? ... how many of us can even say we know ourselves?" An orphan's story about enslaved children, describing their behavior as "unpredictable and bizarre ... as with all true men, *who do not get their parts beforehand*" (emphasis added), suggests that these characters are escaping from the author's control, and seconds later the "orphan's" old father is telling his story.

Roilant learns nothing useful. Not even Cyrion's startling white hair will help identify such a master of disguise. Scuffles break out as guesses about Cyrion grow increasingly extravagant—he is the fat priest or the sage who reeks of goats or the harlot. But the harlots, after a brief trip upstairs, reappear as men. The soldier, drunk beyond coherence, is mysteriously sober when his chance comes to tell a story. And the storytellers alter details as they go. Roilant pounces on a toothless, old beggar man, thinking he is Cyrion, then sits down "to listen as his penance, but for the very last, to a tale of Cyrion." Even the author is losing patience: "It was said (O, oft repeated and irritating phrase)...."

This version of *The Canterbury Tales* never reaches the road. The motley cast are too drunk to leave the inn. Cyrion only appears in the flesh in the last, long episode when the soldier follows Roilant outside and is "recognized at once, for who else could look like this? One of the hellish angels of Lucefael."

As the weary Roilant congratulates Cyrion on his trick, Cyrion remarks, "I should perhaps tell you there was more than one," suggesting the reader should perhaps double back to count.

Cyrion's tricks persist throughout the tallest tale of all amongst a welter of false identities and mistaken assumptions. When Cyrion impersonates Roilant, wearing cheek-pouches (described in loving detail) and a ginger wig, the reader is only enlightened when cousin Eliset, whom Roilant has loved since early youth, detects the fake. In this convoluted story of inheritances, murders and witchcraft, Roilant is unhappily betrothed to another woman whose life appears to be threatened by Eliset's sorcery. Reverting to his former promises to Eliset, he expects to be murdered after the wedding, but chivalrously prefers death over harm to the fiancée in Heruzala. At Eliset's crumbling estate, Cyrion-as-Roilant thwarts a poisoning, fakes death, unmasks a supposedly dead, wicked sister and uncovers a cult of hags living below the house who drink the blood of men to secure rejuvenation. (Rather unsuccessfully, it would seem.) These multiple reversals are as entrenched in the language and characters as in the plot. When Cyrion explodes a ship with the hags on board, the wicked sister "felt a dreadful release, as if a bar of lead had dropped from her soul. And with the release, a fearful loss. And with the loss, a malign delight. And with the delight—" etc.[10]

Cyrion also enjoys mixed feelings, although his contradictions are quickly resolved if understood in the context of courtly love. When Roilant (in an unusually bad temper) leaves to keep his promise to the fiancée in Heruzala, Cyrion meets Eliset in an orchard. A conversation on flowers and the habits of birds obstructs Eliset's efforts to explain her role. Without doubt, Cyrion is wooing Eliset. Talk turns to her penetration of his disguise.

> "What gave me away?" he said.
> "Your kiss betrayed you."

The analysis of this kiss adheres to the central doctrine of courtly love that the woman's decision and her pleasure must be paramount. Cyrion asks if Eliset had feared he might "claim a husband's rights."

> She said, "Not afraid of that. A succession of men have forced themselves upon me."
> "And I merely one more."
> "And you, at last, one I would have chosen gladly."

It is now also strictly within the conventions of courtly love that Cyrion should make love to Roilant's beloved, and so he does: "As his arms came about her, she drifted, and just for an instant remembered that pleasure is only the passing of a season, before she forgot everything save the man who held her."

But this is not the end. Cyrion goes to Heruzala, where Roilant's other fiancée confides her wish to pursue a career in magic, not marriage—she, of course, produced the magic effects intended to force Roilant to marry Eliset. Ignoring her father's wishes, she refuses Roilant and becomes a "young woman, who was no one's lady now, save her own." This is another character we have met before.

Eliset decides to marry Roilant, for whom she has felt "a sort of love ... for many years." As she tells Cyrion, "It would be stupid to love you.... Gods and angels both are noted for their transience. You would leave me." The text here debates the usefulness of heroes to happy lives. Hero's deeds are deeply inconvenient; a kindly if slightly portly husband does not come second to the hero, and the mock-heroic does precisely what it says.

And the scholar has already given us his analysis of the mythic hero: "The very fact that he has become the subject of myths says much of Cyrion. And, who knows, the tales may be true."

Sung in Shadow: The Renaissance world

Appearing a year after *Cyrion*, *Sung in Shadow* is a version of *Romeo and Juliet*. Lee's parallel Sana Verensa fills the empty spaces of an Elizabethan stage with the dense colors, smells, sounds and appurtenances of a Renaissance city. Each fortified family palace is "a planet peopled as if by a unique race, mostly contemptuous and in loathing of others." Sudden violence erupts as young men trade claustrophobic insults. Old men stay indoors reciting unenforceable laws against ancient traditions of family honor. The protests of Romulan's father, Valentinus, that his son settles quarrels "inexpertly, with a sword," do not acknowledge that death also threatens those not seeking confrontation. Soon after, Valentinus is murdered just outside his gate.

Though initially the Montargos and Chentis have no quarrel, the perilous instability of normal relations between Houses is underscored when Iulet's nurse, Cornelia, expresses relief that no-one in Romulan's family has murdered a Chenti "for more than seven years."[11] The Duke himself is mentioned as a former duelist. Mercurio encompasses the ethos of the age as much as its language rhythms when he says, "Tradition, dear heart. How else do we eliminate rivals in commerce and love? ... Oh, all roads lead to boxes.... My Lady Death, we are before you." He rounds off his speech with a "love song ... like a knell." Love and death keep close company in Sana Verensa.

Mercurio's presence at the betrothal is needed for "a demonstration of unity," and Romulan is invited because "Valentinus may relish the social policy of this." Mercurio accepts when he realizes he has already seen Iulet in the brothel. He makes a spectacularly arrogant entrance—"In uproar, twenty-two males exploded into the quite comparable uproar of the house"—and immediately maneuvers himself into Troian's place as Iulet's dancing partner. The dangerous games of the streets come indoors.

Lee's Chenti is a plain, practical man's man. Shamed when his nephew, Leopardo, starts a quarrel at his daughter's betrothal, he has no qualms that political alliance and the consolidation of property rather than his daughter's happiness are its purpose. This is a familiar theme from Lee's *Birthgrave* onwards. Troian, the intended groom, goes beyond what form requires in describing Iulet as "rich in more than cash."

The women of this book are programmed in repression. Forced to internalize their feelings, young women such as Iulet are kept close and powerless. Already in love with Romulan when she consents to Troian, Iulet is obeying her father from lifelong habit. Lee adds in the fantasies of a very young girl: "...by the implication of this conquest, she dreamed of the effect she might have on *him*. The true implications, being young and bound by others to her youngness, she did not see at all."

Cornelia wisely remarks, "a girl is only goods for market." Iulet's father is grateful that sickness has not spoiled her looks, and she may still be married off advantageously. When her secret marriage to Romulan is revealed, he shouts, "I fed you to be a present for my friend," but he is mainly enraged by her non-submission: "...you prefer to carve for yourself." Mollified by her "homage of fear," instead of murdering her he merely casts her into the street with Cornelia.

Though Chenti regrets his anger, to Electra her daughter is pure commodity. "Iuletta ... had shown her only possible worth in alliance-promoting beauty." Lovelessly married at thirteen, "raped and used and left to freeze for so many years," she is only twenty-nine when she is engulfed by an excruciating appetite for her nephew. Lee captures the age's particular concupiscent torments as Leopardo, beholding 'the essential duality of eroticism under him," has "a vision of Hell ... Hell was Electra, not a punishment of horror, but of pleasure which *was* horror." The passage concludes with, "as if he bled to death," and he rushes out, deliriously butchers Mercurio, and falls to Romulan's sword. Electra's desire implodes into an obsession for vengeance and Romulan's death.

Though not contorted like her mother, Iulet protests her woman's situation and the falsity of lovers.

> [S]he felt herself enmeshed in some terrifying masculine sport, she the target at which all took aim ... each seemed her enemy, mocking her. Even Romulan seemed so. What use were her feeble feminine sorceries against the living freedom of a man who came and went as he required?

Sorcery is a perfectly serious issue here. The girl and her nurse both believe in magic potions. Nor is Fra Laurus the simple friar of Shakespeare's play. Lee fearlessly takes on the supernatural uncertainties of the neo-pagan Renaissance, where divine and demonic were not easy to distinguish, and gives him clearly occult powers that blur the boundaries between natural and thaumaturgical. "[I]t was generally agreed ... that fallen angels took on the form of Pagan deities or dispersed themselves into various parts of the physical universe."[12] Cornelia says, "We are all part of some plot of his that none of us can devine." Iulet speaks of how Laurus "treats men and women like game pieces, either he or God to move them, and they mean as little to him." He is eventually revealed in the lineaments of another world, his powers and alchemical experiments are proved genuine, but he remains a permanent mystery.

Romulan too expresses metaphysical anxieties. Laurus remarks, "I perceive ... you do not credit Purgatory, or the Inferno." At this, "Romulan beamed. He did credit them, but they were far away. His youth, his vitality and his looks assured him he was immortal...." But a moment later he no longer beams. What has seemed like "a story worth recounting" becomes "a feverish darkness ... the lower register of death.... For, just as disbelief implied belief, so the activities of magic implied the awful and insecure world that had inspired them."

Romulan's spiritual and amorous uncertainties run parallel. A grey cat is "an omen"; he feels "the jaws of a trap closing upon him" and is tempted to leave Iulet to "flounce home to marry idiotic red-haired Troian, who wanted her." Then, meeting her accidentally, he sees "the astonishing stamina that underlay her delicacy.... Had she been a man, Romulan would already have reached for dagger or sword." With this one stroke, Lee cuts Iulet free of her tight confinement. Romulan perceives her "capacity for great liberation. She might have committed acts of enormous immoderation." Iulet possesses the dangerous strength found in other Lee heroines.

Then the familiar theme of transformation through death extends the story in a sharp departure from the Shakespeare play. After expulsion from the Chenti house, Cornelia sensibly dries her tears and reflects on, "mortals, poor worms, slithering hopelessly towards the fiery pit in an effort to keep warm"; but Iulet, believing herself abandoned, experiences "a strange and dreadful elation ... like broken ice."

> She had lost everything, but not in the end the value of her love. And now, in despairing triumph, she knew she would have died indeed rather than leave go.

Iulet, beyond thoughts of warmth or comfort, is ready to make an Orphic descent into the underworld. Several myths, apparently relating to the Dionysian cult of Orphism, are condensed here.[13] Iulet's passage into hell is paid for by Mercurio with a song; Mercurio is Mercury-Hermes, the psychopomp and guide of souls, but he is also addressed as Orpheus. The "Hell-Priest," Fra Laurus, is also Lucifer, "no longer tonsured" and with "a golden breast properly *innocent* of a crucifix" (emphasis added). The *absence* of a cross attests his innocence. Certain details develop retrospective meaning, such as the mosaic floor picturing "Proserpina's poppies" where Iulet once fainted, or Mercurio's subtly hermaphroditic speech about the rebirth of the soul—"A new body and gender immaterial. Sweet Jesus. Think what it must be to be made a woman."—or his kiss, "very much a lover's," in which Iulet "fathomed his eyes and felt some awesome darkness stirring there."

The motif of doubles or twins (both equivalent to the androgyne) comes back into play. In hell, Romulan finds that Iulet's eyes are "his own ... seeking across a huge gulf of night." Cornelia sees Romulan and Iulet, "like two severed halves of a perfect whole, mending." Their faces are described as "similar as plants of one genus: brother and sister."

Where Shakespeare's use of twins and doubles frequently has a romantic significance, Lee's often carries a sacred significance.[14] When Laurus tells Iulet she has the power to raise Romulan from the dead, he may be referring to myths in which the son-lover is reborn through the mother, but the brother-sister relationship emphasizes the androgynous equality of the lovers. Romulan is not Iulet's "good angel, not her slave, nor her master ... but herself. And she was Romulan ... his eyes, her eyes ... she no longer felt her hands, they had become his hands, or her body, for it had become his body. And as she breathed, she breathed for him." Twins and lovers are both holy: Both are reunited with the lost halves of themselves and both are united in the flesh: "...it seems not surprising, nor is it un–Platonic, that Divine Love should in the end have fostered a spiritual cult of the senses."[15]

Lee's "star-crossed lovers" express the struggle between Platonic thought and Christian orthodoxy. Whereas the frigid Electra is condemned to spiritual isolation in a loveless marriage, Iulet, the pagan 'child of the woods', is united with Romulan through a passion that is both sacred and profane.

Volkhavaar

Though Shaina's owner beats her, as the Grey Lady of Cold Crag remarks, "The rod strikes the back, not the heart"; and Shaina, who is hard-working and resilient, takes delight in herding goats in the mountains. But her heart, the Grey Lady tells her, "is ready to be hurt."

In *Volkhavaar*, quaint beliefs and superstitions saturate a "country of devils, sprites and goblins." A rustic god is created and unmade; souls are possessed and released; a corpse is returned to life by unmaking the instrument of its death; astral projection, shape-changing and the interior lives of animals are all described from a participant's perspective. At the same time, the narrative is a precise account of magic *process* and an analysis of the psychological evolution of a magician or *shaman*.[16]

The Russian witch, Barbayaga, is the prototype for the Grey Lady, Barbayat. Volkhavaar is yellow-skinned, presumably Mongol or Tartar since he comes from across the mountains. He is a model of barbarism and cruelty, with a god of roughly carved stone, blackened by sacrificial blood.[17] Intermittently, Barbayat appears as a talkative mossy boulder—"Not everything that walks is a man ... and not everything that lies quiet is a stone." One must look beneath surfaces.

Both Barbayat and Volkhavaar require blood, Volkhavaar to enhance the power of death, Barbayat for modest self-renewal.[18] As Barbayat establishes loving (blood) relations with Shaina, the traditional Russian forms of address—*Mother, Daughter*—become more than tokens. Barbayat "kissed her on the cheek like the mother she had become.... There was a great change in Barbayat ... she had an appearance of Shaina altogether...." Shaina invokes their kinship: "You called me daughter ... I called you mother. Save me, my mother. Keep me in the world."

As a lonely boy, Volkhavaar also bonds with his god, Takerna. Sacrificing rabbits to a stone idol, he feels "a huge surge of *yearning-made-*

power flood from him" (emphasis added). His survival alone in the forest after the death of his mother also seems essential in his shaman's initiation; and during his years in a dungeon, "Inwardly his mind began to discover its own deep kingdom" in which Takerna's "face cruel as an eagle's, black as jet, looked down into his, familiar and beloved as the countenance of a mother."

Emotional deprivation cripples his sexual desire (Eros), and like a number of Lee's other male characters he craves for power and death (Thanatos) instead. But killing grows monotonous—"He wanted to destroy but not precisely to kill"—and he takes up the creation of *illusion*—appropriately, since his power is largely illusory.[19] "He was not immortal.... Neither was he all-powerful.... Master of Illusion, Shape-Changer, Deceiver of Minds." Coveting the illusionistic skills of a troupe of strolling players, he imprisons their souls and enslaves them; and when Shaina falls in love with one of them, an extended lesson in magical practice begins.

Barbayat withholds the information that Dasyel is ensorcelled, though she admits her spell is very dangerous. Shaina can separate her soul from her body and go to Dasyel, but prolonged separation of soul from body results in death. During her first lesson in astral projection, Shaina is put into a tranced sleep, apparently hypnotized by a fox, but when she asks it, "Did you speak?" Barbayat dryly enquires if she imagines she "can hear the language of beasts." Soon she can, and has a further shamanic ability to merge with animals. Other animals enter the narrative. Crows guard her goats during her absences, and her astral journey begins with the traditional image of the soul as a bird: "Metamorphosis. Girl into bird, into air, into dream."

Volkhavaar also becomes a bird as he gives his soul to his god.

> Kernik was a falcon, and the falcon flew up into the air.... More than illusion now, it was reality.... Kernik-Takerna-Volk flew with the sun in his sideways eyes, high over the husk of the black god and the humility of the landscape, and the magician Volkhavaar was born."

Volkhavaar is a fluent shape-changer ("falcon, wolf, black horse, lead-green fish-king"), and Lee examines the primitive belief that illusion, imitation or representation influence reality: "Maybe all this while it was Volk the man who sprang on the lamb and gutted it with his long lupine teeth, Volk the man who only seemed to hunt the little fish in the river deeps. But ... *If the illusion is quite perfect, who is to say it is not real?*" (emphasis added).

7. Folk, Classic and Fairytale 135

A true theriomorphic transformation occurs when a disembodied Shaina takes refuge in a cat. Despite some conflicting interests, girl and cat are united in loathing for Volkhavaar and gradually come to terms.

> She lay curled, barely sane, in the unknown region.... Then came something and brushed against her. Not physical, and not experienced physically. A consciousness.... A thought. Not hers: a cat thought. Shudderingly both.

In "an unlooked-for and astonishing little exchange ... emerging with a kind of peculiar translation into cat-tongue, woman-tongue..." they defer to one another. "Pardon me, I was desperate, as for a fishead," Shaina tells Mitz. "Meow—behold, I am a mouse before your claw." The cat responds with feline anxiety: "Mind where you are putting my tail.... Stretching is good, also washing. Ugh! Do not think, if you please, of jumping in a cold stream. Lick my paw. So much better...."

Food is a major problem: "Shaina finding a dream of dead mice hanging red on claw.... Shaina sick, turning the cat sick, the cat spinning round and biting her own tail.... Shaina somewhere distressfully saying she was sorry." But the animal activity of killing and eating raw flesh is not peripheral. A dividing line between primitive and civilized, it enables humans to remain connected to the animal kingdom in "A type of behavior that, for one or two million years, had been inseparable from the human (or at least the masculine) mode....' In rites of hunting and war,

> Numerous Indo-European and Turko-Mongol tribes had eponyms of beasts of prey (primarily the wolf) ... hundreds of thousands of years spent in a sort of mystical symbiosis with the animal world have left indelible traces ... orgiastic ecstasy is able to reactualize the religious behavior of the earliest Paleohominians, when the game was eaten raw; this happened in Greece, among the worshippers of Dionysus.[20]

The uniting of Mitz and Shaina has a pronouncedly feminine character. It stresses *merging*, not dominance. They share feelings. "Dasyel and a snowy tom co-mingled. Common ground again." They share dreams. "Shaina pursued mice and rolled in the sun, Mitz carried water from the well ... and fell, over and over, in love with a handsome actor." A mixture of feelings gains in complexity when the cat is reunited with her mistress Woana.

"The will of the alien who had invaded Mitz's inner country had proved too strong to evade or resist. And now that will was ... striving to comprehend this relationship between feline and human female that now suffused the cat's body. Shaina's soul ... marveled at this rite of love, and tried also not to intrude, but could not help intruding...."

As she intrudes, roles are exchanged, as they so often are in Lee's work: Timid Woana becomes the embracing mother of the dauntless Shaina present in Mitz's body. In a female rite, all aspects of the feminine become interchangeable. It is another version of the scene with Barbayat when Shaina had felt "the painless mouth sipping so gently, gently," and she "began to imagine that the little grey witch was her child."

But switches of identity also occur in darker contexts. When Volkhavaar, "partial to cats," plays with Shaina/Mitz, he unleashes a complex chemistry. Though the animal world does not celebrate power or cruelty, the man-become-beast can manipulate animal instinct. As Mitz is overpowered, Shaina "held to her sanity precariously.... Caught in the millrace of Mitz's feline terror, she felt old, primitive fibers interweave in her own spirit. Always sensitive, part witch, as Barbayat had said, now her transplanted soul had become almost unbearably receptive."

Shaina's control deteriorates rapidly as Volkhavaar tantalizes Mitz with an illusory mouse. "Shaina darkened her thoughts and steeled herself. Mitz, instinct uppermost, ran a little, sprang, toyed and horribly patted and mangled.[21] Each motion took her a fraction nearer the magician, as he meant it to."

As Mitz purrs and sleeps, Shaina, her mind darkened, "was pulled down after her, purring and sleeping." Shaina's initiation into the animal world is complete. No longer "alien," her animal instincts equal her human consciousness, and back in her human body, Shaina retains what she has learned as a cat. To reach Woana's window, she takes "A cat's way up, and taught me by a cat."

As Shaina offers a small white flower to the bloodthirsty Takerna (because he "looked angry") and converts him back into a little rustic god, she is 'the maiden kissing Death on his cold cheek," and also the mother-daughter of Barbayat, or Nature herself. Transformation is accomplished through use of this symbol of fertility, and soon there is "a bush of white flowers growing there."[22]

Volkhavaar is well aware of the power of symbols, whether in the form of his Black God, the illusions created by his "golem" actors, or his hoped-for marriage to Woana, who has a "symbolic value." "For the magician, as he said, loved symbols, needed them; *the* foundation of his house."

When Barbayat unmakes the sacred bronze sword used to behead Shaina's body during her soul's absence, returning it into copper and tin, she describes the crucial position of belief in a magical world, "This is the oldest magic: what we *believe* Is, what we *believe* Was, and what is To Be *will* be."

Shaina, however, does not allow magic into her personal life. "It is I who loved, not he," she says as she refuses Dasyel's grateful offer of marriage. "It is foolish, you see, for so intelligent a young man to be taking as his wife one he does not love. I have worn enough chains that I never wished to chain up others." She apprentices herself to Barbayat, and "The irony of her story," the tale concludes, "is merely that her love became, in the end, her motive rather than her goal, the doorway rather than the house."

— 8 —

WORKS FOR CHILDREN

Prince on a White Horse, The Dragon Hoard, Princess Hynchatti and Other Surprises, Shon the Taken, East of Midnight, Companions on the Road, The Castle of Dark, The Winter Players, The Black Unicorn, The Gold Unicorn

---

  In Lee's books for younger children—*Princess Hynchatti and Other Surprises, The Dragon Hoard, Prince on a White Horse*—traditional fairy-story conventions may be used humorously. Ordinary shrewdness outwits the less pleasant foibles of magicians. Animals may be gifted with speech, though a horse denys it is talking with the sensible question, "Whoever heard of a horse talking?" In *this same book*, humor becomes a reflexive instrument of healing a world afflicted by acute depression. Elsewhere a prince, believing a swan is an enchanted princess, has a magician turn it into a woman who then glares at him out of "small yellow eyes." Returning from a quest, a prince remarks, "...until you actually have a hundred-man-long dragon to slay, you don't realize how dangerous it can be."
  As the age range increases, so does the level of sophistication. At one point the mechanics of writing and plot meet with typical Lee sleight-of-hand

in a "between place" for storing characters during dormant periods. Reflex fear and persecution of difference is examined, using magically enhanced abilities as the differentiating factor (*Shon the Taken*) or by juxtaposing a magical world and one that largely operates by ordinary rules (*East of Midnight*). As in books for adults, doubles appear—one a prince, one a slave— and demonstrate how merit is independent of circumstances or social class. War is also subjected to close scrutiny. *Companions on the Road* focuses mainly on the inglorious psychological traumas suffered by soldiers, and a large part of *Gold Unicorn* takes place in a hell particular to war. Tanaquil,[1] heroine of the Unicorn trilogy, pierces a fog of stereotypes and extends the meaning of magic into humbler realms as she mends "broken dolls and clocks, music boxes, and even sometimes some of the soldiers' crossbows, or bits of the cannon...." With a talking peeve as her familiar (her grandiose and flamboyant mother "spills magic everywhere like soup. And—the peeve got splashed"), she recognizes the folly of exhibitionistic magic-making and produces results that no one expects.

The Castle of Dark and *The Winter Players* both examine the dynamics of magic and take on the fear of death without evasion or euphemism. Explanation is less full in *The Castle of Dark*, but quite adult issues are confronted. As a musician incorporates a skull-plate from an ancient barrow into his harp, he invokes a "magic to which he felt oddly accustomed." Later, running in pursuit of a dark force, he asks a guard, "...did Death brush by you on the stair?" No philosophical discussion ensues when the baffled guard asks what he means by Death, but the point is clear: He knows what death is; those who refuse to know live in fear.

He takes responsibility for a dark spirit that he lets loose into the world and allows the source of darkness to have access to him. Using a skull-plate from a timelessly ancient skeleton, he gathers the darkness into a spout that streams off into the sky. Lee breaks with custom for children's books by concluding on a note of moral uncertainty. The musician/magician will never "risk saying, unequivocally, if the Force were evil or merely elemental, if he had driven it out upon men, or ... freed the world of it forever." The possibility of differing interpretations is taken a step further with the added comment, "Or if Hell were a wicked place, for that matter, or just a misunderstanding of men...."

The Winter Players analyzes the operation of magic in great detail, as a priestess, Oaive, sets out to retrieve a finger-bone relic stolen from the shrine she tends. The thief seems to have greater magical powers than she does and to have "grasped the fact that he could overcome the illusion by not believing it ... he understood, she realized, the logic of sorcery." Oaive uses this same logic to conceal herself from a pack of murderous hounds:

"She shut her eyes and breathed deep. I cannot see you, therefore you cannot see me. You cannot scent me, you cannot sense me. I am a shadow of the tree. I am not here."

A personal possession, a tiny scrap of the thief's clothing, enables her to pursue him. "She shut her eyes and forced her mind into the fibers of the cloth.... The cloth had memorized the pulse of a wrist.... She could follow him from this moment on...."

Repeatedly, concentration, will and inner resources are represented as the true origins of magic powers. As the thief says, "Spells are words, and words are merely noises.... Anyone can learn the chants and gestures of the occult art; they can get every syllable and wave of the arm exact, but if there's no magic in them, there will be no magic made.... You are the sorceress, not your instructions."

The thief also confesses that he is controlled by an evil spirit that possessed him long ago when he used a spell meant to reanimate the dead. During a struggle between Oaive and the evil spirit, the three "players" return to a time that predates the original finding of the relic. Through the joint efforts of Oaive and the thief, the evil spirit is killed with a sword; but the top joint of Oaive's finger is accidentally cut off. The relic is Oaive's own finger-bone, severed in an earlier, unremembered version of her life.

The events of the later time-stream and the theft of the relic must somehow be short-circuited to prevent an infinitely repeating time-loop. They seem "caught on a wheel of time, turning forever," but if Oaive returns to the moment before the spell is said and forestalls the summoning of the spirit, she also eliminates the relic, the shrine and the meeting with the thief with whom she is now in love. She therefore travels back through time, dissuades him from using the disastrous necromantic spell and, again using the magic of the personal possession, leaves her finger-bone behind. With it the thief traces her to her time and village, and in this version of reality finds her sitting by the sea, with her fingers all complete. The introduction of time travel creates complex possibilities. Contradictory strands must be unraveled and different stakes assessed. Lee's books for children are in their own way as complex as her books for adults and do not avoid either difficult ideas or problematical subjects.

9

EVEN ANGELS ARE SUBJECT TO CORRUPTION

The Blood of Roses

The Forest

The Blood of Roses has many qualities associated with the epic. Spanning an era, it is a myth of origins, to which character and human relations are subordinated[1]; the hero's birth and innate powers are exceptional.[2] Relating to the genesis of Christianity as it emerges from pagan roots, the myth stretches back into an ancient world, itself considered sacred, where animistic rites were celebrated in the forest round a Great Tree. Lee's forests have always been occult. This one abounds with religious significances.

Certain characters, though normal in appearance, have supernatural powers or originate in the mental projections of the preternatural Anjelen. Anjelen's history requires explanation: Sacrificed to the Tree as a child, he fuses with it. Much later, he emerges reborn from the forest, trailing a numinous past. The priests of the Christus regard him as spiritually gifted, perhaps a saint; few of them consider that he may emanate from the pagan religion they hope to suppress.

Gods or demons—there is little clear separation—may be corporeal. They are fearsome supernatural presences, not poetic conceits of divinity.

Where Flat Earth demons had accessible thoughts and feelings, Mechail and his mother Nilya are not yet personal. Modern human emotion has not been born. Love needs to be *discovered*: "So that was love—what he had felt for her. Back across a void of time. That was love. Her fear for him. Grief loss and terror ... were *love*." Emotional terms of reference barely exist. Maidservants do not mention the heart but whisper that Anillia (Nilya) has "no soul." Supernatural takes precedence over human. Divine-demonic beings do not abandon their spiritual past, and death may not mean a humble return to dust: When Mechail and Nilya return to the Tree they are merging with a divine object.

Lee's myth is evolutionary, not creationist. Like Darwin's man, religion does not spring up fully-fledged, but has a long, bloody ancestry. Primitive elements of the sacred are carried into the Christian era.[3] Simple people may be baffled by moral or spiritual questions as they abandon oceanic being for the abstractions of human meaning, but no-one ever doubts that the supernatural saturates everything.

Events often stem from spiritual sources. Magic and metamorphosis are ubiquitous. A hare that dances in the woods may be a boy. A man may become a wolf, but if he does, "what he was by instinct and usage" will also change. "No worrying or gnawing at the form of the self. Men did that, but not a beast." Jasha, following a soldier through the woods, is "pursuing—rather than the captain—the high-pitched note of the supernatural." Babies may be changelings or spirit-offspring. As Mechi's mother goes out at night to urinate behind the woodpile, the embryonic Mechail alters him in the womb and he is born a dwarf—perhaps babies do not yet apprehend the proper structure of the body.[4] Miscegenation between humans and spirits in human form are commonplace. Proper categories have yet to be defined.

Mechail is the son of a backwoods landholder. Crippled in early childhood by a vampiric moth, he is left by his loving, otherworldly mother[5] to an insensitive father who finds deformity repellent.[6] A remarriage produces a brutal half-brother who conspires with an enemy tribe to have Mechail murdered.

Christian iconography surrounds this death. Coins are paid over. Soldiers drink and dice in the chapel where Mechail's corpse is "lying under the crucifix. It cast a shadow upon him. The shadow had a weight, a bar of merciful lead, that anchored him to calm, unthinking quietude." But this image of Christian death swiftly changes. "Because of it [the shadow] his consciousness began so subtly it infused him like mild light." Suddenly Mechail bursts back into life, slays his enemies and, pausing only to sip the blood of a younger sister, disappears into the forest with "the face of a beast-god of the wood."

Mechail returns into a primeval world, where skulls and the bones of men and animals, signifying rebirth, hang indiscriminately from the trees.[7] The wood seems "unholy, deep ... its supernatural quality was dreamlike. Everywhere might be portents, glowing fungus, starry streams, the shake of bird wings clandestine in a pine-top." He becomes a "man-wolf" that hunts for his food with a "wolf-wolf ... their eyes now and then meeting, without inquiry."

In this primitive stage, "The human is barely distinguishable from any other animal species, the spirit-being is as solidly present as the corporeal one, able to eat, drink, give birth and suffer death for brief or long periods of time."[8]

The forest is "a living chapel" or "vast Cathedral," but only a rural priest, haunted by his uneasily beautiful visions of a youthful "God of the Wood," is innocent enough to mistake it for the Garden of Eden. This is not the cathedral of a Christian god. "Was not the world one whole forest ... mother and father, womb and grave, living and extinction. They worshipped the forest, for, being all things, the forest was also God."

The Great Tree is also divine. A tree was the embodiment of a spirit; the felling of a tree might release a demon. Northern European religious practices revolved around a "sacred tree, beside which everything else sank into insignificance ... at its roots the victim was sacrificed ... the spirit is viewed as incorporate in the tree; it animates the tree and must suffer and die with it.... When a tree comes to be viewed, no longer as the body of the tree-spirit, but simply as its abode.... Animism is passing into polytheism ... a tree-soul, becomes a forest god ... begins to change his shape and assume the body of a man."[9]

When a landholder converted to Christianity cuts down the Great Tree, upon which countless victims have been sacrificed, he is committing a murder of enormous proportions.

> [B]lood bubbled up from the stump.... As the framework of a thousand victims had blended with the Tree, grown into it and become the Tree, so their blood, feeding it, had filled the Tree. It was vegetable, but also flesh. Tree, but also man. But also god.... A fountain of blood sprang into the sky, high as (once) the Great Tree ... the pillar of blood sprayed across Heaven and came down again, drenching the grove beneath.

After Mechail's occult resurrection, the priest-exorcist, Anjelen— "Angel of the Blood"—arrives. Using Mechi, spirit "child" of Mechail, as his bloodhound, he follows a spiritual trail through the forest. From a frozen pocket of the summer forest (frozen presumably in time) a pack of wolves, including Mechial, burst from a sheet of ice. Anjelen departs with Mechail and Mechi. Jasha, the daughter of a supernatural mother, emerges from the depths of the forest to accompany them. She recognizes the moth in Anjelen's crucifix as the mark of a vampire.

An interlude in the city contrasts with the pre-agricultural forest world, and the sacred takes on a new role. Evidence of ecclesiastical wealth and culture is everywhere. But sinister notes sound: A Traveller-girl comes up to offer Anjelen her blood; a cloaked female figure of death sings at a funeral.

The narrative moves on to the Christerium, a vast complex by the sea, built by the Knights of God, specifically "for *Anjelen as a god.*" "*The Christerium was itself a sort of forest, with the great Tree being the seaward tower....* The Tree itself had gone to stone ... his Knights of God, they were the grove, the briar hedge that ringed him round. *Should it be needful they would die for him.*" Anjelen seems invincible, but the god-demon released by the felling of the Tree is gradually petrifying, and his works are turning against him. Just as in childhood Mechail defied God—"I struggle against Your injustice and Your Bloody will"—so in manhood he will refuse to carry out Anjelen's purposes. Anjelen's creations will all outstrip him. Nothing will remain of the "perfect" child that was sacrificed to the Tree. The beautiful God of the Woods will be steeped in mindless vice and destroyed by his creations.

Pagans, Peasants and Princes of the Church

When Anjelen causes his "son" Mechail to be born in a remote and primitive area, close to the Great Tree, he displays little concern for the worldly wealth and ostentation that preoccupies the high-ranking clergy. Apart from the single ruby on his black crucifix, he is comparatively plain: "...the fingers had no rings. They were severe, like the face which had no features but forehead, eyes and eyebrows, and no meaning or message but of Mind and Thought."

In this apparently spiritual appearance, Anjelen is nevertheless recognizing the currency of power in the age he is entering. Mind and thought are the great properties of the transition from the holistic, primitive sacred into a regulated and civilized condition. As the sacred is relegated to a mental and abstract domain *outside* the corporeal world, it is accessible only to the priesthood, and intellectual man comes into his own. Anjelen, however, remains a curiously ambivalent transitional figure. He practices alchemy, saying, "What the ignorant term magic is only the science of true things," but he has been cast out of his original, blissful union with the Tree, and never quite recovers from his sense of loss.[10] Asked how he perceives the Garden, he replies, "The world before it was spoiled." The world of the Tree was a prelapsarian Eden, and he wanders through a changed world in progressive *estrangement*.

But even mind and thought, the keys to the incoming age with its *science* of theology are not born out of nothing; like that which cuts off man from animal, they merely become consciously segregated functions in a Christian scheme. An abstract god is excluded from the living-dying, self-renewing cycle. To a sacral intelligence all things are god, the symbol is not divided from what it signifies, and thought is inseparable from thing:

> If in a primitive society some tree or other is regarded as "the Tree of the World" ... it is possible ... to attain a metaphysical understanding of the Universe.... [A] particular object may signify the whole of the cosmos.[11]

It is this participation in "the whole of the cosmos" that has been lost to Anjelen. Even as the beautiful God of the Woods, he is already degraded, stripped of the "perfect" innocence of the child who was made one with the Tree. The child who believed he would soon become a hare, became instead a wolf (the Christian view of the pagan as savage and beastly).

Godbrother Orro, one of the most sympathetic and tolerant characters in the book, with his kind heart, "healing hands," and "sweet, nearly naive piety," encounters Jun-Anjelen in the forms of both god and beast, and is able to accept the paradox that they are the same. When he sees the God of the Wood, "...there were tears in his eyes. It was like a vision. He could not confuse it with anything sacred. It was profane, yet so completely pure neither could he resist it." As the wolf-boy emerges from the cave, other selves emerge in turn from him. "At first, he came out as a wolf. On all fours.... But next the wolf stood up. It stood as a man.... In the cloak of hair was the young god of the wood."

Orro's vision is pagan but his perception of what must be done is Christian. The man must be *separated* from the beast. "Only through the Christus could this fallen creature be salvaged.... Orro laid one hand, healing, on the matted hair, the low wide forehead, the second healing hand upon the plunging heart. And the Devil went out of Jun."[12]

Later, speaking to the Administer, Orro says, "Haven't we a score of saints who came from bizarre and awful beginnings, out of the sinks of the worst crime and depravity? As if the Devil himself had cauterized them in earthly fires. I think, I do believe that Jun, who evidently was a pagan from the oldest heart of the forest, has been brought to the Christus."

At first, there seems to be no insoluble problem. Lee points out that "pagan rites were so often ... wedded to the rituals of the Christus. Who did they see upon the cross of wood, the peasants of the forest, but their old god again, the perfect scapegoat, flawless and dying in consent, to set them free of sin and sadness."

With Christian need satisfied, Jun enters the novitiate. But as he studies with Orro, deviations from Christian doctrine begin to surface. The deviations consist in Jun's interpretations.

> "The Garden," said Jun, "is the Tree. Men are imperfect. One must be chosen who's perfect. He is God. The sin is the sin of loss, the separation from God. God becomes man to bring men back to Him. The Christus dies on the Tree. His blood rains on the ground from the wounds in His hands and feet. The blood's to be drunk. The power of God which can't die enters with the blood into man and the separation is over."

With alarm, Orro realizes that "this was not the orthodoxy of the Christus ... but the ancient pagan religion of the wood ... for Jun the Christus *was* the god of the wood. A fragment of the elder hierarchy, one of millions, a branch of a colossal Tree. The Christus was wondrous, but nothing new, or special, inviolate and unique."

The pigments of good-evil, God-Devil are once again running together, and Orro, making his confession before he dies, perceives a certain inevitability in this fusion.

> "Jun," said Orro, "is a demon ... I was blinded. He blinds us all. What is so terrible, he reverences the Christus—he worships God, as I imagine the Devil also does, irresistibly, in some hidden palace under the ground. How can the Devil not worship God? He of all things, *knows* God. It's love makes the Devil fight with God."

Different characters in the book have different perceptions of the meaning of Christianity. For the soldiers sent to cut down the Tree,

> Conversion to the Christus had scoured the topsoil of the forest from the soldiers of the Raven garrison. In a stone house in the valley, they took the body and blood of god, and forgot those similar

rituals their progenitors had acted. The new god was more stern in some sort, yet also He could be fooled. You had only to confess, and to pay—in a fast or a coin—and He forgave you. With the old god ... forgiveness was not anything to do with it. Wrong was wrong. There was no blame, the god did not sob at your sins. But if there was a punishment you could not buy it off. It was like life itself.... Inevitable.[13]

The landholder who commands the felling of the Tree "was a convert to the religion of the Christus, the tree-god in another form." When Beljunion, the priest of the Korhlen family, sees the God of the Wood, Christianity has moved much further towards completing its work: "He had supposed it was a vision. But maybe it was a fantasy. Afterwards he was by turns proud of it—and unnerved. He took time to learn to see it in his terms of cipher, to explain it away as something other than it was."

Beljunion is not notably gifted with mind or thought. But the young Mechail believes that "*God's in the wood,*" and to the god in the church he prays, "*Hear me, God, I struggle against Your injustice and Your bloody will.*" And Jun, now grown into Anjelen, admits no distinction and argues his views with the sophistic dialectics of a skilled theologian.

> "There's only one God," said Anjelen.... "Since there is only one God, whatever is worshipped, must be God. They come to the ash and hang a skull on it, and spill blood at its foot like the red leaves lying there. The Tree must have blood, but it makes return. What dies for the Tree, who dies for it, becomes the Tree. Man and Tree. Both are one. Both Sacrifice and Lord, victim and master, together. And what else is Christus?"

For Jun there had been no thought of lord or master; he desired only to become one with the Tree. Anjelen is acquiring the thinking of the Church. And, with less skill than Anjelen, but with the gross worldly elitism of a prince of the Church, the Factor requires a god who represents his own class. Lee's political disaffections come through explicitly here.

> Rational always, this man, for the Factor adored the logic and the intellectual soul of his religion. It was this he worshipped in the person of God and took for God. The Christus of the Factor had, of necessity, been a prince, having for speech oratory and wit, having a weapon as a mind, beauty for a voice, an unblemished frame in which Godhead had poured itself—these were essentials of the God-in-man. God could not be shown forth in any other caste.

The son of the carpenter and friend of fishermen has been forgotten. The Factor chooses to ignore Jun's peasant origins. Impressed by Anjelen's aristocratic and pleasing exterior—"You are more than I had supposed"—he forgets his history. Engrossed in a divisive hierarchy, the Factor is unable to grasp the nature of transformation, and Jun represents pure transformation: "When the eyes of Jun opened, in the starry night, something looked out of them that was not boy and was not tree." Fixated on man as the pinnacle of creation, the Factor would find tree-worship unimaginable. He is bound fast in profane Christianity. At least in part, one must assume that it is this aspect of Christianity, garnished with marble edifices, immutable dogmas and fixed hierarchies, that undoes Anjelen. The simplicity of the child is slowly engulfed by the celebration of power belonging to a prince of a worldly church. For Anjelen, *blood*, originally sacred, becomes profane and power becomes his motive.

In the matter of mind, Lee does not allow simplifications. Mind does not originate as a brute, unconscious property which suddenly sublimates into a daintily articulated vehicle for abstract thought. Mind is a microcosm, containing everything, contained by everything.[14] The book brims over with definitions and instances of mind, but the passage that describes the return of Jun's mind from death is especially fascinating:

> The mind that had been a boy's mind once in the heart of the wood, and that had emptied, and that had filled again with the wild abbreviated eternity of the Tree. The mind which had lived as a wolf, a god-thing, to which a decade was one hundred mortal years. The mind that came up from the shadow, and stayed a shadow.

Unfortunately, this shadow—the shadow of man who was still whole, and of a time that Orro calls "spiritual" time—will become lost in the dislocated abstractions of intellectual ability, power over other men, and the addictive taste of blood. But at the beginning, at least,

> The mind of Jun was like a globe of glass. A million things were engraved on it. Lights and midnights played over and within it. It turned, and gave out, like silent chimes, all that it knew, had learned, had lived, and, too, it kept in, withheld, stored, and wasted nothing. Like a globe of glass, its clarity. And yet, like a forest also, dense and convoluted and *full*.

In its struggle to create an absolute separation of Christian from pagan, and to repress and excise pagan thought from consciousness, the new religion is corrupted. The next chapter will focus on that corruption.

Seduction to Corruption: Blood

As symbols replace religious realities, former rites degenerate into confused folk traditions. "Every year the tree must be slain, the three men ... beaten black and blue, until the bladders of weasels' blood tied about them split and spilled. It was a blood offering to the earth, a peacemaking with the forest...."[15]

A Christian priest caste that excludes women supersedes simple woodman-priests, though Magister Anjelen poses as plain Godbrother to visit the Korhlen estates. He misleads an inept priest, troubled by continuing blood-sacrifices. "Blood sacrifice is neither alien nor outlawed by the Church. You will find the Book threaded with it ... it must not be profaned by the *unlearned and vulgar*."

And Lee plays with time again: Anjelen creates an illusion of the Tree on its old site to incite the Vre to reinstate the sacrifice of prisoners; the young son of this Vre will become Mechail's father (a sermon on Abraham's sacrifice of Isaac foreshadows Mechail's later murder/sacrifice), but, as Anjelen tells Mechail, "Here's the riddle that you are also my son." Anillia is his creation. However, he also asserts fatherrights, "This is my blood. For I will make you into what you are.... You will be myself. As, in her way, she was, your mother. Take my blood. And after you will drink in remembrance of me."

Many such biblical fragments proliferate (as in *Malice in Saffron*).

Anjelen is a hybrid, perverted whether pagan or Christian. He is "the Christerium, yet dissociated from it. Knight of God. Wolf, Angel, priest, sorceror ... no part of anything, but like the moon which pulls the tides." He is Mechail's "*devil*" and resistance seems useless. Anjelen becomes the wolf with which Mechail hunted in the forest and presses him to the ground in wolfish dominance. Mechail, who hates "God and his men," suffers illness and amnesia in a "labyrinth" of hallucinatory horror.

As the Knights of God[16] drink the blood of a boy in the Christerium chapel, Mechail's revulsion conflicts with a horrible "*thirst*." Anjelen asks how he perceives himself—"A night thing, a vampire which craves human blood?" Mechail thinks he may be dreaming. Anjelen says, "Dream and reality. In the world of life, the barrier is slight between them." This sums up the consequences of extracting symbols from their sacred context.

Dream also supplants reality as Anjelen offers Mechail his blood.[17] He "drank until ... *he was no longer human* ... until the sun blazed in him. His flesh seemed clear as glass.... The soul was what he was, and the flesh adjunctive, malleable. There was nothing of himself he might not command, and little of the world."

These are the sorcerous temptations of abstraction. Mechail becomes a god-like object or image of himself. Craving the blood that was previously sacred to god, he feels the desperation of a vampire and seeks Anjelen, "like a lover." But instead he finds Jasha, the daughter of the spirit (the non-corporeal aspect) of his mother. The narrative hinges on the father's weakening hold.

Jasha is about to be burnt as a witch, and Mechail snatches her out of a bed of flames. "Perhaps it was some story Nilya had told him as a child.... To rescue the burnt girl and ride away with her." United with this aspect of his mother, he "turned his back upon Anjelen ... turned from the excitement of the blood like a drunkard from his flagon." A motif of longing for death suggests remorse: "...the dream faded to ... depression and despair ... *that was death he wanted, not sleep.*"

Mechail is not Anjelen's sole disappointment. The first wife he makes for Mechail's father is defective.[18] The misshapen Mechi is also his. His Knights are "dross." Nevertheless, he commands their adoration, and when he fuses himself with an illusion of the bleeding Christus, a jealous knight kisses the "feet of his redeemer" and the Father Factor appreciates him: "His voice could make or break the hearts of humanity. Already the novices, and half the priests here, were under his sway. He was a radiance it would be idiotic to ignore."

To Egar, teacher of alchemy, at first he seems like "the last light, before the night fell down.... God had sent Angelen to take up the torch of understanding." But when Egar tastes blood, not wine, in the chalice, he observes that Anjelen, "might do as he wished, suborn, destroy, hypnotize ... the learning of alchemy was merely for convenience.... Never, even in his meditations on God, had Egar glimpsed a supremacy like this."

When the Factor investigates rumors about blood, he tastes only "the spirit of God" in the cup, but he eagerly offers his own blood to Angelen and soon resorts to the "recent affectation among the Knights" of wearing a high collar. He builds the Christerium, "a palace of God on earth," specifically for Angelen. But Egar, though old and feeble, still recognizes that "evil had taken root, spread its leaves, grew up and pushed against the roof. The Cathedral was filling, day by day, with its spicy, pleasing perfume.... There was no defence."

Lee reflects Anjelen's vices in the mirror of a mediocre intelligence, that of the jealous knight Wedsek. "We're God's and he instructed us," he proclaims, and soon a handful of Knights are seeking out blood-victims in the town. "Blood is life," said Wedsek. "Only Anjelen can judge me." When a shadowy "nameless Knight" starts to pursue him ("This one's craving was obviously cannibalistic"), "Wedsek stumbled out of one court of madness into another." The exsanguination of a prostitute is an irrecoverable transgression against the brotherhood. Female blood contaminates male purity.[19] "The blood of women—it was unthinkable, unspeakable, and forbidden, that the lawless and unclean gore of women be associated with the flawless male blood of the Sacrifice."

Wedsek is claimed by the Cathedral. Their view of his sin is less esoteric: "Woman the temptress ... had worked her mischief. If there was blood it was immaterial. The act of horror was unchastity."

The misogynist Anjelen also warns Mechail against women, but he has less power to seduce and suborn them. He resorts to repression among females, something that will have severe consequences for him.

And after several hundred years, "Longevity had begun to impress on him a man's occasional mortal symptoms.... The hint of wormwood." The elderly Anjelen is becoming disagreeable and spiteful. When he comes across a deranged and ruined Wedsek, he scolds him, "always I hear this intruding step which is yours.... It irks me, Wedsek. You always in my way.... Your gross buffoonery, your acts of mindless inaccuracy.... You can grasp nothing." The population of an entire village is expended to punish Wedsek, as men, women, children and dogs all rush upon him, pouring out their blood.

But the aging Anjelen increasingly resembles his shadow, Wedsek. His vampiric indulgences have turned him into another mindless addict. The eyes and forehead, Mind and Thought, have gone: "His face had no meaning but for the mouth.... That was all it was, and all the face was. The gluttony of a drunkard ninety years of age and always at his cups.... Thirst incarnate."

Anjelen's death is also marked by disgusting excess. Jasha penetrates the Christerium. Believing she is Mechail, Anjelen mutters snatches of old ritual, impatient to get to her blood. When he discovers that a woman has penetrated his male sanctum, he turns upon his last few withered priests and drinks each one dry, like a senile Saturn devouring his age-enfeebled children. But his orgy utterly incapacitates him. "He was bloody.... He was bloated, swollen. His skin looked red, as if it must crack on redness ... and his half-shut eyes bulged, sightlessly."

Lightly prancing on the altar, Jasha attends to the proper procedures for slaying vampires. In a startling inversion of the biblical creation of Eve, she plucks a rib out of his body to stake him through the heart. Traces of the Tree are still subtly present in Anjelen. His ribs retain some qualities of branches, "encircled, ridged and ringed."

Bizarrely, his corpse "did not bleed. His blood stayed in him, seeming to lapidify.... He must transmute, as any god in any story. In the night, before all candles were extinguished, it seemed that Anjelen was changing into stone." In death, this "god" who has spent so long in self-idolatry becomes a stone icon of himself. Stone, least transmutable and most monumentally dead of substances, lies outside the cycle of things that die and can offer themselves up to be renewed.[20]

Women

Before the Christus era, women fulfill certain sacred functions, especially in relation to the ritual care of the dead. Village men "kill" the tree, women bury its remnants, "speaking their own charms" and singing their ancient song with its refrain, "All that lives must die."

But Christian attitudes towards women vary. The Factor is comparatively liberal: Women are more irrelevant than dangerous.[21]

> Women ... should be allowed to touch the hem of the garment of the Christus.... They had their part, as did the animals, and women had souls too, for the Christus had said so, but not souls as men had them. That was not reasonable.

This religion has little to offer women, and many of Lee's female characters, like Lady Crel, practice the old rites clandestinely, as do slaves—a loyal slave sheds his revitalizing blood over the bones of Anillia—and, in their style, Travelers.

The *struggle* between the sexes in this religious dimension uses a remarkable range of women. Veksa pacifies men, believing that spiritual power is unprofitable, worldly power is a male monopoly, and sexual manipulation can secure her interests. Although with Anjelen "Veksa recollected caution, and that the world was in charge of them, these men," she still thinks like her forebears: "These idiots, thinking they could control their masculine world. But the trees were full of supernatural humors."

At the opposite extreme, Lady Crel endures her husband's attentions only when obliged to and values her small daughter far above her son. "Suppose this thing within her now was another boy. She did not like to dwell on that, this absolute closeness of a male. She had prayed for a second daughter." As she confides this to the elderly nun who educated her, "there was between them still the unvoiced other creed of womankind" (note the word *creed*); but concerning memories of girlhood offerings to the Tree, the nun admonishes her, "See that you forget, and forget once more, if it happens again that you go into the wood."

9. Even Angels Are Subject to Corruption   153

In the forest, while Lady Crel prays, "*Let me only be freed somewhat from men,*" her little daughter, Anillia, is spirited away. Thirteen years later, Anjelen will have the Anillia he has created pose as the lost child. However, Lady Crel's gentle example and maternal love will contribute greatly to his eventual ruin.

The Handmaidens of the Christus, one of the many sisterhoods proliferating in the forest, welcome the new-created, amnesiac Anillia into their midst. All "dewed by the pagan elements of the forest," they are radically different from the censorious nuns of the Doma. The priest perceives them as "frowsy sluttish women"; they see him as an "old prude." Unlike women who embrace the new religion, they have no desire to curry priestly favor, but the Administress of the Doma is driven by "terrible self-doubt, a reasonless dread" to beat herself regularly into submission with a spiked rod, curiously unaware of its obvious reference to the male sex organ. When she finally beats herself to "a swamp of fleshy slush," the rod lies "pulsing" beside her corpse with a "milky fluid" trickling from it.

Meaning generally evades the Administress. As she reads from a prayer book before the auto-da-fé, "Jasha caught snatches of meaningless words. God was the redemption and the Christus the Saviour, and there was no death, all was according to the will of the Lord. What could such phrases have to do with Jasha at this moment?"

Phrases have little significance for Jasha at any time. Born from Anilla's spontaneous remaking of herself, owing nothing to Anjelen, the theoretics of the Christus are pointless to her. The book opens with Jasha's conception in the forest where, described as "the lizard daughter," she grows up beside Anillia's grave.[22] "An earth-mound was Jasha's mother, her father a crippled hermit." Her daily nurture is the supernatural. She spends time in a village and begins "to take on the proper mortal contours.... Now she had beings to model herself on, other than the rodents, animals and insects." She tries "to be as like a mortal woman as she could," but "Jasha was practical. Mostly life was superfluous to her process of living." When she sees Mechail, "The beauty of his body did not enthrall her any more than the fine aspect of the tree." Aesthetic emotions are too obdurately human for her. Only the primal links with Nature and her dead mother signify.

Anillia is more obviously human. She develops an intense personal attachment to her son, but recognizes that, "delivered of the flower," she has become "superfluous" and must surrender Mechail to her husband and still more to Anjelen. She longs to protect Mechail—"'While you need me,' she said to the sleeping child, 'while I'm able,' and to her amazement, her human tears spilled across the shawl that covered him." Returning later from the dead, "What brought her back was love. Love's name was Mechail." But hate is equally powerful. "Anjelen was the man, the sterile sword, the erect phallus that killed.... *Hate's name was Anjelen.*"

Anillia dedicates herself to revenge. Anjelen is "God, honor, chastity, discipline. She was woman, chaos, disorder, rebellion.... He spoke contemptuously, a man's voice now.... 'Go to sleep,' he said. 'Go to sleep, Anillia.'"[23] She replies, "Whatever it is you want.... I'll take it from you. You shan't have it. Then I'll sleep."

Lee is again representing the struggle for possession of the child. Anillia and Anjelen argue quite childishly over who is the rightful parent. She refers to herself as Angelen's "daughter," but he counters her insinuation of incest—"Fashioned from a rib of my mind"—and claims spiritual above corporeal kinship. This makes the scene where Jasha destroys him with his own rib doubly ironic.

Mechail's need for constant explanation provides an insight into Anillia's grievances: "We're all the creatures of Anjelen, or the creatures of what he is. Even he is the creature of that. And the man, that priest formed by others, that inquisitor and magician, acting by human rote, losing sight of himself.... His chastity, his father's ambition, those you and I will ruin."[24]

But when Anillia says to Jasha, "now I think we have no purpose but to be, and to continue to be," Jasha merely smiles. "Her instinct—like that of any fox or wolf, lizard, cat, flower, tree, stone—had always known as much." Also by instinct, Jasha carries out her mother's wishes. She first hears her dead mother's voice singing at a funeral. Later, in the Doma, guided by a dream of this song, she moves like a somnambulist—"Jasha served her mother, brain-blind, soul canny"—to a chest containing Anillia's bones, which she reassembles and clothes in her own green dress. These actions lead to accusations of witchcraft and her burning.

The only meeting between Jasha and Anillia comes late in the book, but she dreams about her mother: "...she traced over Jasha's face, stroked the thickly growing hair. Her breath was real and fresh, and touched Jasha's forehead, cheek. Nilya's eyes were lit and alive. Jasha was pleased.... She gave herself to the scrutiny and caresses as does a young cat to its mother's attention."

Jasha comes close to human feeling here, but also experiences "a low note of jealousy, primal as the ground" when she is "left behind in the snow." Nilya and Mechail form a pietà which excludes her. "Mechail lay against her, his head under her neck ... saint's faces on a screen of cloak and hair and dark." Jasha's dream-self fluctuates. "Shall I go out again and wait, lady?" she asks. However, "She was not humble...."

The narrative now splices sacred and profane indiscriminately together. Time goes backwards. With their temporal cycle completed,

Mechail and Anillia return to their sacred origins. "She was the earth, and he became the Tree which rooted in her." As mother of life and death, she returns into nature. "She pointed like a sword towards the single tree.... 'There is what we are,' she said. 'The root of our life. The one coffin that will hold us safe.'"

Jasha is not yet so iconic or so able to recognize herself. As she hides behind a bush, watching the mother and son return into Nature, "She did not suspect herself of constancy, or envy, or need, or trust." Jasha, who "might bite and bark" or "speak and sing," is "lawless as they had not been, no, not even Anjelen," but she will pass ten years as a slave in a village hovel before her part is ready.

> [I]t was as if the seed she had taken with her from their Tree had asked her latency, the opaque soil wherein to germinate.... She was the fox that had received the *dual soul of a man and a woman* [emphasis added].

However, she earns herself a freedom that the less heterogeneous Anillia never could. Female, yet androgynous, she is a new phenomenon, a breaker of cultural chains: "...she was a rogue sapling. The mutant plant."

When Jasha enters the Christerium calling herself Eujasius, Anjelen believes Mechail has returned, though kinship does not dull his blood-thirst. Jasha is intent on total ruin. She "stepped about the altar, parading herself" naked. She taunts him. "Woman's blood," said Jasha. "*Forbidden.*" As Anillia predicted, she ruins his jealously-guarded chastity. "This was no different to the penis of any man. Jasha knew quite well what to do with it. She bowed over him, the Angel of Death, and put her woods girl's mouth around him."

Jasha is last seen diving into the sea. The sea is likened to the forest: The Christerium tower resembles the Tree; Anillia speaks repeatedly about the sea; Jasha craves for salt fish. The sea dissolves form and bears new life; and the oceanic expresses animism naturally, washing away the individual, whether man or god. As the androgynous yet female Jasha enters the sea—"One day she must rise from its depths, with the winged wave at her back. Angel of Storms"—Lee is promising another cycle, another story.

Mechi/Mechailus: The Dwarf as Artist

Coming from the underclass, misshapen and small, Mechi possesses the traditional skill of dwarves. His skill in tricks is immediately noted by the Travelers. However, his greatest skill is for survival, as he endures his barely human existence in an unquestioning, latent state and bides his time during the long narrative. Like Jasha, he exemplifies slow evolution.

Mechi is a chattel. As a changeling, the villagers give him to the forest where travelers find him and teach him a repertoire of tricks before selling him to Mechail's brother "without a second thought." Angelen declares him the *property* of Mechail. At the Christerium, his evolution is as gradual as his masters' devolution, but "priestly rite did not trouble Mechi. The world had never made sense." His structural function is as the contradiction: "It was the Devil's imp. It served God."

He experiences companionship only when sharing a kennel with a starving dog at the Korhlen estate. "The dwarf and the dog slept spine to spine.... It was the dog which whined as they bore the dwarf away." He is put on a leash like a dog to sniff out Mechail in the forest.

Lee turns again to the genesis of the artist: The *artist* emerges from play, and the whole man from the artist[25]: "...the dwarf created himself almost in his own image." Without either strategy or desire, he waits for a stimulus—"a reflex, perhaps." What "they had achieved through sorcery, will, madness, dream, Mechi came to as an artist, a pragmatist." Stealing into Anjelen's room, he plays with his paraphernalia: "Mechi had paused to look into the globe of quartz.... Mechi saw his own reflection. It amused him, for through the medium of the curved crystal, by shifting here and there, he could alter his shape. And in this manner, Mechi refashioned himself in the glass nearly in the shape of a man."

"Game" and "play" cluster thickly as Mechi plays with the mirror, then creates an independent shadow and plays with that. "The game inaugurated for him himself. (He was also learning *not* to be a slave.)" Mechi feels "a weird new excitement, *glee*, an embryo which might at last harden to malice and joy beyond the capacity of any ordinary hating, laughing man."

Genuine, easy laughter has been noticeably absent until now. Mechi's impersonation of Mechail in the dining hall at Korhlen elicits drunken ribaldry; Jasha's laughter as she dispatches Anjelen has the sound of cackling. But after escaping the Christerium, Mechi "would go off roving, a man now, nothing to be picked on, and come back just before sunrise, always amused at something." He is reaching full stature so naturally, "they had not been able, at any moment or hour, to lay hold of it—for this was the subtle development of the plant in the sun."

At Korhlen, Mechi-Mechailus, like a returning Odysseus, is recognized by the dog with which he had once shared a kennel. She grows young and strong again and shares his bed, "spine to spine with him, for he had sent the woman away after their dalliance that the dog might slumber easily." Mechailus amuses himself by "naming her Veksa, really to joke."

As Vre at Korhlen, Mechi-Mechailus is "enjoying, not harsh." "All Mechail had denied in himself, that was Mechi. But now Mechail denied nothing ... he had every capacity for pleasure Mechail had put away.... For he had had to wait in chains."

— 10 —

Entering a More Familiar World

Sabella, Lycanthia, Heart-Beast, Elephantasm

Sabella

Written ten years before *The Blood of Roses*, *Sabella* is already germinating many similar signifiers. Wolves and blood-drinkers prowl through both texts. A cultural conflict between an extinct, indigenous race and recent colonists represents religion as destructive of nature. The "vampire," whose primary need is to accept animal instinct, finds her own Christ in a "vampire" lover. This gentle consideration of a vampire's plight is far removed from *The Book of the Damned*.

The colony's history is short and simple. The confidential, first person narration seems straightforward. If Sabella does not have all the information, she keeps no secrets and is not an excessively complicated person. However, her biological needs are so unusual she considers herself a pervert and addict and excludes herself guiltily from society.

Totally reclusive, needing since puberty to feed exclusively on blood, she hunts for deer in the hills. Despite intense efforts to control her instinctive craving for the blood of male humans, she accidentally exsanguinates several men lured into range with offers of sex. When her aunt dies she attends her funeral in the city, drawn "as if by suction back into the world."

After a brief, blood-drinking liaison, a young man pursues her back home; and when she inadvertently causes his death, his brother, Jace, comes searching for him. Fleeing in panic, Sabella is reduced to prostitution in the city,[1] but Jace finds her and acquaints her with their true history: They both died in childhood in the burial cave of two members of the extinct Martian race who took over their identities.[2] This is the same theme of differing unawares from the apparent body that appeared in *Electric Forest* a year earlier. Sabella too gains liberation through retrospective knowledge—and in a symbiotic romance with her resurrected Martian partner.

A subtext of sucking runs right through the narrative and reaches its climax in the symbiotic feeding patterns of the Martian race. As Jace feeds Sabella with his blood, he obtains "the sensual pleasure of a beast giving suck" and she becomes a suckling infant.[3] "For all I'd cried I wasn't a child, I was glad enough to rest there in his arms ... he moved my head until my mouth was against his throat...." Lee captures the sensuality of infancy: "...when the film of the great silence of the well I had been drinking at seeped off me, and my eyes unglazed, he put me down beside him, and for a while, we were quiet, as if after the other act of love."

Feeding as a metaphor for love or the longing for it is the central motif of the book. The plot moves along a line dotted by Sabella's encounters with food sources. The male seeking only his own sexual gratification is hostile, part of "a league of gentlemen against that dreaded witch, a woman alone." Emptied of mother-love, the sexual act becomes a pleasureless power struggle, though Sabella always tries to give some return for the blood she needs.[4] "Even with the basest of them, I feel a concern to make them happy." With Jace she feels the pulse of relationship. Love "requires a careful pairing, a creation of partners, who could permit in love what never could be permitted in greed or hate."

Sabella's blood-drinking is carefully distinguished from popular vampirism. She says, "Who told you it was messy? Great gouts and slobberings—no. A slender trickle from one (why more than one?) minuscule wound." Nor do Martian vampires differ from humans in the ways suggested by popular lore.

> I can see myself in mirrors. The idea that I might not comes from the same myth that says vampires cast no shadow. Shadow and mirror image are both primitive ciphers for the soul. The myth implies a vampire has no soul. Maybe I haven't, but I've met others who surely haven't too. We all cast shadows, all show in glass.[5]

The "vampiric resurrection" of her victims is "another myth" but the sun is an "X ray," its beams are "razors." "The sun harms me. I think it's my blood.... The radiation of the sun, which would kill you if you were close enough to it, can kill me from a distance."

Although non-human, Sabella suffers severe human guilt. Recalling her problematic adolescence, she still blames herself for her mother's death: "It killed her. I—killed her." Nevertheless, she has the innocence of an animal. Describing the men she feeds upon, she says, "The excitement ... I don't know what it's like at this time, have nothing to compare it to, drink or drugs, or sex or religion." Her own excesses belong entirely to her nature. Her senses scan people with animal accuracy—"their breath smelled of sugars, proteins and digestion." When a man approaches her, she says, "I could scent his life through his skin. I could scent his blood." And as he comes up behind her, she remarks, "You get to know one certain step from all the others, the step of the deer, picking its way towards you through the wolf-dappled night."

Sabella's relations with the deer she hunts are deeply tender. "She comes after me instantly, her delicate steps pattering on the stones among the moss by the water.... Don't be afraid. I stroke her neck, whose nap is prickly velvet.... I feel gratitude, comfort and boundless love." But she tells Jace, "When I take blood from a man ... it isn't the same as when I take it from an animal." Sabella is extending animal experience into human consciousness—which is precisely what creates male frenzies of desire. She never underestimates the animal energies of people. Faces at a Revivalist meeting are "burning as if the great light were about to shatter out of them." The vice-ridden hunting ground of the city is also a biblical "Pillar of fire by night," and though she has no use for Revivalism she evidently believes in God.

> Does it surprise you that a vampire has religion? ... Jesus Christ, after all, was a vampire. They drank blood at the last supper, and then the priests impaled him on a stake of wood.... When he was dead they buried him, but he resurrected the way a vampire is supposed to.

The Blood of Roses can be seen stirring here.

She continues, "Not a dove on an altar, but Jace. Not prayer, but Jace. Not Jesus." Jace becomes J.C.; Sabella finds salvation in her opposite, "light to my dark, his wide outward gaze to my introspection."

She pulls together the text's personal, religious and political themes with the idea that "Men don't own this world."

> [M]aybe the planet is a vampire too ... waiting for its resurrection from the deadness of a desert before it whispered to its inner dead in

their obscure burial places, Come rise up, taste of the oxygen in the skies, and the poured out waters, and the spilled dreams of men.

Though Novo Mar is reconstructed to resemble Earth, with a consumer society of postmen, lawyers, supermarkets, churches and funerals, and has flora that is "all earth-import ... mostly so is the fauna," Old Mars endures. "There are still real Martian wolves in the hills ... catch the glare of their eyes at night, disembodied blood drops seemingly framed in stars, and know them for what they are." Colonists hunt them but Sabella hunts alongside them. The original wilderness to which she belongs is receding before the advance of man. Back in the town of her childhood, Sabella comes upon "a new white fluorescent road by the rims of which *wild flowers still clustered*" (emphasis added), but she sees beyond polarization to integration. Rather than cutting her links with artifice, Sabella incorporates it. "I have none of civilization's taint. A landscape of steel towers against hills of concrete sings to me as does a landscape of rock pinnacles and gullies." As she goes about her unavoidably bloody business, she is returning an animal element into the human world: "...my natural prey strides through the steel prairies, rides the golden mountains of the cities, the neon caves of the towns. There are wolves on all the hills, even the hills of glass."

Lycanthia

In this book (as in *Heart-Beast*, which follows) the beast, the werewolf, is an aspect of identity that rational man prefers to forget he once possessed. Playing opposite the protagonist in *Lycanthia*, its proximity to humans is emphasized; in *Heart-Beast*, where it is the protagonist, a crack opens between the consciousness of beast and human.

In *Lycanthia*, a pianist, conspicuously named Christian and supposedly dying of consumption, goes to an ancestral chateau which unexpectedly reverts to him. In this feudal context, he plays the seigneur with the bourgeois incomprehension of a self-obsessed rationalist. He is unattuned to the pagan environment or the "unholy and magic trinity" that the peasants fear may spring from reuniting the seigneur with a pair of werewolves from the forest.

Christian is essentially a *performer*, a pianist who also plays upon his fatal illness. Though equipped with a suicide pill, he has no idea of death's reality—"the disease, which riddled him like a piece of rotten meat, had, before his arrival at the chateau, only heightened his glamour." When cold brings tears to his eyes, he wonders if he should "assume some overmastering sorrow"; but the servants at the chateau are not impressed, and his fatal consumption is exposed by a commonsensical country doctor as a minor malady.

Christian cannot grasp anything beyond his own civilized world. The eyes in the garden are merely those of a dog; the couple in the forest only imagine themselves to be werewolves. "It implied a world where magic might triumph over fact." He fares no better in action. He is dominated by the housekeeper. His seigneural attempt to rape the servant girl results in impotence. Worse, he lacks the strength to protect the shapechangers from the peasant mob that storms the chateau. Contemptuous, yet relieved at his ineffectuality, the peasants expel him from the region.

Though the still semi-pagan peasants are not likable, they are authentic. Christian never finds a genuine identity and emerges from his odyssey unchanged. He grudgingly admits that the human-animal nature of the werewolves excels his own but is neither enlightened nor ennobled by contact with them. He constantly resorts to self-pity. He is "a stranger in his own unfamiliar house ... he must go insane too. No scrap of dignity or self-reliance or amour-propre must he be allowed to keep." Dependent on self-esteem and admiration, Christian is guilty more of strutting stupidity than hubris. His image matters more than the realities of his situation. In Christian, *Lycanthia* produces another variant of anti-hero.

The housekeeper regards Christian with "Not a trace, either of pity or appetite." When he sulkily refuses dinner, Madame Tienne scolds him unsympathetically. Hungry in the night, he creeps to the kitchen, where he finds the servant girl, Sylvie, half-undressed and tantalizing a "dog"—with only its eyes visible in the dark—with a joint of raw meat. But Sylvie is no more sympathetic than Madame Tienne. When he tells her, "You ought to be sorry for me ... when you're cozily married to some local farmer.... I shall be dead," She emits "a short solitary yap of derision." Miserably unequal to his part, Christian cannot reach climax. Embittered, he terms himself "Uninvolved. A scientist."

He fares little better with the werewolves. Before he tracks down the ostracized Luc de Lagenay[6] he has already seen "the aura of unsafety ... beyond all mortal probability," been attacked by a wolfish animal on the road, and seen Sylvie killed by a beast. Still he maintains it is only a dog. On his second visit he carries a gun and half-believes the legend of lycanthropy when, at the sight of him, passing villagers make a sign to ward off werewolves. In Luc's hut he finds Gabrielle in bed and once again presumes upon his seigneurial rights. She responds by savagely biting his ear. He is about to fire at her when Luc arrives. Just for a moment he sees himself as "clownish" and "disgusting." "At some inexplicable level of consciousness or self, he had been wounded. Beside this damage, the torn ear was nothing."

His preoccupation with his illness vexes Gabrielle. "What do you know about any sort of pain, of the body or the soul? ... Wrapped in swansdown from the day of your birth." Nevertheless, she offers him maternal comfort as he cries like a baby—until this also becomes mere performance: "What a scene, as if from a sixth-rate melodrama." For an instant, Christian imagines Luc experiencing "the ghastly agonizing spasm of the physical metamorphosis crying also in her arms for comfort. But Gabrielle—who had rocked and who had comforted *her*?"

His impotence vanishes with Gabrielle's "mythology, her very doubtfulness." He spends the winter snowed in at the chateau with the two shapechangers.[7] "They lay relaxed, the three, loosely curled together. The wolf pack."[8] It seems as if Christian may after all complete the magic trio. Or learn something about love.

But his winter idyll provides him with neither insight nor resolution. In a scene evoking *Mary Shelley's Frankenstein*, the chateau is invaded by an angry rabble, pitch torches in hand. Christian knows the de Lagenays do not kill humans, but lacks the authority and courage to keep the mob at bay. Even at this point he struggles to keep up appearances and says to them, "I'll deny that you're here. Someone has to stand in their way...." He is "sickly amused by what he had just said. He visualized himself, a hero ... defending his hereditary property like some demented medieval prince."

Gabrielle sneers at his posturing, but La Tienne, who now admits to being her mother, returns to exercise some control—"traces of a matriarchy remained." Latent goddess-worship is also revealed. Tienne confirms that Sylvie was sacrificed to the goddess: "We've learned to propitiate such powers as exist." "The Lady of Lilies"[9] is in reality "The wolf-goddess ... feared and propitiated in this region since pre–Roman times."[10]

During the ensuing exorcism, Christian is tied to a chair while Gabrielle and Luc are staked to the ground and beaten almost to death. Even as a spectator he fails, overturning his chair and falling face down in the mud. He is released when freak weather interrupts proceedings, but the mother and son are left to die. As Tienne comments, "The true purpose of the exorcism is to kill."

However, the two shapechangers, though horribly wounded, do not die. They return to their forest hut while Christian is packed off to the railway station. Gabrielle's final verdict on Christian is, "You are the wolf. Feeding on us all."

Christian learns nothing from the place either. In the obelisk of the wolf-headed goddess he sees only "distorted shapes, something like a gargoyle craning out," and in the sign against werewolves only a misshapen cross. Cairns of stones mean nothing to him. His original response to the village, "*I can return to the city. None of this matters,*" becomes his final one also. When he finds Gabrielle—in wolf-form since it is after sunset—lying on the ground too injured to move, he cannot think of her as anything more than an animal: "He tried to lift the she-wolf a little, but she was heavy with her own laxness, and as he gained leverage on her body, she whined in agony. He could only think of her as a dog. He could not remember that this was Gabrielle."

Heart-Beast

Lee's literary borrowings here dip deep into the by now substantial resource of her own work. After committing *parricide*, Daniel is living in a distant land. A pockmarked *street-magician* tricks him into accepting *a large diamond* that contains a flaw resembling a running wolf. Shortly afterwards, Daniel finds the man's dead body in his room and the diamond gone. However, its influence remains, although Daniel has no memory of metamorphosing into a werewolf at full moon.

He ships out, pursuing the stolen diamond, and when the beast slaughters everyone on board, he begins to recognize his darker aspect. The *ship is wrecked* and he *wanders for a long time in a wilderness*. He does not recognize the dead street-performer in Julinus, whom he meets near *a crusader castle*, but he sells him the diamond, hoping to be rid of its effects. One of Julinus' men shoots Daniel.

Then, like Julinus, Daniel is *resurrected*. An old man takes him in and, ignoring his warnings, is inevitably murdered at full moon. Taking the old man's treasure, Daniel returns home to his *beloved mother*. Soon he meets Laura, with the fatal diamond hanging at her neck, a present bought from Julinus (now posing as a merchant) by her husband, Hyperion.

The rest follows like the unfolding of a curse. Daniel murders his drunkard brother—like their father, he abuses the mother—and becomes Laura's lover. His mother dies, and he is *snowed in* with Hyperion and Laura at their country estate. A *comet* falls to earth, and after the murder of Hyperion, Laura, discovering that Daniel can be killed by "nothing of earth," stabs her beast-lover with a shard of meteorite.

Even this brief résumé reveals multiple elements from other narratives: the fatal jewel, the parricide, the resurrections, the cheap magician, the crusader castle, and so on. Like the amulet in *The Book of the Beast*, the jewel is eventually drowned in the waters of a lake beside which, lantern in hand and watched in the dark by a beast-cum-werewolf, Laura walks like another Dunizel.[11] Daniel has the animal potency of the wolfish Ahzrarn, who bites the hand of Dunizel; and Laura, like Dunizel, is aware of her lover's nature but caught in transpersonal events. She is "metamorphosed" into "a soul-creature"—though it is not a gentle soul like Dunizel's. Daniel's mother says, "I have the Devil in me. But I never gave it life." Laura, however, becomes an avenging Nike.

When Daniel's mother dies, she is "translated into Laura" for him. Overtly Oedipal elements mingle with echoes of the brother-sister love of *The Book of the Mad*.[12] As Daniel tears apart Laura's husband, oranges spill everywhere, as in Leocadia's painting. Felion and Smara are recalled as Laura makes Daniel and Hyperion a last supper of twigs and stones—"in keeping with dark conversation, shadows, isolation, metaphysics, and snow." Snowscapes dominate both books.

The Blood of Roses is evoked as the beast leaps upon an eccentric nobleman who is just about to net a large black moth. *The Book of the Dead* surfaces as Julinus produces apparitions to entertain the guests at a London hotel and disappears as mysteriously as the Conjurer in *The Book of the Dead*, who spirits away the bride-to-be. The importance of the moon in this text is indicated by a quotation from the same source—"The moon is a mask"—and the beast floats away like the bewitched Owlsa towards a huge full moon. This incomplete list establishes the author's tendency to self-quotation here. "Repetition is always involved in giving integrity to what is repeated. It is the second mark, a mark of sameness or difference, that endows the first mark with being and that begins the possibility of infinity...."[13]

Lee's actual praxis here becomes an extension of her interest in eternal recurrence: Writing on a veil of illusion composed of symbols, characters and themes from other texts, she is simultaneously describing her own work as a continuous cycle. The games with time, space and the nature of fiction take on deliberate elements of fairytale in a book that also contains some degree of realism. Laura is Beauty to the Beast, but before that she plays the part of Cinderella, complete with ugly sisters and rescue by Prince Charming. However, when the maid hired to take on Laura's work poisons the entire family, she is clearly acting for the avenging Laura.

Spatial disorientations and fluctuations of size are frequent also. As Daniel leaves his employer to board a ship, the world suddenly contracts: "The court seemed tiny and the fat man like a figure of paper ... the diamond shone, a stone of brilliance in the forest of sunlight, space and time." When Hyperion purchases the diamond, Laura is swept into an alternative space. "She felt a dart of fear, and then a strange sensation, as if she stood in a high place, the wind whirling about her ... and below the cities of the plain before judgment fell on them." Later, cut off by winter from the outside world, she notes, "the snow was like a Biblical calamity.... She felt herself very small, visible to something that watched from above." And as Daniel's mother lies dying, "The fire was miles below, in the hollow of a hill, faint as a breath of rosy mist. As she ascended from it she heard a door opening in another dimension."

The more literal spaces and distances of a sweeping countryside are strongly reminiscent of Hardy's Wessex, especially in a scene where Laura, as "milkmaid," is almost run down by Hyperion's horse. The housemaid is swallowed by a vast landscape; distance makes simple visits portentous and chance meetings fateful; deep snows ensure Hyperion's death. Class misalliances and the exploitation of working women also echo Hardy. When Hyperion falls in love with Laura, she expects betrayal. As her family encourage his advances, she reproaches her father for selling her "for a horse and a packet of tea." However, instead of abandoning her, Hyperion proposes marriage. Finding him a friend, she accepts in a rational spirit.

Cultural niceties are observed abroad also. When Daniel reacts "coldly" to a story about the murder of an unfaithful wife, his employer teases him about Western prejudices: "You are uncouth, you Europeans. Cruelty, too, has its loveliness." The affable, broad-minded merchant notes Daniel's "cicatrice of darkness," but makes no moral evaluation—"God in his omniscience knew what it was, this shadow." Daniel will cease "to accept notions of God"; Hyperion will lose his faith; even as Laura avenges the death of her husband as if from moral duty, "Daniel, not God was omnipresent."

Educated to Western, rational morality, initially Daniel recognizes neither his own passions nor the inexorable forces unleashed by parricide: "...his emotions had been mysterious, and ruled him. He gave way to them, controlling only their outer show in order to protect himself from others. There had come that moment, in the cold land he had left, that moment when he had crossed over from reality to sin, and so to feeling."

Sin here implies the chaos wherein reason no longer rules. The werewolf, truly a *heart-beast*, belongs to this region of passional unreason. Trying to reconcile the *beast* with civilized values, Daniel tells Laura he has, "no purpose. This is something I learnt on my travels. Simply to be." More enmeshed in the "real" world, she replies, "I'm too naive to understand your Eastern mysteries."

The consequences of his sin appear slowly. At first the beast is "innocent and timid still, unschooled in its powers, and all this place a wonder to it." Daniel claims that the diamond is his "by some law more insistent than religion," but it will be a long time before he begins to know himself properly. The old man who cares for him after he has been shot believes the Bible will subdue the beast, but Daniel "*felt* a great depression. He would kill Bernardin." Yet when he explains that the beast cannot be appealed to and is "some portion of me that my humanity keeps buried," he is still giving priority to the man in himself. Much later he will recognize that "portion" of himself as his "true life."

Laura is often motivated by a desire to escape. She escapes her family by marrying Hyperion and submits to his seduction whilst fleeing from the sight—or maybe apparition—of a wolf frozen inside a block of ice. This wolf is an omen of her coming meeting with Daniel and confrontation with a frozen aspect of herself, but she does not submit voluntarily. Hyperion says, "I think a net has been thrown over you. You struggle and resist, but the net isn't broken."

Daniel is too deeply possessed for escape or denial. He warns Hyperion openly about himself. Hyperion glimpses the demonic world but still maintains, "There has to be some reason, some logic in the universe." Nevertheless, he writes in a letter to his dead aunt, "I do not believe, although I am going where you have gone, that I will meet you there." As he loses sight of his God, his eyes open to his destiny: "Tonight is the first night of the full moon. Tonight it will happen."

Where Hyperion expresses resignation—"I won't fight for what's already lost"—Laura comes from a class accustomed to struggle. She tells the doomed Hyperion, "I wished him dead the moment I met him.... I drowned him in a story. Don't you remember?" Hyperion is fatalistic: "This is a fairy tale ... and the nice part is over." But Daniel, cleansed of conscience and remorse, is beyond metaphor. "Human thoughts came to Daniel in bursts.... For a moment it was bizarre to him, the journey he had taken. He saw it as if through a tunnel of light."

Daniel brings together light and darkness, but, where dual beings like Dionysos or Chuz belong in the realm of gods and demons, Daniel is a man struggling to understand his entire nature. He questions his mother closely regarding the beast's character and appearance. The beast demands his total dissolution, "a quag of tissues ... a cauldron, a stew of stuffs...."

Hyperion, Laura and Daniel are singled out by their will to confront the deadly aspects of nature. For Laura and Daniel, the deadly is also godly. Laura's face is "stern," an "Athene face." Shortly before killing him, Daniel tells Hyperion[14] he experiences "The liberty of lawlessness without the guilt," though conceding it is a "sin" to "rule" oneself. Daniel is more than a demon, as Laura discovers from an inscription on the comet-shard which means "*The Sacrifice.*"[15] His blood will be spilt for ritual purposes. Dionysos is about to appear as a beast, and Hyperion sits "waiting for night to step in over the sill." His death has a ceremonial quality beyond regret or remorse, and in death his face is still smiling.

When Daniel, become beast, kills his brother, his mother says, "It was my victory. A champion out of the night. It was as if it came from the dark of me. My will ... a creature that had been coiled at the base of the heart and the spirit.... All of us ... If we could." She comments, "we are animals too, but clutter ourselves with feeling." The beast's rage is "her own.... The serene world, which had been indifferent to their suffering, should pay now in coins of blood."

Others more often regard raw nature with distaste. Ada, a typical daughter of the gentry, consults Julinus (now posing as an itinerant fortune-teller), and when for a moment nature exposes itself undisguised, something "struggled wildly inside her and she crammed it down ... for an instant the whole world was naked and horrible before her. But she *put down at once the veil*" (emphasis added).

Elephantasm

Explicitly concerned with class, race and misogyny, *Elephantasm* interweaves Victorian England and the Indian Raj. Whilst in England, a court revels in the execution of an impoverished young woman who has stabbed an abusing husband—without proper control, women "might become wild beasts. And men hunted down the wild beasts"—in India, an army officer, with classic colonial disregard for non-whites, plunders Hindu temples, rapes "a shadow animal-woman of the heathen dark," and massacres her brother and all his people.

Like Aradia before her, Annie is orphaned (twice over) by the death of her gentle, flowerlike sister, Rose. Though savagely beaten and forced into prostitution by a drunken husband, Rose is still a protective presence for Annie. Fleeing from sexual harassment in the street, Annie thinks, "*Well wasn't I a silly fool* ... in an inner voice that resembled her sister's." Internal voices suggest coexistent realities. After Rose is hanged and Annie put in service on a country estate, she continues to hear her voice. Even when the eldest son of the family forces himself upon her, she hears "*Rose's vocal rhythm*" in his voice. As Annie gains strength, Rose seems to take on bodily form.

Internalized and repressed feelings—especially women's—are a major theme. When she takes refuge from the street in a curio shop where the Indian proprietor sells her a tiny elephant amulet for a penny, "Tears sprang into Annie's eyes, surprising her. She denied them. They slid away back into her heart and left her there, hard and young, pale and dirty, trudging home in her cracked boots." Suppressed screams cannot "get out of her. They roiled in her belly, stuck." Women are called "hysterical and uncontrolled," but Annie's attempts to speak at Rose's trial are sternly silenced, though she wants "to fill the space with raging shrieks." She is forced to keep to herself endless, unbearable images of her hanged sister, "falling like a flower from the chain of time, falling on and on...." Only once does Annie give way freely to grief.

The East, India and various Hindu deities are indicated well before Annie arrives at Sir Hampton Smolte's fake Indian palace in the English countryside. At the shop where her placement is arranged, a small statue of the Madonna resembles the Goddess of the park in *A Heroine of the World*: Her "dress was eastern, rich with gold, and she had a golden crown." However, meaning alters according to context: With her infant replaced by a plate of sweets, this Madonna represents not love but addictive craving. In India, a plate of sweets in the hand of a statue of the chubby elephant god, Ganesh,[16] or his statue gleaming "as if streams of honey ran down it," are both charming images, but the dubious Withers' love of sweets is totally unwholesome—like his insatiable greed for jewels, stripped clandestinely from jungle temples.

Annie begins service as a kitchen maid and is cruelly persecuted by the spiteful Tiff until she is moved "upstairs" for use in Rupert's bloody sexual rituals. When Annie plunges her sewing needle into Tiff's arm (Rose killed her husband with sewing scissors), her retribution is quasi-religious. Tiff dies of blood-poisoning, hallucinating that Annie is "black and her hair as snakes and there's dead heads on her and there's blood running off out of her mouth." She is clearly seeing Kali, *The Dark One*.

Luksmi, Lady Flower Smolte's personal servant, notices Annie's "great strength."[17] "[T]he goddess has touched you," she says. Luksmi, though brought up in a Christian household, has privately retained her mother's Hindu beliefs. The sexual property of Rupert's younger brother, she warns Annie, "We are slaves." Later, as she tends to Annie's wounds with her Indian salves, an intimacy grows between them and Annie begins to absorb Luksmi's Eastern interpretations.

Luksmi believes that Annie's little elephant amulet protects her. Annie has "been through a gate."

> What nonsense, Annie thought. She thought: *He stopped. I made him.*
>
> But she would not think of Rupert. One more image to be shut away.

Explaining the nature of karma to Annie, Luksmi tells her that she owes a debt to Urquhart from a former life. She remains faithful to this duty even beyond Urquhart's death by providing proper Hindu rites.

Further explications of Hindu thought come from Darius, the groom.[18] Though white, he was abandoned in India as a baby and grew up more or less wild there. Though "Smolte's property," he really belongs to nature and the rukh.

When Annie takes Darius the broken geranium[19] salvaged from the slums of London, he plants it in front of a bronze statue of Indra,[20] where it twines rampantly through the god's wheel of life, prefiguring the Indian jungle that is about to erupt on the estate. "It was no longer Annie's.... It was the god's." Indra is, "The god of heaven. Of the lightning. The god of warriors." His wheel is the wheel "of life," Darius explains. "It turns. And lives follow lives. We pass through everything, all happiness, all pain, and in the end are free of it."

Quite unexpectedly, Annie announces, "My sister's dead," and with equal suddenness, "She cried as never since a baby had she cried." Darius assures her that Rose's death is merely *appearance*. He says, "If you were blind, the rose would still be shining on the tree." But Annie walks away: "She did not trust Darius and his luminous voice, [once again, the voice] nor Luksmi. They had let her suffer, say what they might." She is still unready to recognize the nature of Kali, the creator and destroyer.

A Heroine of the World traces Aradia's long and arduous reconciliation with the Death Mother as the partner of love. Annie takes on—or comes to terms with—this goddess in the form of Kali, who *takes* lives and metes out retribution and justice. When Annie tells Luksmi that her sister murdered a man, Luksmi replies, "perhaps it was he who owed her a death.... The world is pain and illusion.... But there is much more than the world," expressing the Hindu belief that the purpose of any single life is not necessarily visible, and justice therefore is possible only through the repetition of lives. Tiff's death also should be weighed on the scale of *divine* justice.

The release of emotion seems to unleash other repressed contents. Annie saves herself from possible fatal injury by realizing that her only escape lies in retaliation. Rupert's sexual perversities make "him feel a little sick," but Annie remains a victim even when she succeeds in reversing their roles. She feels "the birth of a desire ... now forever destroyed, the beginning instead of horror and guilt." Her sister faced the same dilemma, forced either to violence or victimization, and damaged in either case. However, as Darius tells Annie, "the goddess herself is many things. Perhaps you have been the Dark Mother, but now you are soft and kind, with pearls in your ears, the Bright One."

Both reincarnation and the polytheistic Hindu pantheon permit the gods to appear in many forms and aspects. The wheel passes "through everything." With nothing omitted, even the struggle of opposites against each other is passing and illusory: Death and life, dark and light, evil and good are merely giving way to each other. Lee imbues numerous small details with opposition and contradiction. Two cooks prepare the Smolte family's discordant dinners—one for English food, another for curries—and belowstairs are inextricably caught in love and hate and occasional thoughts of marriage. Smolte feels both intense ardor and irresistible loathing for India, and especially its women—even the colors of their saris give him migraine. In a contradictory attempt at repression, his wife, Flower, becomes merely "a screen between himself and India," whereas the beautiful and chaste Indian woman whom he rapes is a "bitch" and "slut." "She had sucked the soul out of him," and it is her fault that he murders the raja he is employed to protect and remorselessly slaughters his people.

Colonialism contains subtler horrors than the desire for material gain. Western moral superiority requires the debasement of the culture, especially the religious culture. The people, particularly the women, are animals. The white man is entitled to absolute mastery over both, and Smolte's dining room is typically festooned with hunting trophies.

When Smolte returns to England, his history is rewritten: "...news had altered and amended itself, they were heroes without doubt, who had stopped a conflagration spreading across India. And Hampton Smolte was, of them all, the best, a gallant Englishman...."

But the Smoltes are all haunted by the precariousness of their own humanity. Even the vapid Flower has an illuminating vision of a latent animal in each of her children. "*One is a pig and one a rat and one a cat.... Don't the Hindus say that? A man can be reborn as an animal. Then why not an animal as a girl? My daughter is a cat.*"

One of several subplots directly involves the domination and de-repression of animals. When a hired entertainer seats his Indian monkeys at the dining table among Flower's guests, they are impeccably repressed and trained to decorum, but in the middle of the night they caper about, wearing the heads of the animals that Smolte has shot. This monkeys' uprising appears to trigger the final phase of the narrative, as the whole estate reverts to nature and the repressed truth about India. The temperature soars; the grounds become a jungle full of the wild animals of the rukh. "The fabric of Maya, of solid-seeming unreality, was giving way." Annie, "under a spell," asks Darius, "Is it a dream?" "The world is a dream," he replies.

According to their kharma, individuals experience these unnatural phenomena differently: Smolte reaches for his gun. Flower dithers helplessly. Urquhart goes out to join the hunt. Elizabeth scales a tree with her ferine cat. Rupert mistakes a tiger for his ayah and dies in paroxysms of pain and pleasure. Only Darius and Annie remain calm. Annie helps Flower from the collapsing house, appropriately, by the back stairs. The tiny amulet, lost some time before, has grown into an immense white elephant which pursues Smolte indoors. Darius puts a bullet through the head of the mortally wounded Smolte. The wheel comes full circle and a straggle of dazed survivors return to the outside world. Hand in hand with Darius, Annie departs, taking nothing with her but a small pot of geraniums.

— 11 —

THE BLIGHTED FUTURE

Eva Fairdeath

This early book was belatedly published along with a foreword by the author. Lee describes its location as "a future world polluted to the point of anarchy and dissolution" where the "social fabric has broken down almost completely." A classic narrative of revenge accompanies the general trappings of a western. Steel invokes gunslinger culture as he tells Eva he is "selling a man's death." Wanderers travel by wagon, beset by horse thieves and plunged into bath scenes amongst atrocious plumbing. Painted whorehouse women flaunt themselves beside the pub/saloon. Money changes hands over cards, and an itinerant preacher dupes country folk.

Lee comments that, "Eva merely *experiences*, and acts." She is "only just learning, by accident as it were, how to break loose." Others are largely obstacles, frequently overcome by biting and screaming. She kills without forethought or hesitation, using whatever means comes to hand. She attaches herself to Steel largely because he represents a way out of her village.

Lee's theme of like attracting like depends here on the fact that Eva and her two lovers are mutants who have adapted to the polluted environment with similar biological traits.[1] The narrative moves through social and interpersonal hostilities towards their joint recognition of solidarity. As Eva brings Steel and Sail together, she is simultaneously establishing her equality with both men and struggling with idealization of Steel. Starting from extreme naivety and inexperience, she is slow to realize "that he and she were initially built of the same material. Surprised, she became aware that he also, as Sail and she were, was merely a human being." It requires Sail to point out that Steel's obsession with hunting down and killing anyone who resembles his parent's murderers is clearly abnormal. "Didn't it ever occur to you that he was crazy? ... obsessed with death. You set him up like a bloody great god.... But he's a killer," he says. But Eva, preoccupied with seeming "cool," says "nothing. It was a trick she had learned."

Initially, she lives almost exclusively by tricks. Since women have no recognized rights in the inbred community she comes from, and the superstitious villagers consider the albino girl a witch, Eva grows up to a moral code of survival. She avoids a father's sexual abuse by encouraging his fantasy that she is a virgin. Steel and Sail remain undeceived, but with other men her trickery and contradictions are remarkably successful. As she is waiting for Steel, a passing man's attentions are "irritating but nevertheless made her feel alert and self-aware. She hoped Steel would come out and find him pestering her." But although she enjoys inciting jealousy and violence, she can never bear to please. In a pointedly offensive gesture, she throws a cigarette offered by a suitor into the river. Later she agrees to an evening out with him for the price of a dress she likes, but ends the evening by denying him entry into her house. When Sail is arrested for stealing, Eva, well aware that he will not get out alive, charms her way into the anteroom where her cheated suitor sits guarding the prisoner. She seduces him, smashes a wine bottle and cuts open his throat. The text remarks briefly, "Johnny goggled at her. She had always managed to astound him. Now, astounded yet again, he fell back and bled among the Sauterne-soaked cushions." As she steps outside the conventions of a society that regards killing as an exclusively male activity, Eva is freed to kill in whatever way carries least risk to herself. Her contempt for male standards concerning a fair fight merely gives her the advantage of surprise.

The rejection of conformity to gender stereotypes is a salient feature of all the main characters here. Even Angel, who befriends Eva briefly, seems to be a figure of authority amongst the townsfolk mainly because, as a lesbian, she falls outside their prevailing gender codes. This questioning of codes becomes something of a measure of intelligence as Angel provides Eva with an instructive commentary on events. The lure of the clothes, cosmetics and high-heeled shoes available in Oiltown also fades quickly. Eva soon complains: "Her feet hurt from clopping about like a horse and from standing still to be admired in various poses." She refuses the position allocated to women who, as Lee's foreword points out, have "fallen back into the role of object and adjunct," and instead plays a dangerous game "as User of Men." Although he is oblivious to gender conventions and neither "buys" nor exploits her, apparently she partly intends this as "obscure revenge on Steel," whose impenetrable self-possession maddens her. She questions him "endlessly," "tortured" by his lack of response. "It was an indication of her worship of him, her misunderstanding, her blindness, that it never occurred to her she might also be torturing him."

Where Steel is strong, silent and unbendingly manly, Sail, with his physical resemblance to Steel, is a trickster like Eva. Thief, con-man and womanizer, he has a glib tongue. He is fascinatingly accessible, and when he becomes sick and vulnerable, Eva succumbs with a rush of almost maternal feeling. Sail's weakness gives her a sense of power, impossible with the invincible Steel.

No other female in Lee's repertoire seems quite so plagued by indecision. When she flees from Oiltown in company with Sail, and they are joined by Steel, "She wanted to shout at Sail to go away, but the second she looked at him total confusion overcame her, because she had the same overpowering desire to embrace him and be one with him that she had just experienced for Steel."

Choice is hampered by the fact that the two men represent different aspects of herself.

It is when these two aspects of herself turn away from her and towards each other that Eva grows desperate. She has learned some ways of dealing with male codes of dominance and honor but is naturally disadvantaged in the matter of men's codes of loyalty to one another. Lee's foreword comments on Eva's "fear of the male bond of friendship." Afflicted with a fierce jealousy of any intimacy between them, when Steel picks up the ailing Sail and physically lifts him into his wagon, Eva feels a "red-hot, icy and oddly shameful tide" run down her body. A moment later, alone in the wagon with Sail, she is "amazed to find herself unbearably sexually aroused ... in some oblique way by the episode outside." What appears as "oblique" to Eva is less obscure to the reader. She has just glimpsed the potential of sexual attraction between two men.

Eva's emotions and the sexual reverberations that follow are extremely complicated. When she discovers Sail and Steel sleeping in each other's arms, "each become for the other what she had been for both of them: a lover," she retreats, sick to the core. "At the doorway she slid out backwards away from the farm, her eyes fixed on the half-open door, as if some monster would emerge from it to pursue her, though she was already irreparably in its power." Her reaction is so extreme it triggers nine days of illness before she and Sail can follow after the "crazy" Steel, whose current killing mission is hopelessly dangerous.

The troubled relationship between the mutants is close to resolution. There is no question of deterring Steel. Instead, they unite and both Eva and Sail kill on his behalf—Eva once again using broken glass. In the final shootout, killing binds them more tightly together than sex ever could, and the three at last are seen to overcome their differences.

Whilst the ruined world creates mutations in increasing numbers, the xenophobic hatred of those who claim to be normal increases proportionally and seeks to deflect blame for environmental catastrophe onto its victims. Meanwhile, the mutants—one of them is observed casually donning the sunglasses of a man who has just been shot—are impervious to the moral dictates of the system that spawned them. Their instinct is correct: Moral culpability belongs to those who practice values that have already made the world into a sulfurous hell. Eva's fascination with a train sums up her essential pragmatism. She loses "her soul on the train, as bygone travelers had lost their umbrellas." For Eva, a soul is just a peripheral possession.

Lee's western neither celebrates unspoilt wilderness nor especially laments its passing. Her point is that mutants have become the natural inheritors of a devastated earth. Eva's non-cerebral orientation is appropriate as she moves through a landscape from which nature and meaning have both been stripped. She must take what she needs from experience that is raw and unfiltered. The deluded standards of a disintegrated civilization no longer apply.

—12—

The Blood Opera

Dark Dance, Personal Darkness, Darkness I

Dark Dance

In the Blood Opera sequence, vampirism is largely metaphoric. Lee links *bloodlines*, or genetic recurrences, in an ancient, claustrophobic and mutant family to reincarnation. Named Scarabae after the Egyptian symbol of immortality, they live beyond their proper time and are corrupted by power.

An unorthodox alchemical subtext fuses *White Queen*, or elixir of life, with the White Queen of *Alice Through the Looking Glass*, places the *Androgyne* in a transvestite lover, originally assumed to be a woman, and religiously cremates Scarabae dead in alchemichally transformative *Fire* as their mansion burns down.[1] Colors—red, white, black, gold—carry alchemical meanings. Like substances in alchemical procedures, characters may remain *inert* for long periods. Egyptian settings and a dream of an Egyptian burial on a pyramid-pyre of books refer to the history of alchemy.[2] *Opera* also indicates *The Great Work* of alchemy.

In accordance with a publisher's request, the Blood Opera has a contemporary setting, and Lee approaches the problem of modern, semi-imperishable, quasi-vampiric, alchemichal characters from several angles. Books create an alternative to the material world—the disaffected heroine even works in a bookshop. A slow tempo and dense textures allow new symbolic identities to develop within realistic contexts—amidst trite conversation, vodka and a platitudinously ordinary English landscape, a train journey ends in a killing which is clearly a ceremonial sacrifice; a dogfight organized in a disused underground station represents Hell.

Rachaela is often *inert*. She never plunges into confrontations out of passionate curiosity. Initially shrouded in a London fog, she is anonymous until her employer, "who remained as thankful a mystery to her as she remained a provoking mystery to him," addresses her by name. She can be almost non-(or pre-)verbal, even slightly infantile,[3] as she rejects conversational gambits, preferring to be home alone, immersed in books, music and the (covertly Egyptian) subject of her dead cat. Among the Scarabae, who live for unspecified numbers of centuries, "she was unique, exciting, like a newborn baby." She behaves "like an obedient child" and nervously secures her door before getting into a bed that is a "cradle."

An introductory quote from Lewis Carroll—"'How do you know I'm mad?' said Alice. 'You must be,' said the Cat, "or you wouldn't have come here'"—reverberates more gloomily in the text: "The world to Rachaela was mostly horrible.... She expected only onslaughts on her privacy, her person." She reveals her name "as if admitting a dangerous secret." Wishing to be autonomous, not family property, she uses an alias, refusing both the Smith of her mother and the Scarabae of her absentee father, Adamus. Rachaela's willful inertia is also a rejection of inherited character. In Anna's remark, "*Life* offends you. You are Scarabae," she hears a manipulative attempt to embed her in the family. The Scarabae household is a "prison" where the abrasive modern world gives way to a stifling atavism. But she still wins small victories. When her watch stops, by noting the hour that she wakes—as if for work in London—she uses her own body-clock to identify real time and triumphs over her reduction to a means of Scarabae genetic continuance.

The "normal" world from which Rachaela has already disaffiliated herself gives way to an isolated mansion where the outside world is totally obscured by stained glass windows picturing scenes "from a Bible of hell." Somehow, despite a "warped and irate" mother who was "a weight of iron," Rachaela has "stayed light as air." But the Scarabae do not permit airiness or lightness. Literally made for her role, she must now be molded to their requirements. The "priestly" Adamus is the only male Scarabae young enough to serve as a parent. That they are father and daughter deters no-one. As Ruth remarks, it serves to "keep the bloodline pure."

Adamus has several features in common with Angelen. Both create daughters intended to bear them sons. With a face "cruel as an angel's," Adamus is "The Prince of Darkness," and the image in Rachaela's bedroom window of a "golden Satan" tempting Eve foretells Adamus's nocturnal visit as it falls across her bed. Adamus and Anjelen both drink blood. Adamus's smaller habit is attributed to a rogue vampiric gene. Possibly Rachaela's tendency to alcoholism is also genetic. Though "magnetized" by Adamus, who is "an externalization of herself," after he makes love to her, "She lay back in the chair and he went out of her like ... the brief tipsiness from the glass of vinegary wine." Without liking or love, her "primal terror ... older far than the Scarabae" is followed by an inevitable distaste for the resulting child. "It had enslaved and damaged her. Now it was to rule her life. Why should she love it, this demon?"

When Rachaela escapes from the household where "twenty-one ancient beetles crept and slipped about their shadowy pursuits," she knows she is not in reality upsetting the master-plan of this ancient-world Mafia. "All the wide world could not afford her sufficient crannies to hide from them." Her efforts to abort the baby fail, and it is passed to a minder while Rachaela goes out to work. When serious illness strikes, Rachaela admits she had "hoped that Ruth would die."[4] But Ruth clings to life—if not to her mother—and they live at uneasy arms length in a tiny flat. Rachaela watches grimly and offers occasional protection as Scarabae traits surface in her daughter. When Ruth disappears at puberty, wanted to produce another generation of Scarabae, "the twelve years of idiocy" are not over. Rachaela follows, knowing "she must face Adamus." "She is our saviour," the matriarch, Anna, proclaims, scorning Rachaela's protests at the compounded incest and her "jealousy" and "sleeping life." As future propagator of the clan, Ruth has no independent meaning.

"You were the rogue flowering, Rachaela," Anna says. Any autonomy indicates a "rogue." Adamus is the good son who stifles personal feeling. The extreme of repression, Sylvian scores out the contents of all the books in the library: "Words mean nothing ... gather like the dust.... I correct them." Years later, Rachaela finds a scattering of intact words, the sum of admissible Scarabae history: "*We have fled before them.*" The rogue of the family is Camillo, said to be about three hundred, once locked away for twenty years after murdering his bride. He gives Rachaela dubious gifts—a dead mouse tied in a ribbon, a crumbling bit of driftwood with "tiny creatures" running from it. She dreams he holds the *key* and goes to him for help and family stories of pogroms and persecution.[5] Unusually, he is not afraid to face daylight or express his nonconformist dislike and mistrust of Ruth.

Ruth's room is ominously red, like the "blood of menstruation and the torn maidenhead. The red of the womb ... of the blood drunk at a feast." She wears an antique, blood-red dress for her ceremonial betrothal to Adamus. Rachaela perceives the dangers of sexual awakening without consummation. In the clutches of the Scarabae, Ruth begins to look like an ordinary, unhappy child, but she forestalls Rachaela's plans to take her away by driving a knitting needle, like a stake, through Anna's heart and murdering several others.

Ruth is locked in the attic. Rachaela determines to release her—"there was some bond between them. Like the umbilical cord, unsevered." Adamus commits suicide, and Ruth finds his body and sets fire to the house. More Scarabae die in the fire, and Ruth, "scuttling like an imp," escapes into the night, "her work accomplished."

The real horror in this *operatic* work lies in the leaden pressures of genetic destiny, as Rachaela seeks liberation at the micro-level of her own genetic makeup. She struggles to escape from what she is made of with the strange inertia of someone literally trapped inside a body.

Personal Darkness and Darkness, I

After the fire, the surviving Scarabae move to London and monied modernity, complete with phones, televisions and horror videos. Books, which Eric is annotating in tiny, "insectile" writing, are being replaced by films. Here, film consistently contains hints of fraudulence. Rachaela, still with them, turns forty, looks twenty, feels "like a child.... Held fast in nostalgia." She begins to perceive herself as "an insect, new-born, hardened ... death was not for her.... Was she trying to understand them at last ... or only herself?"

The narrative's tempo grows erratic. Bursts of activity rupture the slow motion of protracted lives. Rachaela's second child, Anna, bypasses childhood (perhaps Ruth has already lived it for her) and reaches a physical sixteen at two. But Scarabae age always was uncertain, and even Althene prevaricates here: "Suffice it to say our dresses swept the floor." Absent since the fire, a rejuvenated Camillo rejoins them. Clad in leather gear and riding a motor-tricycle, he camps in the garden with a gang of bikers, one of whom starts a flirtation with a visibly younger Miranda. All this *going backwards* again suggests a Looking-Glass world.

Camillo remains oddly sympathetic as he engages with drunks, sleeps rough, marries a vagrant, tries it all. A trickster—"madness was his garment but he had put it on so often it claimed him. The mask had become the skin"—he reaches the acme of Scarabae contempt for ordinary individuals at a rave among "the real young," whom he reduces from their

Ecstasy high to whimpering terror. Lee emphasizes the demonic by conflating traditional myth and modern imagery: "They raised their arms to the white heart of the strobe, like antique worshippers to the core of a sun. Dionysos, Cybele...."

Other family aberrations are more serious. Ruth is busy killing, robbing and burning, but passing over some households like an angel of death. Tabloids christen her "the black vixen." "Poor little girl," one woman remarks maternally, but a victim thinks "of things in horror movies that had to be invited over the threshold." Ruth also believes she is a "monster." She sips a little blood "because she was a Scarabae, a vampire.... It was a sort of duty." However, Althene ascribes Ruth's babyhood illness to a desire to die. Reasons for pitying her accumulate.

The distraught family send for reinforcements, who descend like gods from their helicopter. As Malach and Althene[6] cross the moonlit lawn with two huge dogs, an "owl floated from the treetop like a demon on silken sails. It came to him, settled on his wrist." Whilst Althene's *malachite* globe associates her with alchemical transformation, when Malach goes in pursuit of Ruth, Rachaela fuses chess and alchemical terminology, remarking, "white knight to take black queen."[7]

Malach finds Ruth about to be put to work as a prostitute. At first sight, she calls him "Daddy," but, unlike Adamus, when he locks her in a room he re-educates her. Killing must be just. "The priest kills for God. The warrior kills for his legion. But ... Ruth kills for Ruth." When Ruth says, "I'm evil," he responds, "You're Scarabae.... Forget epithets from horror films," but privately he feels the horror and vomits "the bitterness of centuries and two thousand lies."

Where Adamus only served the family, Malach falls in love. Ruth seems transformed. "*He has created her*," Rachaela observes. "*Is that the reason for love?*" She is including parental love here as something essential to evolutionary progress, and she too is evolving emotionally, experiencing real sorrow when Althene has to leave. Althene comforts her with thoughts of redemption: "Though you have committed atrocious acts, you needn't continue to transgress. Change is possible. Is *allowed*."

Unhappily, Ruth's redemption is flawed. When she kills again, Malach renounces her. "You're not mine. Go into the furnace. Burn up. Finish." *Furnace* suggests both alchemy and hellfire. Rachaela recognizes an enduring genetic pattern here—"*These words come out of vaults of time. Spoken over and over.*" As Malach descends into "hell" to break up a dog-fight underground and returns to "the city that was like all cities, and the time that was like all times, and the agony and tedium and loss that had no end," Rachaela feels "torn open, as if Ruth had been born again out of her body."

Rachaela is dreaming about Ruth's burial as *Darkness, I* opens. Snow is falling round a pyramid of books, some of which are modern paperbacks, combining Egyptian myth and everyday reality. Rachaela is sitting in a dentist's chair as Ruth's *ka* rises out of a sarcophagus, a small flame issuing from its fingertips.[8] Rachaela's mouth opens, and she swallows it. She is pregnant again.

Rachaela still fears the Scarabae "trap" but the alchemical Androgyne signifies healing, and personal attachment is healing her. She neither knows nor cares whether she wants "Althene the woman, or her hidden maleness." "*I am the one having the child. I am not the child,*" Rachaela thinks, and yet she also thinks, "*She is my mother. He is my mother.*"

But Rachaela, forced to share this newly found mother, is jealous of Althene's love for the child—which might anyway change to sexual desire. Despite Anna's flaxen hair and calm nature, a tiny birthmark at the site of Ruth's death wound seems to confirm Ruth's co-presence in her. But she gradually adjusts: "Am I falling in love with my daughter? ... She's mine, after all."

But Althene's father, Cain, wants Anna for his mate and kidnaps her. Althene, in pursuit, falls foul of her own mad mother, who imprisons and gradually poisons her. Rachaela finally pulls herself out of a drunken stupor and, shedding her long inertia, embarks on an explicitly alchemical sea voyage in search of Althene.[9]

As she tears the sick and incontinent (infantilized) Althene from her mother's clutches, Rachaela's feelings become protective and parental. "I *am* Scarabae," she declares and wonders in silent amusement, "Adamus or Malach?" Rachaela is suddenly mother and warrior, double-sexed, a healing androgyne. But as Althene's mother lunges forward with a knife, Rachaela sees the "mother" from the film *Psycho*, with the spurious double-gender of a man disguising himself as his mother.

Similar gender doublings and inversions appear elsewhere. Cain kisses Anna "like a mother. Like the first father she ever had." But doubleness of gender starts giving way to split identity. In Cain's Antarctic facsimile of an Egyptian palace, Anna is renamed Ankhet-Persephone.

This Egypt on ice is riddled with travesty. A "Greek, zippered dress," goes "over white silk knickers and bra with Paris labels." Anna thinks, "*Cecil B. De Mille insisted even the underclothes were authentic.*" This is even more fake than film. Using modern cosmetics, supplied with contemporary novels, the grotesque cast behave "like diners in a fashionable West End restaurant."

Anna asks the "Mother" in the palace why she doesn't speak in the language of Ancient Egypt.[10] "Or the Semitic tongues, or medieval Russian, or the French of the eighteenth century. I've forgotten them all, like fear. I remember my childhood.... I played in the mud, and my sister brought me little colored animals she made, hippopotami and crocodiles. And I remember three rivers." She is clearly implying that the Scarabae have achieved the goal of alchemy, eternal life.

Cain stages an orgy. He rapes a man chained to a pillar, then bites out his throat and drinks his blood. Just as he is urging Anna to join him in his feast, Malach appears.[11] Anna abruptly remembers her former life as Ruth, including Malach's final "betrayal," which is "forgotten but not forgiven." She spits in his face, saying, "Tie him up and hurt him. For me." Cain tortures Malach and tries to rape him.[12] Finally, Cain sacrifices a group of children, then becomes Anna's lover. She, "neither quite Ruth nor, definitely, Anna," is left emptily fearing only a fast-approaching boredom.

The last scene in the book undoubtedly leads on to its unwritten sequel. A raddled, old fortune-teller is telling Malach, "'She is white as snow, but the child in her womb is black. Black as coal....' She lifted her head and added, to the silent entity of the room: 'A *new* darkness.'"

"The Genes Are the Immortals."[13]
Genes and Memes

The Scarabae of Lee's sequence are "insectile": With super-human powers of survival and a blind drive for self-perpetuation at whatever personal cost, they resemble an insect species that is a symbol of eternal life.[14] At the same time, Lee associates them closely with genes. She speaks of throwbacks. Scarabae family members have a prodigious similarity to each other: "...to have any impact on the world.... Each entity must exist in the form of lots of copies, and at least some of the entities must be *potentially* capable of surviving—in the form of copies—for a significant period of evolutionary time. Small genetic units have these properties."[15] Individual Scarabae may reappear in others after their death—most notably Ruth, who returns in the person of Anna—putting their already huge lifespan beyond assessment. "Genes ... have an expectation of life that must be measured not in decades but in thousands and millions of years."[16] The twentieth century has pathways for pursuing eternal life besides those of alchemy and reincarnation.

Anna describes Scarabae existence in terms of a dance—"A changing of partners through time"—an exact analogy for genetic transmission in a sexed species. The history of the Scarabae also pursues a genetic theme: The pogroms and persecutions that litter their past are clear attempts to excise genetic information (i.e., genocide). Even Scarabae vampirism, though it is presented as a genetic aberration, can be read as a metaphor for the gene as a parasite which is sustained by the life/blood of its human host. Certainly, Scarabae disregard for the individual typifies "the gene's universal law of ruthless selfishness."[17] The early, less-evolved Scarabae are without a speck of concern for any except their own, and even that falters at the first sign of deviancy from the norm.

However, Scarabae choices do not always accord with standard eugenic wisdom. They practice incest of the closest possible order. Lee seems to be studying the impulse towards incest from the point of view of the gene, suggesting that a gene's desire to replicate itself as closely as possible could produce an instinctive preference for incest. She does not ignore the danger of reinforcing of the "bad" or "lethal" gene—Cain all but parodies the bad gene—but the "bad" gene's determination to replicate itself is, nevertheless, no less pressing than that of any "good" gene.

Alongside his exposition of genes, Dawkins also proposes another kind of entity, which he calls the *meme*. Close to the traditional notion of the *zeitgeist*, this is a force of culture, not nature, that spreads invisibly and very rapidly and has the same apparent powers of replication as the gene. Throughout her work, Lee has often seemed to assert that myth and religious belief have precisely this sort of ability to persist and resurface with alterations in smaller or larger details, according to their environment.

The Blood Opera pastes together a dauntingly complex collage of components: myth, ritual, sexuality, reproduction, incest, the desire for immortality imprinted in the gene, the influence of memes, the endurance of cultural beliefs, family history and the politics of power. Here, the forces of fate are not merely internal, as with a swallowed jewel, but innate from conception. In the midst of this, the single individual appears small and frail. Lee is once again telling the story of the search for a personal identity, this time putting the quest for transformation through alchemy in play alongside it.

At the root of the narrative, and pivotal to it, the gene expresses its built-in hostility towards change, outside influence or meme.[18] Sylvian's activities in the library, the family's fear of typewriters, telephones and electricity, take on a different aspect if they are seen as expressions of the conflict between particular genes and memes. In putting themselves as far from the modern world as possible, the Scarabae are attempting to isolate exact genetic replication from the mutating effects of memes. Rachaela's presence, contaminated by her contact with modern culture, only slightly disrupts their lives. Ruth's presence destroys them. The move to London produces a flood of mimetic input: The previously quarantined Scarabae are substantially altered. The speed with which a meme may be transmitted is described as Camillo overpowers a crowd of Ecstasy-primed ravers only with thought.

Beyond simple genetic survival, the Scarabae also desire to be *dominant*. This is the basis of Rachaela's struggle with both Adamus and Ruth. Althene, however, seeks to support both Rachaela and Anna. At many junctures, human feeling directly opposes genetic drives. Rachaela loves Althene whether she is male or female, and thus whether or not she is reproductively viable.

Malach tells Anna, "You're free to choose. That's why I came to find you." As Dawkins comments, "We are built as gene machines, cultured as meme-machines, but we ... alone on earth, can rebel against the tyranny of the selfish replicators."[19]

Lee also puts the matter of timing into play. Nature only moves when she is ready. Rachaela's long period of inertia is a dormant phase preceding change. The Scarabae are linked with butterfly as well as dung beetle. As Rachaela takes Anna out into the garden, a yellow butterfly lights as if spellbound on Anna's outstretched hand. Camillo, too, is "changing like a butterfly." "*Change is possible.*" Finally, the individual's sources are as complex and as mysterious as, to use Lee's strangely haunting phrase, "the chemical composition of the sea."

Conclusion

Regrettably, space has not permitted commentary on any of Lee's numerous short stories and novellas. I especially regret omitting *Madame Two Swords*, a novella that is a personal favorite and that, in its treatment of recurrence, transformation and love, underlines most of the contentions made in this book. Nor has it been possible to discuss Lee's more recent work.[1] Tanith Lee has had about a dozen more books reach print since part three of The Blood Opera appeared.[2] Some of Lee's recent work moves through a world we recognize readily: *When the Lights Go Out* is set by the more or less contemporary English seaside. *The Gods Are Thirsty* (though written approximately a decade before its publication) belongs to the genre of historical novel. In her novels *Faces Under Water* and *Saint Fire*, she has produced another parallel city—Venus/Venice—to match her Paradis. *Law of the Wolf Tower* was shortlisted for the Guardian Children's Fiction Award and has already acquired a sequel. A third Unicorn book has appeared.

From all of these books, images stick in the mind. A man carries his dead warhorse up the stairs and heaves it onto his great bed (*Vivia*). A girl's hair bursts into a halo of spontaneous flame (*Saint Fire*). A dog, starving in a London slum, is transported into the heavens (*Reigning Cats and Dogs*). Lee's version of Snow White, *White as Snow*, will appear before the present work does.

This book has not attempted to tell more than a part of the story. Language, humor, even character and plot structure, not to mention many more down-to-earth themes and subject matters, have been largely subordinated to Lee's more esoteric preoccupations. There is space for a great deal more work on this author. I conclude with the hope that this gap will be eventually filled.

An Interview with Tanith Lee

Much of the material in this interview relates to the preceding text. Conducted by letter, the interview seems to fit well with a predilection for letter-writing that Ms. Lee and I share.—MH

M.H. You've written books referring to a wide range of different matters. Can you say anything about what interests you particularly at present?

T.L. The base of all my interest is, always, people. I despair of men and women both, in many cases, and yet I have an innate and enduring belief in Mankind. I am generally addressing these two embattled opposites, in one way or another. Also, I am in a phase of great anger at the injustice of it all. Not only the individual wrongdoing, but the flawed scheme by which the world tries to run.

Of course, I have written of utopia-dystopias. But there the so-called perfect worlds are not perfect, despite the fact that illness and the fear of death, ugliness, handicap and inequality have ostensibly been removed. (I am thinking here primarily of *Don't Bite the Sun*.) People also seem to need challenges. I myself feel these do not have to be challenges of violence, power or pain in order to be fulfilling. I had wished, after DBTS and its sequel, *Drinking Sapphire Wine*, to write a third book, in which I would try to set out an alternate life-style, adventurous and stretching to mind and heart, but still, and importantly, free of the retributions of unprotected life. I did and do think a world would be feasible which gives pleasure and safety alongside excitement and development. One of the saddest messages that has come out of so much (wonderful) SF is that freedom in a brave "natural" world must be paid for by primitive punishments—disease, death, want. One element should not have to exclude the other, even though we are taught, it seems, that they must.

(Unfortunately I hesitated too long to write this third book, and by the time I was ready, I was actively discouraged—the moment, apparently, had passed. One day I may try for it in another form.)

M.H. After reading *Elephantasm*, I was surprised to discover that you had not visited India. What sort of sources and methods do you use when researching locations? How do you prepare for a book? How much is researched in advance? Also plots: Are they more or less fully formed in advance of writing, or do they alter as you proceed? And do your characters tend to surprise you at times? How much do you rewrite? What stage of writing do you enjoy the most? I know you start in longhand; does much alter between pen and typewriter? These are a lot of questions.

T.L. Yes, a cannonade of questions, I'd say. Let me take them one by one in order.

My methods of research are fairly ordinary. I read books about the place, and sometimes watch films set in the place or era. Sometimes too I just rush in and try to find it all out by instinct. *Elephantasm*, for example, was a compendium of books and dreams, that is, daydreams.

Normally I prepare a book by saying, I'm going to start so-and-so tomorrow ... or tonight, or whatever. A title may be enough, a phrase, an image. At other times I plan something of where I am going, but usually not even to the half-way point, let alone the end. Where an end has suggested itself it frequently changes. My books come out of the people in them.

If there is a lot of research needed—for example the Egyptian sequences in *Darkness, I*—I read a lot as I approach that point and continue to read as I write the scenes.

My characters always surprise me. They are real for me, and they do what real people do, constantly altering, changeable. The kindest and the best do wicked things, the evil suffer spasms of sweetness and altruism. Some who are destined to die refuse to do so, others fling themselves into the abyss when not expected. And suddenly, frequently, they learn something of themselves that is a revelation to both of us.

I usually only re-write to tidy up repetitions of words. Or to juggle the odd sentence to make it a little more clear. If the book is coming, then it comes "right." Once or twice I have struggled for days with two or three lines. Most of the time it rushes through and out of me like a river in spate. I will not do re-writes for editors—few have ever asked—unless, of course,

I have made a mistake of some kind. This stance has doubtless won me a reputation for appalling arrogance. Actually it isn't. I prefer to make my own way, and speak with my own voice. For good or ill, I suppose. In this way I never denigrate my earlier works. I have enjoyed them all and learnt from them all, and the way to learn is to do for yourself. However, I am careful. I work hard in attempting to bring out of myself the correct work, and if ever I felt I had not succeeded, to the best of my ability at that time, I would not offer it for publication. Really it is a sort of raucous honesty. I want my books to be mine.

I enjoy all stages of writing. Everything. It is one of the best things in my life. (Along with many other best things, I confess.) Yes, I write everything first in longhand, and by now my writing on a book is completely unreadable, sometimes, in spots, even to me. When typing, it is a final chance to catch repetitions and tidy a little, but only a little.

M.H. I know that you are a very meticulous writer who pays great attention to detail. Does the rushed environment of publishers, editors, etc. ever create problems—e.g. in the form of errors, or changes—for you?

T.L. In some early novels, and stories, I did not get to read the proofs— the slowness of Transatlantic mails made such a delay that publishers tended to shirk this. On reading the printed book, I now and then found a few (usually but not always) minor changes that had been made to my text— without my knowledge. Again time I think was to blame here, and probably the expense, although I found it appalling and heart-breaking. I do feel this should never be done. DAW, however, were very good at trying to correct printer's errors in later editions. One of the oddest matters are the last lines of *The Birthgrave*, which have often been quoted in their original misprinted form. It should read: "And yet, I *have* myself, at last, I have myself...." In fact, I've got so used to the mistake that I no longer worry too much on this one.

Some titles were also changed without reference to me. *Vazkor, Son of Vazkor* and *Quest for the White Witch* were originally one large novel entitled *Shadowfire* (the first volume appeared in England under this title). Don Wollheim coined the title *Night's Master* for the first of the Flat Earth books, and I liked this so much that I made it the format for all the subsequent titles. The last (to date) book, *Night's Sorceries*, was to have been called *Night's Daughter* (as two volumes of the series are in the SF Book Club version). However, this clashed with another author's work, also called *Night's Daughter*, apparently, so it was thought better to change it. I selected *Night's Sorceries*, after a chapter name in the first book. *Tamastara* was called by me

The Indian Nights. Don Wollheim dreamed up the adjunct to *Red as Blood: Tales from the Sisters Grimmer,* which tickled me immensely. I had to fight to keep the title *Kill the Dead,* which was reckoned un-fantasy. It is a sign of the merit of DAW that despite misgivings they let me keep it. Many recent titles have been invented by my husband, John, whose facility for this is alarming—and extremely enticing. They include, *Dark Dance, Personal Darkness, Darkness, I, Heart-Beast.* He and I invented the title for *The Blood of Roses,* walking in Richmond park through the devastation of the 1987 hurricane-aftermath. The felled and broken trees seemed to bring it to our minds.

M.H. You have mentioned *Anackire* as a deliberate contribution towards peace. Are there other books that refer so deliberately to (I hesitate to say *political*) events in the (I also hesitate to say *real*) world? How much is your work affected by contemporary events?

T.L. I have to excuse myself for putting my case about *Anackire* wrongly. I can't consider this book as a contribution to peace. If only it could be. I did feel that perhaps the thrust of glorious war (and, hating war, I am not immune to the glamour of it as a [fantasy] spectacle *inside a book*), this glorious war element, as I say, I felt to be due for a reversal. I wanted to work out on my pieces of paper the way the politically and temporally powerless might hope to set at least their wills against a conflict that would destroy everything. *Anackire* was my way of emitting the thought that one can do or try to do something. The weapons for peace of my characters were will and soul. And mine, as usual, the pen.

The personal outrage I mentioned earlier runs rife in a number of books. *Day by Night,* for example, inflamed by all sorts of oppressions, the Vis novels likewise. (Amrek sprang from Hitler, though I am glad to say, Amrek is a human being, albeit of another world.) The whole Flat Earth sequence—of which, one day, there may be another book—wrestles with a deep inner pain at the random horrors of what we call life. And *Elephantas,* fairly obviously, is a prolonged howl against gender and racial injustice and the mindless, thoughtless misuse of animals. One is always reacting against everyday issues, but, working in the medium of fantasy and SF, one tackles them in a parallel format. On the other hand, the Scarabae books— also curtailed before their conclusion—have pounced headlong on so many contemporary shadows, it almost makes me laugh. For there is, as ever, so much of this dark and nasty material to cut into shapes.

M.H. Evil is strongly and very variously represented in your work. Sometimes animals or humans transformed into animals can seem equipped with more moral integrity than most humans, but the Beast (*Heart-Beast, The Book of the Beast*, etc.) is mindless and destructive. Latterly in your books—perhaps increasingly as they enter the modern world—good and evil seem to have become inextricably and inevitably mixed. Since The Blood Opera sequence remains unfinished, would you like to say anything about the direction it is taking, especially in relation to the problem of evil?

T.L. I believe in evil. I do think there are normally explanations for its onset. Often the damage has gone so far it is unlikely a cure can be found. In some instances, I hope very few, it is inherent. Worse than all this, in a way, is the casual and self-blind evil everywhere practiced by those who, if confronted with the truth of what they do, would laugh. But is this laugh that of disbelief, or secret delight?

The Beast in *Heart-Beast* too is not truly mindless. It may be noticed that it never kills an animal. True, it seems to strike at the harmless and polluted human together. But apparently its argument is with the human race. One wonders why...

Good and evil can be mixed, generally are mixed. Only when one is able to tell a fairy tale, as sometimes one can, is it possible to segregate. I think that one of my main theses is that evil is frequently generated by pain. Rachaela is inert from the beginning of the books. Her attempts to be fair spring from her unwillingness to enter the arena of the world (I do not blame her). Finally she is galvanized, and at the end of *Darkness, I*, one starts to see a change in her.

The evil of Cain is so awful because it sees nothing in itself that is unreasonable. The evil is *everyday*.

I am not really commenting on the modern world. The world has always been a dreadful place—and *that* is what I am saying, by playing the history of the Scarabae against a contemporary era. It's not a world to bring children into—it never was.

The Blood Opera sequence remains unfinished because the publishers appear not to want it. This is disheartening, but becoming professional, alas, does not mean plain sailing. My personal ship has been be-stormed and shipwrecked many times.

What I had planned to do with the fourth, and probably last, novel had more to do with loss and sadness than evil. The child of Anna and Cain is the reincarnation of black Faran. Another precocious child, he is intent on unsurprising revenge. Berenice too returns, taking a handy body over after an accident. Meanwhile, the devilish Camillo is settling into a bizarre domesticity with Lix and the court of old, now bathed and well-dressed tramps. While for Rachaela, her peace is shattered utterly in a way

I find so terrible I am not even prepared to put it down outside the flesh of the full book.

The ultimate crux of the work is Anna, with Malach, and the resolvement of their centuries long repulsion-attraction.

Other issues would naturally have come into it. But, working as I do, I cannot say when or how. I would have to write it, and this, for now, has been denied me.

M.H. Finally, was there a moment when you discovered you were going to be a writer, or do you think the germ was always there?

T.L. How could I discover I was going to be a writer? I *was* a writer. This was my function, clearly demonstrated.

You see, not having learned to read until almost eight, by nine years I was writing. I wrote fragments of comedy and drama, about oriental princesses and captains, wicked wolves and brave ducks, cats and castles. I had only needed the knack of written language to begin.

When asked at about seven what I wanted to "be," I had replied, an actress. That then, what I wished to become. But what I was was soon self-evident.

Of course, I was not lucky enough to have anything published until my late teens—a miniature in a horror book, for which I received about two pounds. Later some stories and novels for children were published. Not until I was 27, and blasé with disgust at the "world of work"—an unskilled wanderer, who could not become especially fascinated by insurance, waitressing or selling bras, I earned as much scorn (more) as I felt—not till 27, then, did rescue properly appear in the risk-taking innovator Donald A. Wollheim, who bought *The Birthgrave*—and even let me keep the curious title.

There, if you like, was the moment when I realized that Fate would *allow* me to be a writer, that which I had been from nine years, that which I will be, in some form, until I die.

TANITH LEE: BIOGRAPHICAL NOTES

Supplied by Tanith Lee.

Tanith Lee was born in 1947. She had a grammar school education until 17, and thereafter worked in various jobs, as a library assistant, a clerk, a waitress and a shop assistant. At 25 she gave herself a year at art college.

In 1974 DAW books in the United States bought three of her "fantasy"/SF novels, the first of which, *The Birthgrave*, launched her in 1975 into the true role of professional writer (although she had had children's novels published in the early '70s).

Since 1975 she has worked steadily, producing an average of two (sometimes three) books a year. This is not done as hack-work, but because she loves her trade and is, for some reason, a very fast worker—despite writing longhand and then having to type her own work, since no other can read her handwriting.

In 1987 she met the writer John Kaiine, who is twenty years younger than Lee. In 1992 they were married. They now live on the south coast of England, with one black and white and one Siamese cat, in a house full of stained glass, old books and plants.

She has, to date (2000), written and published 68 novels and collections, as well as five so-far unpublished novels and two unpublished collections. She has written over 200 short stories, and most of these are still in print. The BBC (in the '80s) broadcast four of her plays, and she wrote two episodes of the TV series *Blake's Seven*.

In the first episode of *Blake's Seven* she composed the words and melody of a song (which has appeared in an inaccurate and abbreviated version in a *Blake's Seven* magazine). Also, in her radio play *Death if King*, broadcast in 1979, she wrote two songs: "My Heart Is My Harp" (lyrics and music) and the Dies Irae (music only).

Her own illustrations appear in *Delirium's Mistress* and *Night's Sorceries* (Flat Earth), and *Day by Night*, *The Silver Metal Lover*, the collection *Red as Blood* and in a couple of semi-professional magazines. A front page image of hers appears with the hardback of her young adult novel, *Shon the Taken*.

She never ceases to be grateful for her (still precarious) escape into professional writing and out of the so-called "real world" that crushes so many of the good and the talented.

NOTES

Preface

1. For magazines, note *Interzone, Locus, Foundation,* etc. *The Encyclopedia of Science Fiction,* by John Clute and Peter Nicholls (Orbit, 1993), and *The Encyclopedia of Fantasy,* by John Clute and John Grant (Orbit, 1997), both have perceptive entries on Lee.

2. Mike Ashley in the *British Fantasy Society Booklet* No. 18, 1993: *Tanith Lee, Mistress of Delirium,* edited by David Cowperthwaite.

3. Sarah Lefanu, "Robots and Romance." From *Sweet Dreams: Sexuality, Gender and Popular Fiction.* ed. Susannah Radstone. Lawrence & Wishart, London, 1988.

4. See Rosemary Hawley Jarman's foreword to Lee's volume of short stories, *Dreams of Dark and Light.* Arkham House, Sauk City, WI, 1986.

5. Michael R. Collings analyses of Lee's language in *Words and Worlds: The Creation of a Fantasy Universe in Zelazny, Lee and Anthony.* Published in The Scope of the Fantastic—Theory, Technique, Major Authors: Selected Essays from the First International Conference on the Fantastic in Literature and Film, edited by Robert A. Collins and Howard D. Pearce, Greenwood Press, 1985.

6. Sarah Lefanu, *In the Chinks of the World Machine.* The Women's Press, London, 1983.

7. Joan Gordon, "Sharper Than a Serpent's Tooth: The Vampire in Search of Its Mother." In *Blood Read: The Vampire as Metaphor in Contemporary Culture,* edited by V. Hollinger, University of Pennsylvania Press, 1997.

8. Lillian M. Heldreth, "Tanith Lee's Werewolves Within: Reversals of Gothic Tradition." *Journal of the Fantastic in the Arts.* Spring 1989. See also: Heldreth. Author Profile. *Science Fiction & Fantasy Book Review Annual,* 1990.

9. Women's Press, London, 1989.

Introduction

1. In one story, *The Glass Dagger,* Dionysos appears as a statue standing quietly veiled under a studio dustsheet.

2. "Dionysus ... embodiment of universal vitality, is described variously.... He presents himself as woman-in-man, or man-in-woman, the unlimited personality.... Strength mingles with softness, majestic terror with coquettish glances." Carolyn G. Heilbrun (*Towards a Recognition of Androgyny*. Norton, New York. 1982) quoting Thomas G. Rosenmeyer, *Tragedy and Religion: The Bacchae in Euripides*, edited by Erich Segal. Prentice-Hall, 1968.

3. *Death's Master*.

4. Rosemary Jackson, *Fantasy: The Literature of Subversion*, Methuen & Co., Ltd., London, 1981.

5. Frederic Jameson (as quoted by Rosemary Jackson) seems sure of the historicity of myth: "The great realizations of the modern fantastic ... draw their magical power from their unsentimental loyalty to those henceforth abandoned clearings across which higher and lower worlds once passed." But his confidence is not universally shared. Dr. Juliette Wood, in her paper *The Concept of the Goddess*, provides balance: "Modern feminism provides the context for study of the goddess in the last few decades. Within the context of religion, it has attempted to re-balance or re-define the relationship between male/female aspects of the deity.... The existence or non-existence of a unified Goddess religion is an important issue even among writers who reject or offer an alternative."

6. Dr. Wood clarifies a position, quite similar to that which Lee adopts, when she points out that different functions may be served by different ways of regarding the Goddess. The purpose may be historical or poetic. Wood does not seek to invalidate either approach: "Many scholars distinguish clearly, and quite rightly, between a literal interpretation of the Goddess and metaphorical use of the Goddess paradigm. The former accepts as historical fact that an ancient and unified system of belief and practice characterized by a matriarchal culture and centered on a powerful goddess figure existed at some identifiable historical period. The latter sees the Goddess as a non-historical archetype, or poetic metaphor."

Chapter 1

1. Insects, especially butterflies, appear regularly in Lee's work. They reach their height in the Blood Opera with the Scarabae.

2. The term "hubris" is fully appropriate in this context, but it has also been used to mean arrogance, egomania and craving for power in discussing more modern works. Lee too applies the word outside its era.

3. Whether a "goddess of the matriarchy," or even a matriarchy, existed is a matter of much scholarly dispute. I do not propose to enter this debate.

4. The theme of rights over the child is found in many of Lee's books.

5. The two books were originally written as a single volume.

6. The southeast of the then known world was the presumed location of several early mother-religions.

7. The name suggests sun-worshipping Mithrains, with their twin gods of light and darkness who appear in many forms (e.g., Azhrarn) in Lee's work.

8. This resolution conjures up both the reuniting of Persephone and Deme-

ter and traditions of the renewal of nature through the union of the mother goddess with her divine son.

9. Rosemary Jackson, *Fantasy: The Literature of Subversion*. Methuen, 1981.

10. Vengeance for injustice is a common motif in Lee's work.

11. Myth insists that fertility requires a son for the mother goddess.

12. The legend of Amor and Psyche from *The Golden Ass* is subtly present here, as we now see that it has been throughout the book. This story recurs in many different forms throughout Lee's work. Amor also lifts Psyche up into the heavens when, after anointing herself with immortal beauty, she falls into a deathly sleep. When Rarm, a member of a more evolved race than her own, cleanses Uastis of illusion, like Psyche, she becomes aware of both her divine nature and her beauty. Self-knowledge makes her autonomous and complete.

13. These lines are often misprinted and sometimes misquoted. The author verifies this as the correct reading.

14. The mother-son icon recurs, and will later become a central theme in *The Blood of Roses*.

15. Suggesting Ahura Mazda, Mithraic sun god, twin to Ahriman, Serpent of Darkness.

16. Creon's treachery towards Antigone becomes a much more serious transgression in the light of his infidelity to this code.

17. "[A]ll love is love between mother and child ... everything else in love is merely a game and as such inessential." Georg Groddeck, *Exploring the Unconscious*. Vision Press, 1949.

18. "[M]an is horrified ... when he attempts to penetrate too deeply the secrets of the mother-son relationship. No one can escape the bonds which bind him to the mother ... it shapes us and decides our fates. No man ever overcomes the mother within him." Ibid.

19. The meaning of mother-daughter, in relation to the goddess, is a central theme in *Heroine of the World*.

20. C.G. Jung, *Symbols of Transformation*. Routledge & Kegan Paul, 1956.

21. Dionysos, central among sons reborn in the mother goddess, is of Eastern derivation. Jung comments, "The relationship of the son to the mother was the psychological basis of numerous cults ... the myths of Mithras, Adonis, Attis, Osiris, and Dionysus ... are connected with Mother-Goddesses and either a consort or a female double...." Ibid.

22. Robert Graves, *The Greek Myths*. Penguin Books, 1955.

23. This theme is to be taken up extensively in Lee's later work.

24. J.J. Bachofen, *Myth Religion and Motherright*. Routledge & Kegan Paul, 1967. (Note the reference to *swamp*, recalling the Hesseks, as also the all-but-identical appearance of the two Vazkors.)

25. Laius abducts Chrysippus, which Graves also suggests may have indicated the procuring of a surrogate for sacrifice. Graves, ibid.

26. The White Goddess will reappear in other works. Dunizel in the Flat Earth sequence is explicitly compared to the moon.

27. Juliette Wood, in the paper previously referred to, assesses Graves. Of his White Goddess, she remarks: "Graves never makes clear whether this 'goddess' is

a metaphor or a reality.... He entitled it 'an historical grammar of poetic myth' in which myth is a kind of universal poetic discourse.... The popularity of Graves' work stems not just from its subject matter, but in that it shares, in its orientation to the past and in its attitudes to myth, many of the concepts and assumptions which underpin much neo-pagan goddess study."

28. Graves, op. cit. (Note that here Graves aligns history and myth.)

29. There is an element of sympathetic magic in the notion of gaining power through killing. Contact with death may perhaps achieve some control over it. Lee takes this idea much further by giving both Uastis and her son a total experience of *their own* deaths. The later Flat Earth series takes up the specific question of seeking power over death.

30. Miriam Robbins Dexter, *Whence the Goddesses, A Source Book*. Pergamon Press, USA, 1990, p. 82.

Chapter 2

1. In this capacity he is known as *The Lydian*, an epithet for Dionysos.

2. Joseph Campbell, *The Hero with a Thousand Faces*. Meridian Books, USA, 1966.

3. The mystery is powerful. I was obliged to consult with the author to establish with certainty that Rehger died by suicide.

4. This has its precedents in myth, but in this context, whether this is an effect of belonging to a goddess culture, or whether it is a necessary aspect of the hero as Lee perceives him (or both) remains intriguingly debatable. Though there are many regional variations in the vast landscape of this trilogy, the child-bearing function seems to have universal value. Wherever Anackire is worshipped, women appear to have equal status.

5. A definition of early perceptions of godhead. Joseph Campbell, *The Hero with a Thousand Faces*. Meridian Books, 1966.

6. According to Walter Otto (*Dionysus, Myth and Cult*. Indiana University Press, 1965), epiphanies are perceptions of "the world itself as a divine form, as a plenitude of divine configurations ... all of them ... are at the same time cult practices, that is to say expressions or imitations of the glories of being which appeared at the beginning and established the culture through their appearance." The Vis trilogy explores this phenomenon in race and culture specific detail.

7. Readers will note the similarity to the opening sentences of *Birthgrave*. In a letter, Lee writes, "On the White Goddess in *Birthgrave* and Vis, it's really just the Mother goddess, who is also whore, virgin and warrior, and appears in every culture in some form. Karrakaz of course represents this figure in the Birthgrave trilogy—as do other women (Kotta, Malmiranet). These therefore are rooted also in human female perception, no matter what enormous powers they possess. Anackire really is God—He/She/They and It. The closest is probably the Hindu vision, or the Egyptian.... As I think I said, though, I did eventually realize that the albino Amanackire of Vis were also the Hubristic Lost Race of *Birthgrave* and the Vazkor books." To this Lee added that the Vis world and the Birthgrave world are parallel rather than the same.

8. The Amanackire are undeniably racist. They enslave members of darker-skinned races in order to maintain their otherworldly lives and are obsessed with keeping their own strain pure. Rehger asks Aztira, " 'If your race believes in many physical lives, do they ever fear rebirth as some man of Alisaar or woman of the black Zakorians?"/ Startling him, she laughed lightly; all her youngness was in it./ 'Yes,' she said, "they do fear that. They say it would be self-punishment. Why else must we maintain one body against death, but to elude this truly awful fate?'"

Chapter 3

1. Azhrarn's disguise suggests that story is itself a form of disguise.

2. The child at play "manipulates external phenomena in the service of the dream and invests chosen external phenomena with dream meaning and feeling" D.W. Winnicott, *Playing and Reality*. Tavistock Publications, 1971.

3. "Beneath the lightning flashes of Dionysus grew the certainty that the enigmatic god, the spirit of a dual nature and of paradox, had a human mother and therefore, was already by his birth a native of two realms." Walter Otto, *Dionysus, Myth and Cult*. Indiana University Press, 1965.

4. The name echoes that of Jasha in the later *Blood of Roses*, a book preoccupied with trees and vegetal spirits.

5. The seven sisters, or Pleiades, most commonly known as the daughters of Aphrodite, are also found in several earlier systems as daughters of the moon-goddess, who summon the sacred king to his death.

6. Lee's work occasionally suggests that contact is potentially cruel in itself, as in the short story *Gemini* or Zharet's death by ecstasy in *Delusion's Master*.

7. This seems to be the first appearance of Amor, as in the Amor and Psyche of Apuleius's *Golden Ass*. Since Amor, the god of love, would only visit Psyche in the dark, ordinary mortals believed him to be a monster. This tale flits in and out of Lee's work repeatedly, almost as favorite a subtext as that of the dying god.

8. "[I]t is Azhrarn who is the undoubted hero of the three books, almost, one feels, despite the author's attempts in the second and third books to relegate him to the background." Sarah Lefanu, "Robots and Romance." *Sweet Dreams: Sexuality, Gender and Popular Fiction*, Lawrence & Wishart, 1988.

9. Azhrarn and Chuz-Oloru intermittently appear in female form or manifest "feminine" behavior, such as masquerade, unpredictability and, in Oloru, physical cowardice and spells of fainting.

10. "[T]here is no heterosexual norm. Azhrarn, the demon lover, is imbued with great erotic power, and ensnares both men and women." Ibid.

11. William Blake, *The Human Abstract*.

12. In psychoanalytic theory the infant believes in its own magic powers.

13. (3) Zhirem's second immersion in water in *Delirium's Mistress* will have quite different effects, renewing rather than threatening to dissolve him. "Water is … the element in which Dionysus is at home. Like him it betrays a dual nature: a bright, joyous and vital side; and one that is dark, mysterious, dangerous, deathly." Walter Otto, *Dionysus, Cult and Myth*.

14. Lucy Nixon, in her paper *The Cults of Demeter and Kore* (1994), comments

on "the value of pomegranate as an anti-fertility drug," adding that, "The connection of plants with the cults of Demeter and Kore suggests that control of human fertility—both promotion and suppression—might well have been in the hands of women."

15. "[A] creature without consciousness has no possibility of becoming schizophrenic." Gregory Bateson and Mary Catherine Bateson, *Angels Fear*. Macmillan, New York, 1987.

16. "Metaphysical" as in the Metaphysical Poets.

17. Zharet's downfall already looms as she gives the pilgrims her views about a *goddess*. "It seemed to her that the child of a god would be a son.... How could a god choose to manifest his holy seed in female progeny?"

18. See John Donne's *The Ecstasy*.

19. Note Oberon and Titania's quarrel over the Indian boy. Themes or images from *A Midsummer Night's Dream* appear quite often in this sequence.

20. Stone, representing fixity, has strongly negative connotations.

21. Still living because the citizens of Simmurad had once drunk the draught of immortality.

22. Note the shift in the meaning given to stone.

23. The name Soveh, given by her mother, was Dunizel's name in her own childhood. The space between Soveh and Azhriaz, the name given by her father, is bridged with Sovaz. The suffix "az" denotes sorceress.

24. With a kiss he turns her into a tiny green butterfly. Azhrarn apparently punishes troublemakers by transforming them into lower species.

25. Here Azhrarn resembles Lucifer, but falling stars recur: the comet that was part-parent to Dunizel, the falling stars caught by children when Azhrarn visits Baybhelu, Sovaz's cry, "Helpless as a falling star I am."

26. Each Hindu god has a particular beast as transport or vehicle.

27. The use of the present tense indicates a larger shift, a change of era.

28. They had also brought about her mother's death.

29. The lotus is the Eastern symbol of the goddess, and the "jewel in the lotus" represents the sexual union of god and goddess.

30. These passages strongly evoke Blake's views of reason and experience. The quotation recalls the line, "To see the world in a grain of sand."

Chapter 4

1. Tarrocca, still popular in Mediterranean regions, uses a similar deck.

2. Being a closed circuit, it begins again where it ended.

3. Jane Harrison, *Prolegomena to the Study of Greek Religion*. Meridian Books, Cleveland and New York, 1966, p. 588ff. The Wheel of Fortune and the Orphic Wheel are clearly the same.

4. Jane Harrison, *Themis*. Merlin Press, London, 1963, p. 467ff.

5. Apart from its connection with Diana and witches, Dia is an alternative name for Naxos, the island of Ariadne's abandonment.

6. Maria Louise von Franz, *Apuleius*. Spring Publications, Zurich.

7. Alfred Douglas, *The Tarot*. Penguin Books, 1980.

8. "[I]n the legend of the desertion [of Ariadne] Theseus and Dionysos are obvious doubles." (Jane Harrison, *Themis*, Merlin Press, London, 1977, p.322, footnote 4.) Walter Otto calls Ariadne's myth an "alternation of acute ecstasy with heart-rending woe.... In this we recognize the duality of all Dionysiac being." (*Dionysus, Myth and Cult*. Indiana University Press, 1965.)

9. For a full account of Hermes, see N.O. Brown, *Hermes the Thief*. Vintage Books, New York, 1969.

10. Alfred Douglas. Ibid.

11. The Egyptian-based card of The Wheel of Fortune, meaning reincarnation and the beginning of another cycle, has a jackal clinging to it.

12. The Hanged Man indicates helpless stasis between the world of the living and the world of the dead. Both Thenser and Aradia occupy this position, condemned to death until saved by the other.

13. In the Egyptian Book of the Dead the goddess is represented as a knife. E. Neumann, *The Great Mother*, Bollingen Foundation, 1955.

14. Wiparvet: Wepwawet or Upuaut, an Osirian god of the dead, and opener of "the way." *Larousse Encyclopedia of Mythology*, Hamlyn.

15. The same infinity symbol, a figure 8 that hovers above the head of The Magician, is transformed into a woman's hat on the card of Strength.

16. The wolf, Wiparvet, also seems to be more than himself. It is the time of Lupercalia, which refers specifically to Pan and fertility, and suggests the Roman mother-wolf. Italian folklore enters in the comment that the wolf-god has "left no pawmarks on the ground, for lupins to grow." He is also the dog Anubis, like Hermes, Lord of the Land of the Dead, the dog-like animal that clings to The Wheel of Fortune, symbol of the cycle of death and reincarnation, and the dog that stands baying at the entrance to the underworld in the card of The Moon. Roman prostitutes were known as Lupae.

17. N.O. Brown, *Hermes the Thief*. Vintage Books, New York, 1969.

18. Presumably Wiparvet-Anubis.

19. Like the Buddhist concept of "earth turning into water," this indicates release from a state of constriction.

20. Both in the plot and as aspects of Aradia and Thenser, Irmenck and the boy painter have parallel qualities. The boy oscillates between planes of reality, Irmenck is blamed for non-existent crimes. Helpers and messengers, both fit the role of page. The Tarot Page of Cups is poetic and clairvoyant; the Page of Wands signifies faithfulness.

21. The card of The Chariot shows a man in armor, holding a wand and being pulled by two horses or sphinxes. The cards of Chariot, Devil and also The Hierophant all have *two* attached creatures serving them. Horses and sphinxes refer to the mother-goddess. The card itself can be taken as an emblem of victory—or its opposite, if reversed. The significance of Aradia's "chariot" as she sets out on her final journey is clear.

22. Dolphins, emblems of both Aphrodite and Isis, are symbols of love, both psychopomps and saviors in the soul's journey over the sea of death.

23. Retka's oriental origins are firmly underlined. Thenser tells Aradia, "His granddam on the maternal side was an Eastern princess of Taras with green-black hair," establishing his connection with reincarnation and mother-rites. His name

suggests Seker, the Egyptian lord of death and precursor to Satan. He obviously represents the Tarot card of The Devil.

24. The Virgin Mary (goddess) as tower is recognized in Catholic litanies as 'Tower of Ivory.'

25. See Lee's short story "The Golden Rope" (*Red as Blood*, DAW Books, New York, 1983), with its inverted tower.

26. Ariadne, Cretan fertility goddess, is reputed to have hanged herself. Disjointed body parts were hung in trees in Crete as part of a fertility rite. The Hanged Man of the Tarot is portrayed hanging upside-down.

27. The color blue is significant. A butterfly found on Gurz's windowsill is "tiny and piercingly blue." Gurz requests her to wear her blue dress.

28. For psychological ramifications of this myth see Erich Neumann, *Amor and Psyche*. Routledge & Kegan Paul, 1956.

29. Theseus returning by ship to Attica forgets to change his black sails to white ones and causes his father's suicide. White sails here suggest that Thenser-Theseus has finally remembered himself and his promises.

Chapter 5

1. *Drinking Sapphire Wine* was originally a sequel to *Don't Bite the Sun*. Later published under one title, they are now reprinted in the USA as *Biting the Sun*.

2. Perhaps, once again, this passage might be given a secondary reading as some kind of description of Lee's own perceptions and methodology.

3. If robots can hate, can they also love? The question is examined in *The Silver Metal Lover*.

4. The narrator revives duels out of an *abnormal* interest in history. Abnormal because memory/the past stand in naked opposition to the Sapphire Wine of the title, which induces forgetfulness.

5. Mary Midgely discusses these issues in her book *Animals and Why They Matter—a Journey Around the Species Barrier*. Pelican Original, 1983.

6. Appropriately, *theatre* is also the locus for surgery.

7. Mesmer died one year after Mary Shelley's elopement, and *mesmerism* is linguistically in keeping with gothic science. The theme of *playing god* is taken much further in *Day by Night*.

8. "(Did she know what she was? She was his creation.)" Multiple parentheses blur the boundaries between rhetorical, authorial or scientific comments.

9. The frequent motif of twins appears in many texts and will be central in *Sung in Shadow* and *The Book of the Mad*. Twins serve many purposes.

10. The word "phase" calls to mind the "mirror phase" as used by Lacan and Winnicott and its part in forming an identity.

11. Robots vary from being semi-slaves to respected servers of the gods.

12. This passage recalls Azhriaz's flight into chaos and transformation into a child. Certain sources of madness are clearly stated.

Chapter 6

1. The name Anna is also used in the Blood Opera when a ritual stabbing to the heart leads to reincarnation.

2. The androgyne or hermaphrodite is central in alchemichal change.

3. Lee's fusing of Paris with Paradys aligns itself with the medieval habit of describing cities as *Paradise*—havens of order, refuges from the wilderness. During the Black Death, Paradise becomes Hell on earth.

4. Fero: as in *ferox*, wild or savage, but more importantly as in *ferous*, bearing, producing.

5. Lee may be specifically indicating the Luciferians who believed that Lucifer was the brother of god. The brother-sister pair mirror this relation. But the text seems to intend a composite, and the main issue is the division between good and bad creators. The sister is an enlightened outcast, paralleling Lucifer; the brother clings to the orthodox church.

6. Friedrich Heer, *The Medieval World Europe from 1100-1350*. Weidenfeld and Nicholson, 1962.

7. This type of woman appears again in *Blood of Roses*.

8. The name *Imago* is attached to the Roman occupation of the site of Paris and will reappear as the location for *The Book of the Beast*.

9. Heer, op. cit.

10. The winter Feast of Fools and the Ass celebrates Janus, the twin deity who, like Jhane, has two faces.

11. Berlin associates itself more readily with this sort of gender perversity than Paris, but Louis is on his way to "another city," somewhere further north, and Anna Sanjeanne was also traveling north. Lee confirms the Germanic aspect, explaining that "Paradys is a parallel, partly Paris, partly Alsatian." She puts the date at "a combination of 1910 and 1920."

12. Lee continues: "I remembered the children's game: *Who's there? Who's there? No one is there. Then ask Monsieur No One in.*" In *The Book of the Beast*, Monsieur No One is the name given to the beast by the servants.

13. Lee cites this as a line from Galen, adding: "Caerulei mundi regna was supposed to come from 'Pliny the Other'—I made this gentleman up, though he exists in the parallel world. Galen seems to obtain in both, and so, of course, quotes him. The concept of the Kingdoms above the Sky, Empires of Azure, also mine."

14. Lee returns to the "primitive" in other texts, notably *Blood of Roses*.

15. This explains the momentary appearance of a Roman in *Empires of Azure*.

16. Thot is the inventor of writing, the patron of magic and a being able to penetrate the land of the dead and the underworld.

17. "Prehistoric cults made bears and wolves into Lords of the Beasts." Mircea Eliade, *A History of Religious Ideas*. Collins, 1979.

18. Lamiae have also been equated with Lilith or the daughters of Lilith.

19. The flower of Lilith or Astarte, the lily or lotus represents the yoni, the goddess and the Virgin Mary. It also recalls the ambiguous Marie-Lis of *Malice in Saffron*.

20. Edgar Wind, *Pagan Mysteries of the Renaissance*. Peregrine Books 1967.

21. Marie-Louise von Franz, *Apuleius' Golden Ass*. Spring Publications, 1974.

22. H. E. Butler's translation of *The Metamorphoses or Golden Ass of Apuleius of Madaura*. Clarendon Press, Oxford, 1910.

23. For utuk, see *New Larousse Encyclopedia of Mythology*, Hamlyn.

24. Eliade (op. cit.) explains that the Sumerian world was created from the body of the divine Tiamat, but her subsequent demonization meant that the universe and man's body were made of both divine and demonic substance. The Tiy-Amonet of *Empires of Azure* connects with the goddess Tiamat "the tumultuous sea" and original female-but-also-androgynous waters of the beginning. She creates the world, but also many monsters with claws and the heads of animals. Eventually she is destroyed and displaced by Marduk.

25. Mircea Eliade, *The Sacred and the Profane*. Harper Torchbooks, 1961.

26. The value of such objects varies in other books: The flawed diamond of *Heart Beast* is "priceless"; Sabella's bloodstone is inexpensive; a tiny ivory elephant is sold to a servant girl for one penny in *Elephantasm*.

27. Both stories open with a drowned girl being pulled from the river. Jausande's drowning is genuine, but in *Elle Est Trois* only a clump of debris is pulled from the water. Meanwhile, a poet hallucinates a woman resembling the vampiric Antonina and personifying the death that will follow an orgy of writing under opium. The story also comments that the poet would have provided "some linking device, some cause, a romantic mathematic.... A ring possibly, with a curse on it." Dates of composition suggest this story is an early nucleus for the sequence.

28. See *Empires of Azure*, footnote 13.

29. The soul of Dionysos was trapped in a mirror by the Titans. Perhaps the sculpture is kept covered to prevent a similar entrapment. The image, whether in mirror, representation or photograph, is always dangerous.

30. The "truth of Yshtar" is her beauty, jealousy of which is perhaps the real cause of Valmé's distress. Lee has suggested that perhaps Yshtar is the real object of Valmé's desire.

31. *Down Below* appears in *The House of Fear*, by Leonora Carrington, reprinted by Virago Press. Carrington speaks of being led across "the initial border of Knowledge." During her stay in the hospital, she experiences a cosmic consciousness where her blood is transformed into "comprehensive energy—masculine and feminine, microcosmic and macrocosmic—and into a wine drunk by the sun and moon." Even her suitcase label becomes significant. She *is* "manipulating the firmament," she becomes all things—"the third person of the Trinity ... an androgyne, the Moon, the Holy Ghost, a gypsy, an acrobat" and so on. An injection of psychotropic drugs is "a sacrificial moment." When she recovers her sanity, her "cosmic objects, my night creams and nail buff, had lost their significance."

32. Lethe, a river outside the boundaries of Paradys in *Stained with Crimson*, is now "mercury-colored" (viz Hermes, and his connections with the dead) and flows through the center of the city.

33. For an excellent account of The Salpetriere in the nineteenth century, see Elaine Showalter's *The Female Malady*, Virago.

34. The name *Oblatic* (Citalbo) instantly suggests *oblation* or sacrifice. (Hilde is also referred to as a sacrifice.) The other two names are more obscure. *Samoht* (Thomas) maybe suggests the name of a demon, and Tolehcim (Michelot) has a

Mexican resonance appropriate to the life of Leonora Carrington, who settled in Mexico after her release from hospital. "Smara" means memory in Hindu mythology. One is tempted to rearrange the name "Felion" as "No-life."

35. Maybe in reference to left brain and right brain, he keeps to the left side going into the labyrinth and the right side coming out. A later quotation reinforces this interpretation: "See, the Minotaur has two daughters; call them 'Left' and 'Right.'"

36. Here Felion is equipped with Psyche's traditional weapons.

37. A penguin's amber markings resemble a necklace. The Great Penguin is eventually identified as *Koodjanuk*, whom "The ice peoples invoke ... to heal the sick." Koodjanuk also suggests Mexican gods who were often birds, and Leocadia's penguin has an "obsidian" beak.

38. Johanos is noted for his stage role as "The Roman."

Chapter 7

1. The harp indicates Celtic affiliations.

2. Perhaps it is a little idiosyncratic to read the meaning "funny words" into the name of Parl Dro. But "droll" is also the term for a Celtic wandering storyteller or minstrel—and all of this is rather a tall story.

3. It will be remembered that the similar figure of Vazkor senior in *Birthgrave* felt no erotic desire—his son existed only to further his power. Dro's son is the result of desire, and serves no apparent purpose. Whether Dro "does" or "doesn't" provokes constant prurient curiosity.

4. The Silky is a Celtic fairy or ghost. "The Northumbrian and Border Silky ... is always female.... The tree was long called 'Silky's Chair'." *A Dictionary of Fairies*, Katharine Briggs. Penguin Books, 1977

5. Caesar mentions Celtic/Druid burning of human sacrifices.

6. Like Vazkor senior, Dro also always wears black.

7. Her name suggests Sidhe, the Celtic word for fairy, appropriate to a story so infused with a Celtic and twilight atmosphere.

8. As a version of *Roland*, Roilant presumably refers to Ariosto's *Madness of Roland*. Also note Tasso's *Jerusalem*. References to the genre of Romance and themes of Courtly Love seem generalized.

9. Note *cire*, French for *wax*.

10. Lee's habit of producing a further, closely related text espousing a contradictory standpoint collapses into a single passage here.

11. The Chenti are also known as the Gattapulettas for their heraldic leopard. Iulet is often called "kitten" or "catling." Mercurio reiterates Shakespeare when he refers to Leopardo's "nine lives." Tributes to *Romeo and Juliet* are too numerous to mention, appearing in the dialogue and other forms, as in the transformation of Mercutio's curious speech about Queen Mab in her wagon into Iulet's entrance at the betrothal party, drawn in a snail shell and escorted by insects.

12. E.M.W. Tillyard, *The Elizabethan World Picture*. Chatto & Windus, 1952.

13. A rival to early Christianity, Orphism focused on release from the Great Wheel and rebirth through the underworld Persephone. Its text was the *Descent into Hades*.

14. This is highly explicit in the Vis sequence, where the coupling of twins is required for the reincarnation of the goddess. Although Shakespeare does not especially associate his several sets of twins with incest, it can seem to lurk beneath the surface anyway, as in *Twelfth Night* where each twin is first attached to and then exchanged by a same-sex adult already romantically linked to the other. Certainly Shakespeare was strongly aware of the erotic possibilities of twins.

15. Edgar Wind, *Pagan Mysteries in the Renaissance*. Faber & Faber, 1958.

16. "Ecstasy of the shamanic type ... implies belief in a 'soul' able to leave the body and travel freely through the world ... myths, legends and rites related to ascent to the sky and 'magical flight' (wings, feathers of birds of prey—eagle falcon) are bound up with certain oneiric and ecstatic experiences specifically characteristic of shamanism." Mircea Eliade, *A History of Religious Ideas*. Collins, London, 1979.

17. Like the Black God of the garden of Veshum, in *Death's Master*.

18. In line with the primitive belief that menstrual blood was the source of fertility and renewal of Mother Earth, Barbayat appears to be interested only in the blood of women.

19. A psychoanalytic study of Volkahavaar would categorize his sadism, destructiveness, desire for domination as Reichian. His making of a "god," along with his evident fascination with both theater and illusions, suggest Adler's "fictions," whereby feelings of inferiority are converted into those of superiority. Stripped of *illusions*, he is a pathetic sight.

20. Mircea Eliade, op. cit. See also Claude Lévi Strauss, *The Raw and the Cooked*.

21. In the original fairy story of Barbayaga, the young girl, sent to live in the witch's house, proves her goodness by her kindness to mice.

22. In its simplicity, this resembles Aradia's gift of nettles and chrysanthemums to the black goddess in the House of Night.

Chapter 8

1. Tanaquil is a pre–Roman variant of the goddess Tanit.

Chapter 9

1. Character has been a consideration in its present sense for less than a millennium.

2. Epic heroes often have dead or supernatural mothers, which makes them children of Nature or the Goddess. If we take Mechail to be the hero, he has a supernatural mother; if Angelen, we must say he is, like various pagan deities, born or reborn from a tree.

3. In line with Lee's usual position, this is not literal Christianity. The sacred content here can also be related to other religions.

4. Anymore than the part-formed religion knows the shape it will take.

5. The single exception predating the era when human emotion can be considered as such is mother-love, a feeling common to humans and animals.

6. In ancient thought, deformity always had meaning. Abnormal was also paranormal. Thus Mechi, the dwarf, is seen by the villagers to be "a changeling ...

a demon's slough," but the Traveller girl "took him according to her own creed, for something ripe with potential, the marked of God."

7. Mircea Eliade, *Myths, Dreams and Mysteries*. Fontana Library, 1968.
8. J.M. Frazer, *The Golden Bough*. Macmillan, 1957.
9. Ibid.
10. An aspect of Anjelen's insatiable blood-thirst may perhaps arise from a loss of corporeal existence.
11. Mircea Eliade, *Myths, Dreams and Mysteries*. Fontana, 1968.
12. Viz Jhane's laying on of hands in *Malice in Saffron*.
13. The emphasis on paying and buying has a profane character.
14. In both *Mind and Nature* (Wildwood House, 1979) and *Angels Fear* (Rider, London, 1988), Gregory Bateson extends the concept of mind into "interfaces" that are inseparable either from each other or from matter. "The separation of 'mind' from 'matter' and the *cogito* established bad premises, perhaps ultimately lethal premises, for Epistomology."
15. "[T]he Protestant interpretation of the words 'This is my Body—This is my Blood' substitutes something like 'This stands for my Body—This stands for my Blood.' This way of interpretation banished from the Church that part of the mind that makes metaphor, poetry and religion—the part of the mind that most belonged in Church—but *you cannot keep it out*." Gregory Bateson and Mary Catherine Bateson, *Angels Fear*. Century Hutchinson Ltd., 1988. It is from this sort of position that Lee takes her great leap backwards into a fully archaic world.
16. The Knights of God resemble the Knights Templar in their wealth, their secret rituals, the practice of alchemy, the wearing of swords, etc.
17. Mechail also drank blood when he rose from the dead.
18. She dies choking on a worm/serpent in a bleeding apple.
19. Taboos relating to female blood—discussed earlier—existed in Judaic and Muslim contexts, as well as Ancient Greece. Christianity has partially submerged them, but they persist in churching, a ceremonial cleansing once necessary before a woman could reenter a church after childbirth. The polluting power of female blood is crucial in resolving this narrative.
20. Stone was used in a similar way in the Flat Earth sequence, with the image of Zhirek fixed forever in hatred and rigidity in a desert stone.
21. For a full account of the dangers of pollution by women, especially their blood, see Mary Douglas's *Purity and Danger*.
22. Corresponding with lizards, as used in the *Birthgrave* sequence.
23. *A Midsummer Night's Dream* is negatively evoked in Anjelen's efforts to make Anillia sleep. Lee's forests always seem to evoke this play.
24. In fact, Jasha destroys Anjelen's chastity—thus Anillia's statement includes her in a fusion of son and daughter.
25. See D.W. Winnicott, *Playing and Reality*. Tavistock Publications, 1971. Lee's account of the making of Mechailus uses a range of signifiers that strongly resemble Winnicott's: the mirror, the transitional object (Mechi's projection of himself as dwarf), and others.

Chapter 10

1. The theme of prostitution as in *The Blood of Roses*.
2. Vide the shape-changing Martians of Ray Bradbury's *Martian Chronicles*.
3. "Feeding and sucking play a large part in the perversion of life forces. In the bizarre and sinister 'Sirriamnis' a young slave girl ... becomes a hare and sucks the semen of her lover/master...." Sarah Lefanu, *In the Chinks of the World Machine*. The Women's Press, London, 1988.
4. Lee's short story *Fleur de Fur* also compares vampire favorably with man and contains the same theme of maternal nurture as essential to love.
5. Lee gives her the voice of a beleaguered Shylock.
6. Lagenay derives from "*loups gens aieux,*" which Christian sees carved into the fireplace, as also from *loup garou*.
7. In the Saxon calendar, the first month of the year is the month of The Wolf. This element of the story recalls the wolf god that appears near the feast of Lupercalia in *A Heroine of the World*.
8. An article in Small Press 1989, points out that Lee's werewolves behave exactly like a real wolf pack, headed by a dominant, maternal-reproductive female. Lillian M. Heldreth, *Tanith Lee's Werewolves Within: Reversals of Gothic Traditions*. Orion Publishing, USA.
9. The lily symbolizes the Virgin Mary and, in the hand of the angel Gabriel of the Annunciation, her fertilization also. The name Gabrielle further fuses Christian and pagan entities. (And, Lee comments, also refers to Saki's werewolf *Gabriel Ernest*.)
10. The wolf's maternal function is best known in the adoption of Romulus and Remus. The doctor, referring to the forest goddess, says, "The Romans ... had a name for her." He means the Roman goddess Lupa, whose winter rites were celebrated to ensure fertility.
11. The absence of water near Christian's chateau suggests sterility.
12. Due to be published the following year, *The Book of the Mad*, according to Lee, existed in note form at the time of writing *Heart-Beast*.
13. Susan Stewart, *Nonesense*. The John Hopkins Press, Baltimore and London, 1978, 1979.
14. His name associating him with sun gods, Hyperion embodies Apollonian traits against Daniel's Dionysian characteristics. When Daniel kisses Hyperion on the lips he is expressing a sacred link between the two gods. The name Daniel comes from the triple moon-goddess Danae, also the Three Fates. The name's masculine form is Dan or Dan El.
15. Walter F. Otto, in his *Dionysus*, states that Dionysos possesses "a savagery that is absolutely, without mercy.... He is called 'render of men,' 'the eater of raw flesh' ... we hear not only of human sacrifice in his cult but also of the ghastly ritual in which a man is torn to pieces."

Like Lee's Hyperion, Dionysos, as Pentheus, had his head torn off.

The word Sacrifice, engraved on the comet-shard, resembles the name Oblatic, used by Leocadia's mysterious uncle.

16. Ganesh, a plump, benevolent god with the head of an elephant, is, in Lee's words, "Lord of Beginnings, Maker and Taker of Obstacles, The Mountain which Moves." He is also a god of fertility.

17. Luksmi is a form of Laksmi, goddess of good fortune and consort of Vishnu. The goddess Laksmi is described as brilliant, shining, and is especially honored at Diwali, the festival of lights.

18. The Persian king Darius was noted for religious tolerance. Although Zoroastrianism emphasized the need for women to be controlled by men, and consigned the majority of women to hell, King Darius made no attempt to force it upon his subjects. The Parsees (Zoroastrians) were absorbed when they migrated there. The *Larousse Encyclopedia of Mythology* (Hamlyn) states, "the duality Mithra-Ahura ... corresponds to the duality Mitra-Varuna of the Vedas ... for it is time, marked by the revolutions of the sun, which regulates the alternation of light and darkness."

References to India's overlapping cultures are frequent. The raja is Moslem, his sister Hindu. He says, "...all the gods are emanations of the One.... my sister had a Hindu mother. Am I to dismay my sister?" Smolte sits inert and bored as Withers and the raja recite "their Persian and Greek poetry."

19. Resembling Aradia with her pot of camelias.

20. Indra is a god of both war and fertility.

Chapter 11

1. They are also albinos—as found in several other texts.

Chapter 12

1. Lee points out, "Perhaps it is salient that Ruth was not cremated. Her rotting and partly eaten body is found near the end of *Personal Darkness*. (The family of Lix, however, die by fire, are even burned alive in *Darkness I*.)"

2. "Burkhardt ... traces the transmission of alchemy from before the rise of the Egyptian civilization, through to Alexandria, where it was codified and placed in the largely written form in which it was transmitted both to the West ... and to the East...." Arthur Versluis, *The Philosophy of Magic*. Arkana Paperbacks, 1986. The burning of the Great Library at Alexandria is also relevant here.

3. Lee also comments that to portray Rachaela as infantile is potentially lopsided: One could equally say that "to fail to accept the laws of the world is, rather than childlike, the only sane response."

4. There is often a Looking Glass inversion in names: Ruth, signifying pity, has none; with a biblical namesake renowned for maternal kindness, Rachaela actively rejects children; far from being the first man, Adamus is the last potent Scarabae male.

5. Wearing armor, riding a rocking-horse, or trailing the hobbyhorse which will later adorn his motorbike, reciting long unsolicited tales, Camillo suggests the White Knight of *Alice*. In *Personal Darkness*, Rachaela and Althene are "the Red Queen and the White Queen."

"The White Queen is the symbol of the purification of Quicksilver; the Red King is the symbol of purification of Sulphur, through Fire." Ibid.

6. *Althene* suggests *Pallas Athene*, running together male and female, warrior and mother. Malachi, an O.T. prophet, was concerned with marital fidelity and the Day of Judgment.

7. Surprisingly, Malach is Camillo's father.

8. The *ka* is one of the seven souls, believed by the Ancient Egyptians to be the soul that made it possible for a man to become a god after death. It is a twin-soul, associated with blood and the Mother.

9. The "night sea journey," with its "aim of resurrection," is discussed in C.G. Jung's *Psychology and Alchemy*.

10. Another alchemical reference. The mater, or other half of god, is dormant in the matter of the world, and is thus the *mother* of what is created.

11. Blood as repository of life and vehicle of the soul is central to Scarabae ritual. Even Malach, when offered a chalice filled with blood, makes token participation. He "dipped in two fingers.... These he touched to his lips."

12. Referring to "the male rapes by Cain," Lee says, "In Ancient Egypt ... sodomy of one either unwilling or resisting was a show of power-strength, not so much a sexual act—like female rape, of course. Cain is ... attempting to reduce Malach in a way that will, if successful, defile and lessen Malach on his own terms. Obviously Malach, Cain and Ruth-Anna have struggled previously in Egypt."

13. Richard Dawkins, *The Selfish Gene*. Oxford University Press, 1976.

14. The primitive silverfish is an example of the insect's capacity for exceptional survival.

15. Ibid.

16. Ibid.

17. Ibid.

18. Dawkins points out that the battle for survival also appears in the competition between memes. And genes, desiring to remain unaltered, are also at war with memes, whose basic purpose is to bring about change. His memes "resemble the early replicating molecules, floating chaotically in the primeval soup, rather than modern genes in their neatly paired, chromosomal regiments." Lee's chaotic Scarabae are frequently associated with just such a fluid medium. Their first house stands by the sea; Sylvian is cremated on the beach and returned into the sea. During her *alchemical* night sea voyage, Rachaela refers to the sea as the source of life. "To lie above the sea was to lie in the womb. She had felt this gentle motion before, in the blood-heart-cave of her own mother." A story of the Scarabae past describes a flight by ship, during which Sacha gives birth to a stillborn child which, presumably under the overwhelming influence of the sea, looks like a mermaid.

19. Ibid.

Conclusion

1. The bibliography lists Lee's subsequent works.

2. Lee explains why this sequence remains unfinished in the interview that follows. Another volume with the title *Darker Ages* was intended, and possibly a further volume after that.

BIBLIOGRAPHY

For reasons of space, Lee's novellas, short stories, most collections of short stories and radio and television plays have been omitted here. I have given only first publication dates. Mike Ashley has compiled a much fuller bibliography of Lee's work.

The Novels of Tanith Lee

The Dragon Hoard. Macmillan. London. 1971.
Princess Hynchatti and Some Other Surprises. Macmillan. London. 1972.
The Birthgrave. DAW Books. N.Y. 1975.
Companions on the Road. Macmillan. London. 1975.
Don't Bite the Sun. DAW Books. N.Y. 1976.
The Storm Lord. DAW Books. N.Y. 1976.
The Winter Players. Macmillan. London. 1976.
Drinking Sapphire Wine. DAW Books. N.Y. 1977. (Later published in a single volume with *Don't Bite the Sun*.)
Volkhavaar. DAW Books. N.Y. 1977.
East of Midnight. Macmillan. London. 1977.
Vazkor, Son of Vazkor. DAW Books. N.Y. 1978.
Quest for the White Witch. DAW Books. N.Y. 1978.
The Castle of Dark. Macmillan. London. 1978.
Night's Master. DAW Books. N.Y. 1978.
Death's Master. DAW Books. N.Y. 1979.
Electric Forest. DAW Books. N.Y. 1979.
Shon the Taken. Macmillan. London. 1979.
Sabella, or the Blood Stone. DAW Books. N.Y. 1980.
Kill the Dead. DAW Books. N.Y. 1980.
Day by Night. DAW Books. N.Y. 1980
Lycanthia, or the Children of the Wolves. DAW Books. N.Y. 1981.
Delusion's Master. DAW Books. N.Y. 1981.
The Silver Metal Lover. Science Fiction book Club. N.Y. 1981.

Prince on a White Horse. Macmillan. London. 1982.
Cyrion. DAW Books. N.Y. 1982.
Sung in Shadow. DAW Books. N.Y. 1983.
Anackire. DAW Books. N.Y. 1983.
Days of Grass. DAW Books. N.Y. 1985.
Delirium's Mistress. DAW Books. N.Y. 1986.
Night's Sorceries. DAW Books. N.Y. 1987.
The White Serpent. DAW Books. N.Y. 1988.
The Book of the Damned. Unwin Books. London. 1988.
The Book of the Beast. Unwin Books. London. 1988.
A Heroine of the World. DAW Books. N.Y. 1989.
The Blood of Roses. Legend. London. 1990.
Black Unicorn. Macmillan Atheneum. N.Y. 1991.
The Book of the Dead. Overlook Press. Woodstock, N.Y. 1991.
Dark Dance. Macdonald. London. 1992.
Heart-Beast. Headline. London. 1992.
Elephantasm. Headline. London. 1993.
Personal Darkness. Little, Brown. London. 1993.
The Book of the Mad. Overlook Press. Woodstock, N.Y. 1993.
Darkness, I. Little, Brown. London. 1944.
Eva Fairdeath. Headline. London. 1944.
Vivia. Little, Brown. London. 1995.
Reigning Cats and Dogs. Headline. London. 1996.
When the Lights Go Out. Headline. London. 1996.
The Gods Are Thirsty. Overlook Press. Woodstock, N.Y. 1996.
Red Unicorn. Byron Press. USA. 1997
Faces Under Water. Overlook Press. Woodstock, N.Y. 1998.
Law of the Wolf Tower. Hodder. London. 1998.
Saint Fire. Overlook Press. Woodstock, N.Y. 1999
Wolf Star Rise. Hodder. London. 1999.
Islands in the Sky. Basset Series. Random House. N.Y. 1999.
White as Snow. Tor Books. N.Y. 2000.
Queen of the Wolves. Hodder. London. 2000.

To come: *Wolf Wing.*
           A Bed of Earth.
           Venus Preserved.

Works by Other Authors

Apuleius. *The Golden Ass.*
Ashley, Mike. "The Towers of Tanith: Aspects of Imagery in the Fairy Tales of Tanith Lee." *Tanith Lee, Mistress of Delirium*, edited by David Cowperthwaite. British Fantasy Society Booklet No 18. 1993.

Bibliography 213

Bachofhen, J.J. *Myth Religion and Motherright*. Routledge & Kegan Paul. 1967.
Bataille, Georges. *Literature and Evil*. Calder and Boyars, London. 1973.
Bateson, Gregory. *Mind and Nature*. Wildwood House. 1979.
Bateson, Gregory, and Mary Catherine Bateson. *Angels Fear*. Rider, London. 1988.
Blake, William. *The Human Abstract*.
Briggs, Katharine. *A Dictionary of Fairies*. Penguin Books. 1977.
Brown, N.O. *Hermes the Thief*. Vintage Books, N.Y. 1969.
Campbell, Joseph. *The Hero with a Thousand Faces*. Meridian Books, USA. 1966.
Carter, Angela. *Wise Children*. Vintage. 1991.
Clute, John, and John Grant. *The Encyclopedia of Fantasy*. Orbit. 1997.
Clute, John, and Peter Nicholls. *The Encyclopedia of Science Fiction*. Orbit. 1993.
Collings, Michael R. "Words and Worlds: The Creation of a Fantasy Universe in Zelazny, Lee and Anthony." Published in *The Scope of the Fantastic- Theory, Technique, Major Authors: Selected Essays from the First International Conference on the Fantastic in Literature and Film*, edited by Robert A. Collins and Howard D. Pearce. Greenwood Press. 1985.
Dawkins, Richard. *The Selfish Gene*. Oxford University Press. 1976.
Dexter, Miriam Robbins. *Whence the Goddesses, A Source Book*. Pergamon Press. USA. 1990.
Douglas, Alfred. *The Tarot*. Penguin Books. 1980.
Eliade, Mircea. *A History of Religious Ideas*. Collins. 1979.
Eliade, Mircea. *Myths, Dreams and Mysteries*. Fontana Library. 1968.
Eliade, Mircea. *The Sacred and the Profane*. Harper Torchbooks. 1961.
Eliade, Mircea. *Shamanism: Archaic Techniques of Ecstasy*. Bollingen Series, Princeton University Press. 1972.
Fraser, J.M. *The Golden Bough*. Macmillan. 1957.
Gordon, Joan. "Sharper than a Serpent's Tooth: The Vampire in Search of Its Mother." From *Blood Read: The Vampire as Metaphor in Contemporary Culture*, edited by V. Hollinger. University of Pennsylvania Press. 1997.
Graves, Robert. *The Greek Myths*. Penguin Books. 1995.
Groddeck, Georg. *Exploring the Unconscious*. Vision Press. 1949.
Harrison, Jane. *Prolegomena to the Study of Greek Religion*. Meridian Books, Cleveland and New York. 1966.
Harrison, Jane. *Themis*. Merlin Press. London. 1977.
Hawley Jarman, Rosemary. Preface to *Dreams of Dark and Light*. Arkham House. Sauk City, WI. 1986.
Heer, Frederich. *The Medieval World Europe from 1100 to 1350*. Weidenfeld and Nicholson, London. 1962.
Heilbrun, Carolyn G. *Towards a Recognition of Androgyny*. Norton. 1982.
Heldreth, Lillian M. Author Profile, *Science Fiction and Fantasy Book Review Annual*. 1990.
Heldreth, Lillian M. "Tanith Lee's Werewolves Within: Reversals of Gothic Tradition." *Journal of the Fantastic in the Arts*. Spring 1989.
Jackson, Rosemary. *Fantasy: The Literature of Subversion*. Methuen & Co., Ltd., London. 1981.
Jung, C.G. *Psychology and Alchemy*. Routledge & Kegan Paul. 1953.

Jung, C.G. *Symbols of Transformation*. Routledge & Kegan Paul. 1956.
Larousse Encyclopedia of Mythology. Hamlyn.
Lefanu, Sarah. *In the Chinks of the World Machine*. The Women's Press, London. 1988.
Lefanu, Sarah. "Robots and Romance." *Sweet Dreams: Sexuality, Gender and Popular Fiction*. ed. Susannah Radstone. Lawrence & Wishart, London. 1988.
Midgely, Mary. *Animals and Why They Matter—a Journey Round the Species Barrier*. Pelican Original, London. 1983.
Neumann, Erich. *Amor and Psyche*. Routledge & Kegan Paul. 1956.
Nixon, Lucy. *The Cults of Demeter and Kore*. Seminar paper, delivered to series—Gender Studies: The Ancient World. Oxford, 1994.
Otto, Walter F. *Dionysus, Myth and Cult*. Indiana University Press. 1965.
Rosenmeyer, Thomas G. *Tragedy and Religion: The Bacchae and Euripides*, edited by Erich Segal. Prentice-Hall. 1968.
Showalter, Elaine. *The Female Malady*. Virago, London. 1987.
Stewart, Susan. *Nonesense*. The John Hopkins Press, Baltimore. 1978.
Tillyard, E.M.W. *The Elizabethan World Picture*. Chatto & Windus. 1952.
Versluis, Arthur. *The Philosophy of Magic*. Arkana Paperbacks. 1986.
Von Franz, Maria Louise. *Apuleius*. Spring Publications, Zurich. 1974.
Wind, E. *Pagan Mysteries in the Renaissance*. Faber & Faber, London. 1958.
Winnicott, D.W. *Playing and Reality*. Tavistock Publications, London. 1971.
Wood, Juliette. *The Concept of the Goddess*. Seminar paper, delivered to series—Gender Studies: The Ancient World. Oxford, 1995.

INDEX

alchemy 72, 150, 177, 181, n210
androgyne 42, 177, 182, n196
Ashley, Mike n195, 213

Bachofhen, J.J. 20, n197
Bateson, Gregory n200, n207
Bateson, Mary Catherine n200, n207
Blake, William n200
Brown, N.O. 81, n201

Campbell, Joseph 28
Carrington, Leonora n205
Clute, John (& Grant) n195;
  (& Nicholls) n195
Collings, Michael R. n195

Dawkins, Richard 183, 184, n210
Dexter, Miriam Robbins 26
Dionysos 3, 31, 37, 44, 58, 66, 70, 74, 135, 167, n195, n196, n197, n198, n201, n204, n208
Douglas, Alfred n200, n201
Douglas, Mary n207

Eliade, Mircea 116, 118, 135, 143, 145, n203, n204, n206, n207

Fraser, J.M. 143

Gnosticism 5, 72
Gordon, Joan 2
Grant, John n195
Graves, Robert 20, n197, n198
Groddeck, Georg n197

Harrison, Jane 72, n200, n201

Hawley Jarman, Rosemary n195
Heer, Frederich 108
Heilbrun, Carolyn G. (quoting Rosenmeyer) n196
Heldreth, Lillian M. 2, n208
Hermes 74ff
Hinduism 26, 169, 170, 171, n198, n200, n205
hubris 6, 8, 13, 25, 26, 29, 102, n196

incest 10, 14, 17, 18, 21, 63, 154, 178, n197, n206

Jackson, Rosemary 4, 11, n196, n197
Jocasta 20, 21, 89
Jung, C.G. 19, n197, n210

Lefanu, Sarah 2, n195, n199, n208

Midgely, Mary n202

Neumann, Erich n201, n202
Nicholls, Peter n195
Nixon, Lucy n199

Oedipus 8, 9, 15, 16, 17, 21
Otto, Walter F. n198, n199, n201, n208

Psyche 50, 89, 107, 116, 117, n197, n199, n205

reincarnation/resurrection 3, 6, 8, 9, 26, 28, 29, 30, 35, 41, 60, 62, 67, 96, n199, n201, n203, n206
robots 90, 91, 95–99, 103, 104

Showalter, Elaine n204
snakes 23, 24, 30, 32, 34, 35, 46, 86, 116ff, 169, n207
Sophocles 9, 20ff
Stewart, Susan n208

Tillyard, E.M.W. 131

vampirism 100, 106, 107, 142, 149, 150, 151, 158ff, 160, 177, 179, 181, 183, n195, n204, n208

Versluis, Arthur n209
von Franz, Maria Louise 73, 117

Wind, E. 116, 133
Winnicott, D.W. n199, n203, n208
wolves/werewolves 32, 78, 81, 145, 158, 161, 163, 164, 165, 166, 167, 181, 184, n195, n203, n208
Wood, Juliette n196, n197

www.ingramcontent.com/pod-product-compliance
Ingram Content Group UK Ltd.
Pitfield, Milton Keynes, MK11 3LW, UK
UKHW041955140426
5217IPUK00015B/811